Confronting Visuality in Multi-Ethnic Women's Writing

Confronting Visuality in Multi-Ethnic Women's Writing

Angela Laflen

palgrave
macmillan

CONFRONTING VISUALITY IN MULTI-ETHNIC WOMEN'S WRITING
Copyright © Angela Laflen, 2014.

All rights reserved.

First published in 2014 by PALGRAVE MACMILLAN® in the United States—a division of St. Martin's Press LLC, 175 Fifth Avenue, New York, NY 10010.

Where this book is distributed in the UK, Europe and the rest of the world, this is by Palgrave Macmillan, a division of Macmillan Publishers Limited, registered in England, company number 785998, of Houndmills, Basingstoke, Hampshire RG21 6XS.

Palgrave Macmillan is the global academic imprint of the above companies and has companies and representatives throughout the world.

Palgrave® and Macmillan® are registered trademarks in the United States, the United Kingdom, Europe and other countries.

ISBN: 978-1-137-41303-1

Library of Congress Cataloging-in-Publication Data

Laflen, Angela.
　Confronting Visuality in Multi-Ethnic Women's Writing / Angela Laflen.
　　pages cm
　ISBN 978-1-137-41303-1 (hardback : alk. paper) 1. American literature—Women authors—History and criticism. 2. American literature—Minority authors—History and criticism. 3. Visual perception in literature. 4. Visualization in literature. 5. Feminism in literature. I. Title.

PS151.L34 2014
810.9'9287—dc23   2014005799

A catalogue record of the book is available from the British Library.

Design by Scribe Inc.

First edition: August 2014

10 9 8 7 6 5 4 3 2 1

Contents

List of Figures — vii

Acknowledgments — ix

Introduction: What's (Still) Wrong with Images of Women? — 1

Part I   Coming-of-Age with Mass Media

1   (Re)Visualizing History in Toni Morrison's *The Bluest Eye* — 21

2   Transforming Culture and Consciousness in Bobbie Ann Mason's *In Country* — 43

Part II   Witnessing Visual Manipulation

3   "There Were Signs and I Missed Them": Reading beneath the Image in Margaret Atwood's Speculative Fiction — 65

4   The Politics of Vanishing: Bearing Witness to the Wounded Family in Louise Erdrich's *Shadow Tag* — 85

Part III   Spectatorship in an Expanded Field of Vision

5   Against Visual Objectivity in Gish Jen's "Birthmates" and Chitra Banerjee Divakaruni's "The Ultrasound" — 105

6   Queering Spectatorship in Alison Bechdel's *Fun Home* — 123

Conclusion: Confronting Visuality in the Digital Age — 143

Notes — 149

Works Cited — 169

Index — 191

Figures

Figure 6.1	Panel from page 17 of *Fun Home: A Family Tragicomic* by Alison Bechdel	132
Figure 6.2	Pages 100–101 from *Fun Home: A Family Tragicomic* by Alison Bechdel	133
Figure 6.3	Page 161 from *Fun Home: A Family Tragicomic* by Alison Bechdel	139

Acknowledgments

When I first began working on this project over a decade ago, nearly half of the literary works discussed in this book had not even been published. The project has, therefore, of necessity, been a dynamic one, and I have accumulated many debts to colleagues, family, and friends during the years it has taken to create this book.

I am grateful to Nancy J. Peterson and John N. Duvall for encouraging me early on that there really was something worth exploring about women's writing about visuality and thoughtfully responding to the earliest versions of these chapters.

I am indebted to my colleagues in the School of Liberal Arts at Marist College for providing the time and support to finish this book. I have particularly appreciated the encouragement of Dean Martin Schaffer, and a research leave during the 2013–14 academic year provided the time I needed to complete the project. Additionally, Eileen Curley, Kristin Bayer, and Lea Graham were patient and engaged audiences for discussions about these ideas. I also thank Don Anderson for helpfully advising me at key moments of the publication process as well.

As always, Joan Ferrante, Robert Wallace, and John Alberti provided much-needed support and enthusiasm for this project and generously devoted time to reading parts of the manuscript as well.

I extend my thanks to my editor at Palgrave Macmillan, Brigitte Shull, and editorial assistant Ryan Jenkins, both of whom were enthusiastic about my project and patient with my questions throughout the publication process.

Chapters 3 and 5 are revised, updated, and extended treatments of issues I explored earlier in scholarly articles. I am grateful to these journals for providing permission to reprint the revised chapters here and for their initial encouragement of my work. Chapter 3 originally appeared as "'There's a Shock in This Seeing': The Problem of the Image in *The Handmaid's Tale* and *Oryx and Crake*," *Amerikastudien/American Studies* 54.1 (2009): 99–120. Chapter 5 originally appeared in *Mosaic: A Journal for the Interdisciplinary Study of Literature* 41.4 (2008): 111–27. I am also grateful to Alison Bechdel and Houghton Mifflin for permission to reprint images from *Fun Home*. All images in Chapter 6 are from *Fun Home: A Family Tragicomic* by Alison Bechdel (Copyright © 2006 by Alison Bechdel) and are reprinted by permission of Houghton Mifflin Harcourt Publishing Company. All rights reserved.

My family has also been patient with me and supportive during the time needed to complete this project. I give thanks to Harold and Linda Vaughn for their seemingly limitless generosity. J. Brandon Laflen has been a constant source of conversation and inspiration about these ideas in addition to offering the best technical support imaginable. My three children, each of whom was born during the years it took to develop and write the book, have provided me with considerable impetus for the project, allowing me to witness firsthand how we are each interpellated into visuality and come to see and be seen, from our earliest days, through the lens of gender. It is to them that I dedicate this book, with the hope that the world into which they grow might be characterized by more equitable and generous looking relations.

Introduction

What's (Still) Wrong with Images of Women?

Confronting Visuality in Multi-Ethnic Women's Writing argues that women's literature has an important role to play in bridging a divide between critical analyses of women's images and the reliance on objectifying structures in mainstream media. The works considered here were published between 1970 and 2010, a period during which visual representations of women came under intense critical scrutiny, and as a result, representational practices evolved, though not in ways that early feminists would have anticipated or approved. Throughout this period, writers (in addition to feminist scholars, media workers, and activists) sought to understand, as Griselda Pollock put it in the title of her 1978 article, "What's Wrong with Images of Women?" and to intervene directly in visual relations to change the ways women were represented, the low status afforded to "women's genres," and working conditions for female artists and media workers. Despite this intensive engagement with visuality, however, women's very real social and political gains have been met with a "postfeminist sensibility" in the media that draws on feminist ideas and rhetoric but frequently puts these to the service of decidedly antifeminist aims and representations (Gill 247).[1] However, these developments have made it more difficult than in the past to respond to problematic media trends from an explicitly feminist perspective, and this problem is compounded by a growing sense of uncertainty among feminist media critics about the proper subject for feminist critique. In contrast, I suggest that women's literature has largely avoided these problems because instead of "fixing into images," as Sue Thornham suggests much feminist media criticism has done (52), it situates images of women within larger contexts of visuality and in doing so provides a fuller picture of how images serve the interests of dominant power structures. Additionally, women's literature offers a way to make the rich history and theoretical vocabulary of feminist critique accessible to readers in a way that theory alone often cannot do. Though the cross-cultural tradition of confronting visuality in women's writing has been largely overlooked for a variety of reasons, this tradition is increasingly relevant in an age when more explicit feminist critiques of media are met with suspicion and hostility and when feminist criticism itself sometimes seems uncertain about "what—if anything—should be the target of critique" (Gill 271).

Certainly, performing feminist media analysis today is increasingly challenging. Following what Andrea Stuart has referred to as a split within feminism between "professional feminism" and "popular feminism," the feminism made popular by the media came to combine feminist values and rhetoric with antifeminist aims and representations. "Popular feminism" seems to rely on feminism primarily as a way to "inoculate" against charges of sexism, creating confusion about what the term *feminism* really means in contemporary media culture. This confusion is evident in recent debates about nostalgic television shows such as *Mad Men* and *Game of Thrones*.[2] Though the "old-timey, misogynistic societies" at the center of both shows differ,[3] what both shows provide is, essentially, "a chance to see people do misogynist, racist things without facing consequences" (Doyle). Nevertheless, despite the fact that female characters in the shows are routinely subject to bigotry and sexualized violence, debates about these shows focus less on whether they are sexist and more on whether they are actually feminist.[4] Fans and critics argue that the shows are feminist based on their "complicated, edgy female characters" (Zeisler), with some even suggesting that the misogynistic settings allow the strength of the female characters to emerge—a sentiment Tracie Egan Morrissey voices in discussing *Game of Thrones*: "While the realm that [Martin] has created isn't exactly woman-friendly, the hardships and limitations it creates for its female inhabitants lends itself well to the rich development of their characters." Feminist critique of programs like these is challenging because they "suture" together feminist and antifeminist ideas (Gill 270). Thus the female characters are depicted as active, sexually desiring agents in the stories even as they are also harassed and exploited on the basis of their gender and though male characters in the programs are free to voice and act on sexist ideas with relative impunity. Judith Williamson calls this "sexism with an alibi: it appears at once past and present, 'innocent' and knowing, a conscious reference to another era, rather than an unconsciously driven part of our own" (1). However, Rosalind Gill also notes that in this context, "[feminist] critique becomes much more difficult—and this, it would seem, is precisely what is intended" (268).

Indeed feminist scholars and activists have struggled to respond to today's postfeminist sensibility (247). Even Gloria Steinem has recently seemed uncertain about how to interpret the "resexualization of women's bodies" (Ross 62). When Steinem was asked at a 2010 conference if she felt discouraged that "young women today can dress like hookers and be OK with being treated like a piece of meat, whether it's in a music video or in social situations," she replied, "my question to the young woman who is dressing as you describe is: Is she doing it because she wants to? Is she body-proud? Is she sexuality-proud? Because then, I say, great. Is she doing it because she feels she has to? That she won't be popular otherwise? Then, that's wrong" (qtd. in Strachan).

Though Steinem's response perfectly reflects the core feminist values of female agency and sexual empowerment, it overlooks the extent to which these values have been co-opted—and distorted—by popular culture and contemporary media. Indeed in today's media landscape, men no longer objectify women, but women are instead presented as active, desiring sexual subjects who choose to present themselves in a seemingly objectified manner because its suits their liberated interests to do so (Goldman; Ross 62). However, as Gill points out, the fact that the "resulting valued 'look' is so similar" belies the fact that women are "just pleasing themselves, and following their own autonomously generated desires" (260). Nevertheless, the confusing combination of feminism and antifeminism in contemporary media has resulted in a situation in which feminists increasingly seem unsure of how to respond, and those who do object to this state of affairs are subject to inevitably personal and vitriolic attacks (Gill 268; Ross 87).

It would seem, then, that four decades of feminist critique and intervention into visual relations has resulted in a kind of critical impasse where, despite having a "more secure institutional base than in the recent past and a vocabulary of theoretical languages" (Gill 271), "the very sophistication of media studies makes it harder and harder for feminists to actually object to any kind of representational practice" (Viner 20–21). Liesbet Van Zoonen concludes that the "theoretical and empirical sophistication of feminist media studies has not only jeopardized its relevance for a critical feminist media politics but also diminished its potential as a comprehensive cultural critique" (26). For example, as we acknowledge the pleasure that some women can derive from watching shows such as *Mad Men* and *Game of Thrones* or the sense of agency some women might achieve by dressing in sexually provocative ways, it becomes difficult to find justifications for critiquing these practices as part of the hegemonic construction of gender identities.[5] Indeed in this atmosphere, some have argued that terms like *objectification* and *sexism* are outdated and in danger of losing meaning entirely (Williamson 1).

Nevertheless, the prevalence of sexualized violence against women, increasing numbers of women with eating disorders, and a burgeoning demand for cosmetic surgery among even very young girls,[6] along with the fact that women today are so systematically objectified, attacked, and vilified in the media, illustrate the need for a feminist response capable of connecting the rich history and body of feminist work on media with today's media practices and viewers. As Gill contends, the challenge is to "articulate the politics that can engage effectively with this new [postfeminist] sensibility, and move forward to more open, equal, hopeful and generous gender relations" (271).

Women's literature has an important role to play in making the connection between feminist criticism and today's media culture and consumers. *Confronting Visuality* focuses on multi-ethnic women's literature that has moved in tandem with feminist media studies throughout the contemporary period. However, works by Toni Morrison, Bobbie Ann Mason, Margaret Atwood, Louise Erdrich, Gish Jen, Chitra Banerjee Divakaruni, and Alison Bechdel are also able to deal differently with issues of gender and visuality than are feminist media studies. These writers have unique tools to work with in considering what it feels like for women to be immersed in American media culture and can use the identification between readers and literary characters to foster greater critical awareness in readers about how issues of gender, race, and sexuality become visible (or remain invisible) through contemporary visualization practices and technologies. Via literature, writers are able to situate images of women within larger contexts of visuality and provide a fuller picture of how images serve the interests of dominant power structures. In the texts considered here, the point is not to change any given image, which women may or may not even agree is problematic, but to change the entire context for viewing women and the ways that women see and relate to what has been called "the shared legacy of women's images" and their meanings (Henninger 5). This is particularly relevant in the current "postfeminist" climate that makes critique of individual images of women so difficult as well. Rather than arguing for or against specific representations of women, the writers instead actively oppose *visuality* itself and claim the right "to look at that which authority wishes to conceal," particularly with regard to women (Mirzoeff, "Introduction" xxx). I follow Nicholas Mirzoeff's definition of visuality as "a specific technique of colonial and imperial practice, operating both at 'home' and 'abroad,' by which power visualizes History to itself. In so doing, it claims authority, above and beyond its ability to impose its will . . . Visualization demonstrates authority, which produces consent" ("Introduction" xxx). Visuality has three component techniques as a means of authoritarian control: classification, separation, and aesthetics. Mirzoeff explains that "when the three components work together, they form . . . a complex of visuality, in which the sense that the arrangement is right reinforces the classification, makes separation seem natural, and, in turn, what is right comes to seem pleasing, almost beautiful" ("Introduction" xxxi). Though the works included in *Confronting Visuality* emphasize different components of visuality, they all consider the way that aesthetics supports the work of classification and separation. In other words, in these works, images are interesting not in and of themselves but because of the ways they aestheticize the classification and separation of individuals and groups on the basis of gender, race, class, sexuality, and so on. Focusing on images, therefore, is a way for these writers to confront the operation of visuality more generally and make visible the power structures that sometimes remain unseen or attempt to hide behind irony or even the rhetoric of feminism.

The writers included in *Confronting Visuality* exemplify diversity in women's writing about visuality and consider specific legacies of objectification. However, common strategies of resistance surface from this diversity. None of the writers advocate either rejecting visual technologies outright or promoting falsely positive representations of women. Instead they take an activist stance with regard to visuality and intervene in visual relations by seeking to train their own readers to be critical viewers of images. This approach rests on two important assumptions. First, it inherently assumes that readers are also, inevitably, spectators and consumers of a variety of media. Second, the writers assume that literature does not merely mirror social concerns but provides a space within which social realities can be transcended and contested.

Although some men's literature also registers the increasing importance of the visual in contemporary culture,[7] the writers included here also share an awareness that, despite the ways that visuality differs depending on other social characteristics, gender continues to distinguish the construction of men and women within mainstream media and to specifically reflect on the difference that gender makes in looking relations. This emphasis on using literature to equip readers with critical vision is also an important way that this group of women writers asserts the continuing relevance of literary forms even in the midst of dramatic social changes to reading practices in the contemporary period. These writers recommend and employ literature as a medium within which to critically comment on issues of visuality, and in their works (which take the form of novels, short stories, and graphic narratives in a variety of literary genres), they bridge traditional divides between image and text as well as high and low culture.

Women, Visuality, and the Pictorial Turn

The ever-increasing body of criticism on visuality and literature has largely overlooked the cross-cultural tradition of confronting visuality in contemporary women's writing. However, this oversight seems to stem from a desire to understand the full complexity of visuality and to avoid suggesting that there is a single, common female experience of visuality. The time during which the works included in *Confronting Visuality* were written saw both images of women as well as the lives of women change considerably, along with the critical tools available to analyze and discuss women's images. Central to the evolution of feminist media criticism was the development of increasingly complex models of spectatorship and audience studies.

The contemporary period gave rise to both modern feminism and modern image culture, and Amelia Jones has described the two as having a "symbiotic relation" with one another ("Introduction" 3). Both arose during a profound cultural transformation that W. J. T. Mitchell has termed *the pictorial turn* and defines as "a postlinguistic, postsemiotic rediscovery of the picture as a complex interplay between visuality, apparatus, institutions, discourse, bodies, and figurality" (Mitchell, *Picture* 16). Although this move toward visualization has its roots in the development of technology that extends the human sense of sight, it has accelerated in recent decades due to the speed with which imaging technologies develop. Additionally, as human sight has become extended in unprecedented ways—out into space and within the human body, for example—contemporary imaging technologies have led to a dramatic increase of images in Western culture.[8] As scholars grappled with understanding the changes brought about by the move toward visualization, feminism proved to be "one of the ways in which we can most usefully come to an understanding of the image culture in which we are suspended" (Jones, "Introduction" 3).

Certainly, for modern feminists, the pictorial turn has had enormous implications. Beginning in the 1960s, second-wave feminists found themselves in a situation where images of women were ubiquitous and media culture was becoming pervasive.[9] Consequently, as Gill explains, "unlike their mothers and grandmothers, second-wave feminists were bombarded daily by representations of womanhood and gender relations in news and magazines, on radio and TV, in film and on billboards" (9). Given this, it is not surprising that media became a major focus of feminist research, critique, and intervention. Betty Friedan initiated a focus on images in *The Feminine Mystique* (1963), which traced the postwar construction of America's ideal image of femininity (what Friedan called the "happy housewife heroine") through media representations she found in women's magazines and advertisement images (23),[10] and in 1966, the National Organization of Women, with Friedan as its first president, declared media to be one of the major sites of struggle for the revived women's movement (Van Zoonen 26). Since that time, a focus on the media and on visual representations of women has been hardwired into modern feminism.

Much of the early work in feminist media studies focused on developing a critical vocabulary for discussing existing images of women and intervening directly in representational practices by creating alternative images, whether by showcasing the work of female artists or changing working conditions for women in media industries.[11] Women also worked to penetrate the burgeoning field of communication studies, which "did not seem to be very interested in the subject 'woman'" even by the mid- to late 1970s (Van Zoonen 25). As the Women's Studies Group of the Birmingham Centre for Contemporary Cultural Studies (CCCS) complained in 1978, "we found it extremely difficult to participate in the CCCS Groups and felt, without being able to articulate it, that it was a case of the masculine domination of both intellectual work and the environment in which it was being carried out" (*Women Take Issue* 11). However, feminist media studies also began to emerge as its own interdisciplinary endeavor via the launching of the journal *Women and Film* in 1972 and the publication of foundational articles such as Laura Mulvey's "Visual Pleasure and Narrative Cinema" in 1975 and Gaye Tuchman's "The Symbolic Annihilation of Women by the Mass Media" in 1978.

While this early work was enormously important in building a foundation for feminist studies of media, it was quickly critiqued for being too reductionist and for failing to account for the incredible diversity in the way the media visually construct women and how women interact with images. Van Zoonen explains how, beginning in the 1980s, scholars developed ever more sophisticated models of spectatorship and a thorough understanding of the ideological workings of aesthetics and media (26). For example, because early work in gender and media focused largely on reception analyses rather than audience studies, critics writing in the early 1980s such as Annette Kuhn suggested that this early work constructed an abstract, ahistorical spectator with little connection to the lived experiences of women who actually view media ("Women's Genres"). A move toward studies of real audiences, such as Janice Radway's 1984 examination of female readers, shifted scholarship from a focus on reception to a focus on audience, and this resulted in increasing recognition that women's viewing practices are inflected by a myriad of factors in addition to gender, including race, sexuality, and class, among others.

The move toward audience studies helped reveal a gap vis-à-vis race in early studies of female spectatorship, which some scholars have attributed to the reliance on psychoanalytic theory in reception analysis. Laura Mulvey's influential arguments about spectatorship were built on a psychoanalytic model to demonstrate how the patriarchic subconscious of society shapes the experience of watching films as well as cinema itself. In the mid-1980s, critics such as Jane Gaines charged that "the psychoanalytic concept of sexual difference is unequipped to deal with a film that is about racial difference and sexuality" and that "the psychoanalytic model works to block out considerations which assume a different configuration" (12).[12] This charge was echoed by bell hooks in 1992 when she contended that "feminist film theory rooted in an ahistorical psychoanalytic framework that privileges sexual difference actively suppresses recognition of race" (*Black Looks* 123). hooks's work, which resisted the psychoanalytic framework of feminist film theory and insisted on the materialist arguments of critical race theory and cultural studies, was itself foundational in helping "to bridge feminist and critical race theory by arguing that gendered viewing practices are also intersected by racial identity" (Kearney 589).[13]

In the 1990s, other critiques began to problematize the assumption of heterosexuality in media texts and reception practices. Writing in 1991, Pratibha Parmar pointed out that Mulvey's model of spectatorship "presumes heterosexuality to such a degree that it often appears to demand it" (20), and in 1993, Alexander Doty sought to reconfigure film spectatorship via queer theory and argued that queerness is central to, rather than subtextual within, mass media texts. Mary Celeste Kearney explains that Doty "encourages scholars to consider the many ways in which consumers, particularly those in the LGBTQI community, reconfigure media narratives in order to find pleasure" (590). Consequently, scholars such as Judith Mayne, Teresa de Lauretis, and Mary Ann Doane began to explore the critical possibilities within traditional and alternative cinema for cross gender identification. As a result of this work, studies of media expanded to recognize ways in which "images in contemporary culture make many forms of address to more than one audience, and allow the possibility of multiple identifications by the spectator" (Evans and Gamman 32).

Essentially, feminist critics came to recognize, as Rita Felski points out in questioning the possibility of a "single, common femaleness," that "the many empirical differences of race, class, sexuality, and age . . . render notions of shared female experience untenable" (182). As a result, the critical focus in feminist studies of media shifted to examining the differences between groups of women and even individual female spectators.[14] From Mulvey's initial assertion that male and female spectators view cinema differently, scholarship expanded to recognize positions for looking that Mulvey did not originally account for in the somewhat simplified structure of the male and female gaze she proposed—including "queer spectatorship," bell hooks's "oppositional gaze" and "black looks," and E. Ann Kaplan's "imperial gaze," among others. By the mid- to late 1990s, work by Beverley Skeggs and Hilary Radner illuminated the important role that social class plays in the way women engage images of femininity, and in the new millennium, Katherine Henninger has demonstrated the importance of region on women's participation in visual relations. The study of visuality thus fragmented as feminist scholars focused in on specific groups or types of female spectators, attending to the differences that race, ethnicity, region, and sexuality make to looking relations.

Literary studies was relatively slow to address issues of visuality raised by contemporary media,[15] but as literary scholars began to publish work throughout the 1990s and 2000s focused on issues at the intersection of literary studies and visuality—including ekphrasis, spectatorship, looking relations, witnessing, surveillance, and spectacle—they tended to replicate the pattern of examining issues of visuality in narrow sociohistorical contexts. Consequently, there are a number of excellent volumes focused on explorations of visuality in specific ethnic or regional groups, such as Henninger's *Ordering the Facade: Photography and Contemporary Southern Women's Writing* and Eleanor Ty's *The Politics of the Visible in Asian North American Narratives*, or on particular literary genres, such as Jane Hedley, Nick Halpern, and Willard Spiegelman's edited collection *In the Frame: Women's Ekphrastic Poetry from Marianne Moore to Susan Wheeler*, or in the works of specific writers, a number of which I discuss in the individual chapters that follow.[16] However, *Confronting Visuality* is the first book-length examination of issues of visuality in a contemporary, cross-cultural context. Yet this cross-cultural approach is important because it reveals that despite the diversity between the writers included, they identify similar concerns about visuality and similar strategies for intervening in it. And these common strategies have the potential to serve as the foundation for a new (or newly recognized) feminist approach toward media, one that navigates some of the pitfalls that currently threaten feminist media studies in today's postfeminist climate.

For example, while recognizing differences in the ways groups and individuals participate in visual relations is important to identifying specific and effective strategies for resisting or embracing visual images, so much focus on the differences between women has also played a role in the current critical impasse in feminist media studies. As Van Zoonen questions, "If meaning is so dependent on context, can we still pass valid feminist judgments about the political tendencies and implications of texts? For we don't know how audiences will use and interpret texts . . . If one interpretation is not by definition better or more valid than another, what legitimation do we have to discuss the politics of representation, to try to intervene in dominant culture?" (37).

Though it is not my intention to suggest that a single female perspective on visuality or even any individual image is possible or desirable or to understate the differences between the writers and texts included in *Confronting Visuality*, I do suggest that all female viewers inherit what Henninger has referred to as a shared "legacy of women's images" (5). As they rework and respond to this legacy, the writers included in this book use literature as a way to contribute to what Van Zoonen has referred to as the "'semiotic empowerment' of female media recipients" (38). In discussing the value of this approach, Van Zoonen stresses that the point of such "empowerment" should not be to make female audiences aware of the "'true' sexist, patriarchal or capitalist meanings of a text" but rather "the pleasures of discovering multiple and sometimes contending constructions in a text" (38). Women writers can help readers see images differently and model alternative ways of reading and negotiating the meanings of images. In doing so, they seek to equip readers with the critical skills to interpret the legacy of women's images, both those they have already internalized and those they will encounter in the future.

The Legacy of Women's Images

Those responsible for producing and distributing media images of women often question the power of a single image to affect female viewers' attitudes and behavior. For example, when Alexandra Shulman, the editor of British *Vogue*, was asked if the fashion industry should assume any responsibility for creating impossible-to-achieve images that young girls measure themselves against, she replied, "Not many people have actually said to me that they have looked at my magazine and decided to become anorexic" ("Fat"). However, while it might be convenient for some media producers to dismiss the power of a single image, this flies in the face of scholarship that suggests that women never encounter a single image in isolation; instead every image builds on every other image a woman has seen, giving images of women what Felski has referred to as "the weight of sedimented meanings" (182). Considering the impact of contemporary advertising on female viewers, for example, Janice Winship explains, "We do not come 'naked' to the ads or to any ideological representation and simply take on those representations. We already have both a knowledge of images of women from other discourses and an acquaintance with 'real' women in our everyday lives. The signification of an ad only has meaning in relation to this 'outside' knowledge of the ideology of the feminine"

(218). It is this cumulative weight of meanings combined with longstanding social narratives about femininity that give images their power. Indeed in her study of female body image, Susan Bordo argues that images have a "homogenizing" and "normalizing" power, and she implicates them in a whole range of contemporary body practices ranging from dieting and eating disorders to cosmetic surgery. According to Bordo, "female bodies become docile bodies" through such practices, in conformity to "an ever-changing, homogenizing, elusive ideal of femininity," and this constitutes "an amazingly durable and flexible strategy of social control" (166).

Moreover, the legacy of women's images ensures that images exert power over women regardless of whether a woman thoroughly engages a particular image or largely overlooks it. As Sue Thornham explains, "looking at these images, we might view them in distracted fashion, often in the form of magazines which may be flicked through, their contents fragmented or re-ordered, the images lingered on or passed over. This does not mean, however, that the moment of vision, of exposure to the image, is any less constitutive of our sense of self" (52). She points to work by Anne Cronin, who argues that the act of vision stretches both forward and backward in time. Stretching back, it is simultaneously an act of interpretation that draws, however unconsciously, on other images, the images of memory and the unconscious.[17] Thornham explains that in this context, "the power of the mass circulation of images which offer themselves often precisely as mirrors of our (idealized) selves will lie in their capacity to evoke these other, buried images" (52). And stretching forward in time, images "offer to stabilize momentarily our sense of self through the act of identification, a sense of self which can then be projected forwards into our daily living" (Thornham 52). However, these images are also "social constructions produced within relations of power"; thus they "bind us into specific, socially, sanctioned senses of ourselves" (Thornham 52). This work helps to explain the curious interplay of choice and compulsion with regard to images that has been the focus of a great deal of feminist criticism.[18] While women often perceive themselves as free to pick and choose among images and indeed are free to some extent, interacting with images also can lock viewers into larger narratives about femininity even when these are not immediately discernible.

The works included in *Confronting Visuality* recognize the power of the legacy of women's images even as they attempt to disrupt this power. By describing and critiquing visual images in their writing, the writers attempt to not only influence how readers see and read actual images but also impact how readers will read images they encounter in the future. And this is true whether or not readers can actually view the images that the writers discuss or only imagine those images based on their long experience with images of women. For example, readers can actually find an image of the wrapper of Mary Jane candy that Morrison describes in *The Bluest Eye* for themselves or watch the episodes of *M*A*S*H* that Mason alludes to in *In Country*, while in *Fun Home*, Alison Bechdel painstakingly reproduces real photographs and other documents from her family's archive. In other works, such as Erdrich's *Shadow Tag*, Atwood's speculative novels, and Gish Jen's and Chitra Banerjee Divakaruni's short stories about fetal ultrasound, the writers describe fictitious images that readers cannot actually see for themselves. Nevertheless, the pervasive visualization of women ensures that readers have experience viewing images similar to the ones described in women's writing and can recognize the visual tropes women writers engage—ranging from the demure Southern belle to the Asian dragon lady, the ambitious career girl to the criminal lesbian—as well as a wide range of media invoked in these works—including portraiture, advertising, film, fetal imaging, and many others.

As they describe characters interacting with images of women, writers focus on the way that meaning is produced and negotiated in visual relations and identify this process of negotiation as rich with critical potential. As Henninger observes, representation is always a negotiated power, and meaning is not inherent in any image but must be "negotiated (or not) between the artist and her subject. Negotiated between the desire of the artist and that of her audience . . . Negotiated between the ideologies or conventions of a culture . . . and positions of acceptance, ambivalence, or resistance to those conventions" (6). By focusing on the process of negotiation in their writing, women writers not only challenge the dominant effects of being represented as women—and more specifically as black women, Southern women, Canadian women, Native American women, Asian American women, and lesbians—in diverse contexts, ranging from intimate personal relationships, to the wider domestic realm, and to the sphere of global politics, but they also depict women as active participants in scopic relations and in processes of visual signification and test alternative patterns of behavior.

Identifying and testing alternative patterns of behavior is particularly important because it demonstrates that although visual culture is influential, it is also contextual, and individual spectators can become able to see differently from the way they are intended and to manipulate and direct the gaze of spectators in potentially useful ways. Additionally, it creates space for recognizing the many ways in which women shape visual culture even as they are shaped by it, both as producers and as consumers.

Reading Texts and Images in Contemporary Women's Writing

Their attempts to render power visible to readers illustrate that many women writers' interest in visuality is not purely aesthetic but reflects an activist impulse as well. That is, while they do innovate literary techniques and themes in response to changing conditions of visuality, the writers included in *Confronting Visuality* also seek to change how readers view images of women by disrupting the visual pleasure associated with visual images and by situating images in sociohistorical contexts. They claim real importance for their writing by using it as a vehicle through which to equip readers with strategies for critical seeing. Indeed a number of the works use metafictional and self-referential strategies to explicitly address the importance of literature as a critical space within which to reflect on the ethics and politics of representation. By using literature in this way, these writers also inherently address ongoing questions about the status of literature in a visual, digital age.

Certainly, one of the most obvious impacts of the pictorial turn on literature has been in transforming the reading habits of the public. Numerous studies have linked the rise in consuming electronic media to a decline in literary reading,[19] and due to the traditional divide between images and texts, this has been interpreted by many critics as an attack on reading itself.[20] There has been considerable anxiety about the "fate" of reading in an image-driven, multimedia age. Headlines such as "Should English Departments Throw in the Towel?," "The Long Decline in Reading," and "Twilight of the Books" cast literature as an endangered species in need of protection by highly literate, well-educated protectors.[21] Some critics predict a future in which individuals are unable to grapple with the more subtle demands of reading text, their imaginations inadequate to the task of deciphering meaning from imagery and metaphor.[22]

Other critics have suggested that linking reading narrowly to literary reading fails to take into account the numerous other ways that people read in contemporary culture.[23] And Kathleen Fitzpatrick contends that Barnes & Noble and Amazon.com have succeeded not by "striving in some altruistic fashion to promote the Arnoldian cultural uplift of literacy against a debasing mass culture" but by "responding to existing markets and creating new ones" (4). Nevertheless, contemporary anxieties about the encroachment of images into the domain of text reflect longstanding notions that these are separate, distinct, and mutually opposed. Arguments for the printed word's temporal or spatial status span the centuries, with Gotthold Lessing asserting in 1766 that inherently spatial plastic arts and inherently temporal literature should never encroach on one another (110) and with Roland Barthes arguing in *Image, Text, Music* that the inherently spatial literary work acts as a container or constraint for the fluid, temporary text of language (156–63, 70). In this view, any elevation to the status of images requires a subsequent decline in the status of text. Moreover, this view assumes that consuming images is a more passive experience than consuming text; hence a decline in literary reading signals a larger social decline in literacy or critical reading practices.

Literature registers the impact of changing reading practices as well. However, while there is a pattern in the writing of some contemporary men, such as Thomas Pynchon, Don DeLillo, Jonathan Franzen, and David Foster Wallace, of adopting an adversarial position toward technology in their fiction (Fitzpatrick 5), the pattern that emerges in the women's writing included in *Confronting Visuality* is recognizing that visual imagery contributes to the ongoing objectification and subordination of women and racial Others, and this is the source of these writers' concern over the proliferation of images and decline in literary reading. While some male writers have tended to claim obsolescence for themselves as writers and for their work, the women included here are motivated to adapt the form and contents of literature to address the pressing concerns they see and, in doing so, demonstrate forcefully the ongoing relevance and necessity of an engaged literature.

Thus Morrison, Mason, Atwood, Erdrich, Jen, Divakaruni, and Bechdel do not adopt an adversarial position toward media images per se out of some perceived loss of status as a result of the increased importance of images. Instead their writing has adapted in important ways to represent visual technologies and practices. In this way, their writing reflects changes in visual practices and technologies throughout the contemporary period as well. In fact, the blending of the verbal and the visual is one of the key traits of the pictorial turn. Mitchell claims as one of his basic assumptions that as a result of the pictorial turn "all media are mixed media, and all representations are heterogeneous; there are no 'purely' visual or verbal arts" (*Picture* 5). The power of contemporary media derives not only from appealing to human sight but also from the careful and strategic combination of modes of communication. Technology enables text and image to work together to more effectively and persuasively communicate information. And in the process, images and texts, and our understandings of them, are altered. In the age of multimedia, digital production, the traditional association of the visual with space and the verbal with time no longer seems to make sense, if in fact it ever did.[24]

In the works considered here, the writers do not so much bridge a gap between text and image as suggest that there is no gap. They reflect Joseph Tabbi's contention that electronic media have changed "not the book *per se* but the way that books can be read now. The end of books is more accurately the end of academic readings that isolate texts from the larger media ecology." This group of writers attests to the power of literature to reach audiences of unprecedented size and scope via a variety of media. The fact that all the authors included in this study have been commercially and critically successful, appearing regularly on bestsellers lists and receiving major awards,[25] signals the success of these authors in communicating their message to a wide reading audience and bridging the gap between academic and popular reading audiences. Moreover, these writers have experimented with popular media in a variety of ways. Morrison, Atwood, Mason, Erdrich, and Divakaruni have consented to have their works adapted to film, stage plays, and opera. Atwood has worked as a visual and comics artist; Bechdel is trained as a visual artist and has worked in the hybrid form of graphic narrative for more than three decades, and Atwood, Morrison, Mason, and Erdrich have incorporated visual elements, such as photographs and illustrations, into their texts. Most of these authors also have active web presences: Atwood, Erdrich, Divakaruni, and Bechdel blog regularly, and each of the authors maintains a website.

These writers emphasize that the practice of reading includes *both* text and images, and instead of advocating for the value of reading text *over* images, they stress that critical reading skills are increasingly necessary in the face of information overload and manipulation, whether for commercial or political ends. They rely on multitextuality and intertextuality to bring together a wide variety of materials and texts in their works. Several of the works included are also multivoiced, and a number of them rely on the rhetorical tool of ekphrasis to create verbal pictures. Mason has developed what has been alternately derided and celebrated as "Kmart realism" to reflect the lived experiences of her rural Southern characters, and she experiments with deep metaphors from film to capture the experience of having one's consciousness colonized by popular media. Bechdel radically experiments with narrative techniques in her graphic memoir to seamlessly meld word and image. Via techniques like these, the writers demonstrate their awareness of the supposed threats to literature posed by visual and multimedia forms and address questions about the continuing relevance of literature. And they do so in a wide variety of literary genres, from speculative fiction to domestic drama, fictional war memoir to autography. In this body of writing, visuality is not a threat to literature; it is an important subject for literary treatment and actually underscores the importance of critical reading.

These writers' commitment to using a wide range of media and genres to reach their audiences further underscores the important work they set out to accomplish by training readers to confront visuality. Although many other women writers have contributed to the development of this tradition in the contemporary period, works included in this book represent key moments in women's confrontations with visuality, when women writers—often responding to or anticipating technological developments—use literary tools to depict the dangers and possibilities of changing visual practices and technologies and develop particular innovative narrative techniques to consider issues of visuality and engage important contemporary theorists. These innovations have helped women's literature evolve, have influenced other contemporary writers, and have helped women's literature earn its status in the contemporary period.

Part I, "Coming-of-Age with Mass Media," examines two female bildungsromans, both of which focus on the impact of popular media on forming female identity and desires and chart the commercial interests that seek to construct particular kinds of gendered consumers. Toni Morrison's *The Bluest Eye* and Bobbie Ann Mason's *In Country* question the way American history has been visualized and dramatically insert alternative stories focused on young female protagonists into prevailing American narratives (of the World War II era and the post–Vietnam War era, respectively). In doing so, they not only insist that these characters are central to American culture but also attempt to make the ideological work of visualization apparent to readers.

The stakes for recognizing the work of visualized authority are even higher in the three narratives included in Part II, "Witnessing Visual Manipulation." Chapter 3 argues that the faultiness of human vision, along with mechanisms of spectacle and surveillance as they have been described by Michel Foucault and Guy Debord, becomes the foundation of totalitarian regimes in Margaret Atwood's dystopian novels *The Handmaid's Tale* and *Oryx and Crake*. And Atwood's insistence that a "multiplicity of witness" is the best way to avoid editing dissident voices out of official histories and records finds a parallel in Louise Erdrich's novel *Shadow Tag*, which refocuses the examination of the ethics and politics of representation in the domestic realm. In addition to belying the notion that contemporary Native Americans have "vanished," *Shadow Tag* explores how gendered relationships and family structures are inflected by visual practices and racial ideologies just as surely as geopolitical relationships are and suggests that one can gain critical purchase on the material artifacts of family only by bringing together disparate, sometimes explicitly contradictory, materials.

The material artifacts of family are also subjects of consideration in the three narratives included in Part III, "Spectatorship in an Expanded Field of Vision." In "Birthmates" and "The Ultrasound," Gish Jen and Chitra Banerjee Divakaruni focus on the complexity of interpreting fetal images since they function not only as family artifacts but also as medical and political artifacts. These stories demonstrate how infused with ideology even supposedly objective medical images are, as well as how culture, gender, class, and other sociohistorical factors complicate a viewing of these images. Alison Bechdel similarly works to destabilize spectatorship in *Fun Home* by demonstrating the profound effect that sexuality has on viewing and interpretive practices. In reconstructing her childhood memories and family artifacts in the form of a graphic memoir, Bechdel places the reader into a queer spectatorial position that undercuts the heterosexist gaze by forcing the reader to avow knowledge of homosexuality and adopt a queer gaze.

In studying North American narratives, I have attempted to discern similarities between writers often studied and discussed in isolation from one another due to differences in the sociohistorical contexts and even the genres in which they write. My sense is that though these differences are undeniably significant to the narratives, there are also important, often overlooked, similarities in the ways the writers respond to the experience of being visually constructed as female. At the same time, this study does not purport to be comprehensive, and there are obvious gaps. I have not gone out of my way to choose representative texts from different ethnicities, and I have not included any Latina or Jewish-American authors. I have also not included poetry or drama in the study. I have instead chosen narratives that stress and illustrate my argument about how women writers can help bridge the divide between critical analyses of visuality and the reliance on objectifying structures in mainstream media and to consider how this constitutes an overlooked tradition in contemporary women's writing. To this end, I have included several texts by canonical writers who helped establish and shape this tradition, especially Toni Morrison's *The Bluest Eye*, Margaret Atwood's *The Handmaid's Tale*, and Bobbi Ann Mason's *In Country*, each of which has received many excellent readings. However, I also focus on four lesser-known or more recent works that illustrate the evolution of women's writing about visuality. Part of my aim in writing about this subject is to create further interest in women's writing about visuality and to foster recognition that women writers have important perspectives to offer the feminist study of media, especially as media respond to feminist critique analysis in problematic ways.

Part I

Coming-of-Age with Mass Media

1

(Re)Visualizing History in Toni Morrison's *The Bluest Eye*

Throughout her body of work, Toni Morrison has been deeply engaged with the ethics and politics of visuality. Morrison's interest in visuality stems from her desire to "bear witness to the plight of African Americans" (Bouson 2), a plight that Morrison has described as "grotesque" (Jones and Vinson 181) and in graphic description as "my people are being devoured" (Morrison, "Language Must Not Sweat" 121). There is a tension also between Morrison's sense that the desperate situation of African Americans warrants immediate attention and the strange invisibility of racial issues in much of American culture. Morrison recognizes that a process of erasure and forgetting has rendered America's racial past and its ongoing legacy largely invisible in American culture—though its effects remain keenly felt and impact the lives of contemporary Americans, both black and white. In *Playing in the Dark*, she indicts literature for its role in this process of erasure, suggesting that though "the major and championed characteristics of our national literature" are "responses to a dark, abiding, signing Africanist presence" (5), "in matters of race, silence and evasion have historically ruled literary discourse" (9). She has also suggested that slave narratives played a role in this process of erasure, explaining that "over and over, the writers pull the narrative up short with a phrase such as, 'But let us drop a veil over these proceedings too horrible to relate.' In shaping the experience to make it palatable to those who were in a position to alleviate it, they were silent about many things, and they 'forgot' many other things" ("Site of Memory" 109–10). Not surprisingly, Morrison describes her job as a writer "to rip that veil drawn over 'proceedings too terrible to relate'" ("Site of Memory"110), to "find and expose a truth about the interior life of people who didn't write it," and "to implement the stories that I heard" (113).

Though issues of visuality pervade her writing, Morrison's first novel, *The Bluest Eye*, which was composed throughout the 1960s and published in 1970, is an important starting point for this study as well as for examinations of visuality in Morrison's later writing because the novel represents a foundational moment in contemporary critical treatments of visuality in literature and theory.[1] Combining feminist and nationalist concerns in unprecedented ways,[2] *The Bluest Eye* manifests a crisis in visualized authority, exposing the generally invisible operation of power. To this end, Morrison makes visible the ideological functions of families, educational institutions, and popular culture, and she seeks a different, though not formal or authorized, place from which to visualize. Significantly, this "different place" is not imagined to be one of racial or cultural authenticity, an issue that perplexed many members of the Black Arts movement and continues to circulate in critical discussions of *The Bluest Eye*.[3] Instead Morrison demonstrates that one does not have to identify a position of authenticity in order to confront visuality.

In *The Bluest Eye*, Morrison "implements" one of her own personal experiences from childhood in order to examine what could happen to "the most vulnerable member" of a community (210), a black female child, in the decades before black became beautiful in the United States. In an afterword she added to the novel in 1993, Morrison describes how the novel grew out of a childhood encounter with a classmate who expressed a desire for blue eyes, her repulsion toward that desire, and her confusion about how the classmate had come to perceive them as more desirable than her own dark eyes (209–10). This childhood experience informed Morrison's subsequent engagement with the Black Arts movement in the 1960s, whose members asserted the beauty of blackness and encouraged black people to reclaim beauty. Though Morrison found these assertions inspiring, she also questioned why it was necessary for blackness to be reclaimed among black people; how was it they had come to accept the dominant view of beauty? (210). Unpacking the complexity of this issue in *The Bluest Eye* led Morrison to create a multifaceted examination of the political and social functioning of visuality, one that attempts to disrupt the dominant visual regime by bringing to light both the operation of power that is generally unseen and the subordinated history of African Americans during the World War II era.

Morrison fashioned *The Bluest Eye* as a female bildungsroman that employs a strategy of paired characters, essentially splitting the primary female perspective in two.[4] Pecola Breedlove, the central focus of the novel, is the abject scapegoat for her community's racial self-hatred, while Claudia MacTeer, the primary narrator, develops a critical gaze as an adult with which she interrogates her own childhood memories and desires. Splitting the narrative focus between Pecola and Claudia allows Morrison to at once depict the full effects of the objectifying gaze in her consideration of Pecola, whose personal devastation is so complete that she cannot narrate her own story, and at the same time, the development of a critical perspective via Claudia. In other words, the novel traces one logical, though admittedly extreme, outcome of the black community internalizing racist ideologies even as it offers a possible strategy to avoid this outcome. Nevertheless, Claudia admits that as an adolescent she also identified with the objectifying gaze and is therefore also implicated in her own critique.

Merging Nationalist and Feminist Concerns in *The Bluest Eye*

Morrison's consideration of visuality in *The Bluest Eye* is uniquely contemporary because of the way she was influenced by thinking about visuality and aesthetics emerging from both the Black Arts movement and feminist media studies at the time. Central to the Black Arts movement was the call for an aesthetics that was distinct and separate from white Western traditions based on, in Larry Neal's words, "a separate symbolism, mythology, critique, and iconology" (29). This move toward a new black aesthetics, the expression of which was an art that reflected a sense of self-determination, meant that the "Black artist," as the poet Etheridge Knight states, had to "create new forms and new values, sing new songs (or purify old ones); and along with other black authorities, he must create a new history, new symbols, myths and legends (and purify old ones by fire)" (qtd. in Neal 30). The Black Arts movement, with its call for a black aesthetic to serve the political and social interests of black Americans, offered Morrison a vision of literature that was politically engaged and able to foster social change. It also directed her to consider the ideological and political functions of aesthetics. As she explains in the afterword, "The assertion of racial beauty was not a reaction to the self-mocking, humorous critique of cultural/racial foibles common in all groups, but against the damaging inferiority originating in an outside gaze" (210). And *The Bluest Eye* was recognized by early reviewers as a "Black Arts novel," which meant that its "engagement with African American psychology was thus acknowledged through Black Aesthetic concepts" (Douglas 153). For example, Ruby Dee's 1971 review of the novel explicitly connects it to the Black Arts movement: "The author digs up for viewing deep secret thoughts, terrible yearnings and little-understood frustrations common to many of us. She says these are the gnawings we keep pushed back into the subconscious, unadmitted; but they must be worked on, ferreted up and out so we can breathe deeply, say loud and truly believe 'Black is beautiful'" (319).

However, while *The Bluest Eye* was legible for early readers in the context of the Black Arts movement, which may have contributed to its acceptance by reviewers as well,[5] Morrison's concern with nationalist issues is tempered with feminist concerns as well, and it is the way she combines these concerns that makes the novel unique in its historical context. Morrison shares the unease of other second-wave feminists ranging from Betty Friedan to Laura Mulvey to Gaye Tuchman with the impact that media images of women have on female spectators, and in the context of 1960s and 1970s feminist media studies, Morrison's focus on issues of female representations and spectatorship in *The Bluest Eye* reflects a larger trend in feminist scholarship.[6] However, while this early work tended to overlook the impact of race on the visual construction of women or women's engagement with images,[7] Morrison foregrounded the way that visual relations are inflected by gender, race, and class. Issues of race would not emerge as a focal point in feminist scholarship until the mid-1980s when feminist scholars such as Mary Helen Washington, Hazel Carby, Judith Mayne, Teresa de Lauretis, Jacqueline Bobo, bell hooks, and Jane Gaines began to insist on the importance of race in differentiating women's experiences, in general as well as in relation to the gaze. These critics emphasized that because black women often "experience oppression first in relation to race rather than gender," they can at times more easily identify with black men than with white women and that black women often experience race, class, and gender oppression as an "interlocking" system (Gaines 16). Morrison's depiction of black female spectatorship in *The Bluest Eye* anticipates this later work and has even been cited by scholars as influencing the development of theories of black female spectatorship. Most famously, bell hooks references *The Bluest Eye* in *Black Looks* when she describes Pecola's mother, Pauline Breedlove's "education in the movies" (Morrison, *The Bluest Eye* 122), as illustrating the need for critical responses to media (hooks, *Black Looks* 121).

Morrison also does not limit her critique to specific images of women but rather situates these images in the operation of visuality more generally. While examinations of women's images tend to focus on changing the way women interact with specific images or types of images without necessarily changing the larger contexts in which images circulate (Thornham 52), Morrison's focus on the contexts of visuality aligns her project with the more recent interdisciplinary work by those in critical visuality studies who seek to change the way events and history are visualized broadly.[8]

Thus Morrison's consideration of visuality in *The Bluest Eye* surpassed most other 1960s- and 1970s-era critical considerations of women and images by situating images in larger contexts of visuality and also by foregrounding the effects that race and social class, in addition to gender, have on visual relations. Thus though *The Bluest Eye* emerged out of the critical contexts provided by the Black Arts Movement and feminist media studies, Morrison combined these contexts in unique and groundbreaking ways. And the fact that scholarship has largely come to share Morrison's concerns with visuality underscores the ongoing significance and relevance of this text to contemporary studies of visual relations. In fact, I would argue that the novel's expansive critique of visuality is only now becoming clear as critical visuality studies evolves to recognize and discuss how the operation of visuality exceeds the work of images as well.

Visualizing History

Morrison herself drew attention to the significance of visual issues in *The Bluest Eye* via the title she gave the novel[9] and in the afterword she added in 1993 when she writes that she wanted the novel to "peck away at the gaze that condemns" blackness as ugly (210). However, while Morrison invokes the language of the gaze in this description,[10] she actually seems to refer less to a specific optical process than, more generally, to "a contest as to who is capable of visualizing events, whether in and as the History proposed by the state, or as alternative subaltern or decolonial readings" (Mirzoeff, "Introduction" xxx). In other words, at stake in *The Bluest Eye* is not only how black female spectators interact with images but also, in a larger sense, how visuality itself naturalizes power relationships and, along with this, whether or not it is possible to identify a different way of visualizing and a different position from which to look that is not predetermined by the existing power structure.

Indeed *The Bluest Eye* stages a contest between the official visualization of American history and cultural citizenship—as this is represented in educational and popular culture narratives—and the underrepresented, often unrecognized, history of racial and gender oppression in America. Morrison captures the official, formal vision of America in several ways, including through depictions of passages from the Dick-and-Jane reader that begin each chapter, Hollywood images that attract Pecola and Pauline, and the "sugar-brown" girls who assimilate into middle-class domesticity. Together, these cultural manifestations represent the white norm of 1940s cultural citizenship that the novel engages and critiques. This norm is marked by the negation of blackness as well as nostalgia for an imagined American past. Lauren Berlant has discussed how complete participation in American public life has always required the "abstract citizenship" associated with an "unmarked" white male body, and she refers to the body's visible qualities, the parts that resist abstraction, such as a black body, "surplus corporeality" ("National Brands" 112–14). Consequently, black individuals are constituted only a position of absence, and abstract citizenship requires the negation of blackness in order to be recognized as a full member of society. The official version of 1940s cultural citizenship is also characterized by nostalgia for an imagined past. Henry Giroux finds evidence of such nostalgia in 1970s Hollywood, explaining that films such as *The Last Picture Show* and *American Graffiti* "resurrected white, suburban, middle-class youth in the nostalgic image of Andy Hardy and Frankie Avalon" (35, 42). In this mythically innocent past, as Debra Werrlein explains, "Domestic unrest evaporates while post-war prosperity thrives, despite such tragic realities as the lynching of fourteen-year-old Emmett Till in 1955" (55). Interestingly, in *The Bluest Eye*, Morrison considers how narratives of childhood are particularly effective at disseminating both the ideal of abstract citizenship and nostalgia (represented in the Dick-and-Jane primers, the celebrity cult of Shirley Temple, and candy wrappers bearing the image of blond Mary Jane). In the educational and popular culture narratives of childhood to which Morrison alludes, white middle-class children and their families are depicted as the norm and invoke nostalgia for an innocent American childhood, which symbolizes, as Werrlein contends, "an ideology of *national* innocence" on racial matters (54). In *Playing in the Dark*, Morrison would ask even more insistently, "What are Americans always so insistently innocent of?," and she writes that the answer is a subordinated "Africanist population" that serves as a convenient scapegoat onto which the "new white male" can project all his fears (45). In *The Bluest Eye*, she demonstrates that narratives of childhood and American innocence serve to occlude the history of racial oppression that the nation is unwilling to look at or acknowledge. In contrast, the narratives of black girlhood that Morrison places at the center of the novel depict a strikingly different vision of postwar American culture and represent Morrison's attempt to bear witness to the plight of the African American community during this period. The novel is, as Morrison has said, "a terrible story about things one would rather not know anything about" ("Unspeakable" 208).

To draw attention to the discrepancy between official American history and the underrepresented history of African Americans in World War II America, Morrison situates Pecola and Claudia at the start of the mythical postwar period. Beginning in 1940, the novel takes place during a time when Americans had supposedly begun to look beyond the domestic worries of the Depression to define America's role in a growing international conflict (Rogin, *Ronald Reagan* 237; Werrlein 195). Michael Rogin explains that although domestic concerns about ethnicity and class had dominated American politics from 1870 to the New Deal, World War II "provided the occasion for the emergence of the national-security apparatus" (*Ronald

Reagan 246). In contrast, though Morrison's novel is set just prior to the beginning of World War II, the war is largely absent from the novel. Instead Morrison focuses on local concerns and subordinates national and international affairs. In Lorain, Ohio, Morrison's own midwestern hometown, characters are most concerned with caring for children, and the difficulties of this task in light of poverty and the lingering deprivation of the Depression displace questions about America's possible involvement in the war. Furthermore, as Werrlein points out, "while 1940 marks the eve of both war and economic recovery in American history books, it also marks the year Richard Wright's *Native Son* kicked off an angry protest movement against racism" (55). Morrison captures this underrepresented aspect of American history in *The Bluest Eye*. As Werrlein explains, "when 1970s America had already begun to assemble nostalgic myths about suburban life during and after World War II, Morrison offers a sharply different version of 1940s family and community, one that suggests that familial 'pathologies' do not simply spring from individual shortcomings" (56). Instead, as Gurleen Grewal explains, the Breedloves emerge from a history of "a race-based class structure of American society that generates its own pathologies" (118). Morrison's challenge in *The Bluest Eye* is to make visible this race-based class structure and the way that it has come to seem so natural that critique is difficult..

Classification, Separation, and Aesthetics

To do this, Morrison dissects the way that visuality is used as a means of authoritarian control, demonstrating that the black community of Lorain is subject to intense visualization from social and political institutions that define individuals narrowly and foreclose, for many, the possibility of even imagining any other social arrangement. For example, educational and social-scientific narratives that subordinate and demean blackness are institutionalized in Lorain in ways that make it difficult for characters to recognize the ideology underpinning the social arrangement, let alone imagine a different arrangement. Morrison alludes to these narratives particularly through her use of the Dick-and-Jane primers, and Morrison's critics have commented on how her references to the primers illustrate the ideological power of visualizing white middle-class family life as the norm. Andrea O'Reilly argues that the books instruct pupils in the ideology of the family (87), while Grewal describes how primers prime, or make ready, and Morrison shows how they prime black subjects (125). According to Werrlein, "by associating white suburban families with prosperity, morality, and patriotism, Americans painted black urban working-class families as un-American" (125). Moreover, in 1965 the Moynihan Report formally labeled the black family "pathological" and in doing so "outwardly dissociated black families and especially black women, from the national ideal" (Werrlein 125).[11]

Certainly, the narrative of white family life presented in the primers contrasts starkly with the stories of racial and sexual oppression and violence narrated in *The Bluest Eye*, a contrast that Morrison draws attention to in order to demonstrate the artificiality of the primer narratives and render them incoherent. As the novel progresses, Morrison "dissects the stories" by compressing words and sentences and by "separating their standardized elements into isolate and unintelligible phrases such as 'SEEFATHERHEISBIGANDSTRONG' and 'SEEMOTHERISVERYNICE' . . . In addition, she complements form with context, filling the 'SEEFATHER' and 'SEEMOTHER' chapters with complex histories" (Werrlein 60). As an example, the SEEFATHER section details Cholly's abandonment by his mother, rejection by his father, emasculation at the hands of white hunters who witness and mock his first sexual experience, and descent into alcoholism and domestic abuse (132–60). Morrison revises the primer by dramatically inserting the Breedloves' stories into it. The fact that the primer becomes illegible in the context of these stories, just as it has become illegible due to Morrison's revisions of its form, illustrates that the idealization of family life and childhood in the primers is inadequate in the context of historical facts and effects of conquest, slavery, immigration, and exclusion. However, her use of the primer also serves to illustrate the social and political power of visualizing. Despite the fact that Morrison's characters, the Breedloves in particular, are completely excluded from the family ideal depicted in the primers, they experience intense pressure to strive for this ideal, and, as J. Brooks Bouson points out, they feel intense personal shame that they cannot achieve it (24).

Morrison makes clear that this "failure" is due not to individual shortcomings but to the systematic exclusion of African Americans by considering the way that specific components of visuality operate and work together to enforce authoritarian control. Nicholas Mirzoeff explains that there are three major components of visuality: classification (creating distinctions such as black and white that are then enforced), separation (physically distancing those so classified), and aesthetics (making the classification and separation seem pleasing and beautiful) ("Introduction" xxxi). According to Mirzoeff, all three components work together, and when they are effective, individuals will not even recognize the operation of visuality. All three components are evident in *The Bluest Eye* and work together powerfully to subordinate the black community.

Classification

Individuals in the novel are classified on the basis of race, gender, and economics, and the borders between these classes are rigidly policed. Significantly, in *The Bluest Eye*, the policing is carried out almost exclusively by members of the community, and community members have actually furthered classified individuals on the basis of skin tone so that those with lighter skin have a higher social status than those with darker skin. For example, Geraldine, one of the "sugar-brown" girls that Morrison describes very critically in the novel, is shown policing boundaries of race, gender, and class when she restricts her son Junior from playing with darker-skinned black boys, because "the line between colored and nigger was not always clear; subtle and telltale signs threatened to erode it, and the watch had to be constant" (87). Junior also recognizes the visual markers of blackness, though he intensely desires them:

> Junior used to long to play with the black boys. More than anything in the world he wanted to play King of the Mountain and have them push him down the mound of dirt and roll over him. He wanted to feel their hardness pressing on him, smell their wild blackness, and say "Fuck you" with that lovely casualness. He wanted to sit with them on curbstones and compare the sharpness of jackknives, the distance and arcs of spitting. In the toilet he wanted to share with them the laurels of being able to pee far and long. (87)

The fact that Junior's desire is articulated in sensual and sexual terms emphasizes the ways that race, class, and gender are interconnected in *The Bluest Eye*. Junior's desire to be physically dominated by darker-skinned, lower-class boys threatens his mother's strict social hierarchy and the binary oppositions of white and black, rich and poor, and male and female on which it is based, requiring her to constantly monitor his activities in order to maintain these distinctions.

Separation

This classification scheme is reinforced by the physical and psychic separations that serve to distance community members from one another as well. Though Lorain is at least a partially integrated community,[12] it is still subject to physical separation based largely on economics, and Morrison attends to the spatial relationships in the town, so that the Breedloves occupy a storefront downtown, in contrast to the MacTeers whose rental home is in an integrated neighborhood, in contrast to the rich white family for whom Mrs. Breedlove works and who live in a lakefront home adjacent to a beautiful, segregated park reserved for whites. These divisions are reflected in the school as well, as Morrison highlights the "politics of the playground" by which even the children in the integrated school practice physical separation along the lines of gender, race, and economics.[13]

The community is also characterized by psychic separation, as members of different classes fail to recognize the essential humanity of members of other classes. This is evident, for instance, when Pecola purchases candy from a white shopkeeper who looks at her with "the total absence of human recognition" that is at once disturbing to Pecola and yet familiar because it "lurk[s] in the eyes of all white people" (48–49). But this psychic separation is not limited only to members of higher classes who look down on those subordinate to them. For example, Claudia and her white neighbor Rosemary completely fail to identify with one another as fellow human beings. Thus Rosemary frequently spies on Claudia and her sister Frieda while they are playing and interprets everything the girls do as "playing nasty" (30), while for her part, Claudia harbors a desire to physically harm Rosemary and all the "little white girls" with whom she interacts (22). Though Rosemary and Claudia live in close proximity to one another, racial prejudice serves to keep them separate from one another as effectively as physical distance would. Similarly, there is a psychic separation between male and female characters. That male characters like Soaphead Church, Mr. Henry, and Cholly Breedlove fail to recognize young black girls as fully human is evident in their sexual objectification of and assault on them, while many of the adult women, though as different from one another as the whores and the God-fearing Pauline, are joined together in a mutual hatred of men (42, 56).

Aesthetics

The willingness of individuals in Lorain to police the divisions between white and black, male and female, rich and poor, and light skin and dark skin indicates that many people in the community have come to see these divisions as natural and right. Morrison suggests that this high degree of acceptance is due in large part to the work of aesthetics in making the classification and separation seem pleasing and even beautiful. And though visuality is "not necessarily or simply a regime of images" (Mirzoeff, "Introduction" xxxiii), in *The Bluest Eye*, mass media images are one of the most obvious ways that sexist and racist ideologies are naturalized and infused in the community. In fact, Morrison's examination of how mass media aestheticizes sexist and racist ideologies is so compelling that this aspect of visuality has received by far the most attention in critical discussions of *The Bluest Eye*.[14]

Morrison's focus on mass media reflects changing conditions of visuality in the United States during the World War II era. The novel registers the growing pervasiveness of media in American culture and everyday life, and Morrison highlights how as characters consume media, they are pulled into the capitalist public sphere. Morrison depicts the capitalist presence in American everyday life by referring, quite specifically, to advertising campaigns, films, and celebrities of the era. But the status of advertising and films in *The Bluest Eye* isn't simply referential or commercial; as Berlant has observed, "By the turn of the century, product consciousness had become so crucial a part of the national history and popular self-identity that the public's relation to business took on patriotic value" ("National Brands" 117).

However, the capitalist public sphere is also racially inflected and does not offer every individual the same level of participation. For example, it constitutes only positions of absence for black individuals and requires the negation of blackness in order to be recognized as a full member of society (Berlant, "National Brands" 112–14). The media Morrison references in *The Bluest Eye* communicate, in subtle and not-so-subtle ways, the message that white skin is better than dark skin and European descent is better than African descent. While the Hollywood films referenced in the novel overtly posit white actors and actresses as desirable, consumer products bearing images that idealize whiteness are also ubiquitous throughout *The Bluest Eye* and greatly shape the desires of individuals. Images aestheticize this system of values, equating beauty with a specific race as well as a set of social and familial practices (including cleanliness, order, property ownership, and sexual restraint, among others). This aesthetic does not entirely exclude blacks but rather includes them in subordinate, demeaning positions. Thus Peola from *Imitation of Life* and Mr. Bojangles, celebrity figures that Morrison references in the novel, also function to instruct viewers in the proper place of blacks in American culture. This position, in its supporting role to white characters, is alternately tragic or comic.

Largely as a result of their constant exposure to visual images, characters in *The Bluest Eye* have learned to value whiteness, and Morrison's light-skinned black characters generally choose to reject blackness in order to participate as fully as possible in a range of social and consumer relations, while her darker-skinned characters, such as Pecola, cannot shed their surplus corporeality and therefore remain, paradoxically, hypervisible as black and invisible as abstract citizen consumers. What is more, the community has internalized the message of inferiority communicated via visual images. Within the community, this takes the form of intraracism based on skin tone—individuals with light skin are more highly valued than those with dark skin. As a result, the light-skinned Maureen Peal receives quite different treatment from the community than the dark-skinned Pecola Breedlove. Maureen is a "high-yellow dream child with long brown hair braided into two lynch ropes that hung down her back." She is "swaddled in comfort and care" and enchants "the entire school," teachers and white and black children alike (62). In contrast, the dark-skinned Pecola is considered ugly even by her own mother, who bestows all the love she has on her white employers' "corn-yellow" haired daughter (108), and Pecola is subject to abuse by her entire community, including her black classmates, who frame their taunts in racial language, referring to her as a "Black and ugly black e mo" (73).

Images of Femininity

In Lorain, the three components of visuality work together powerfully to naturalize the division within and subordination of the black community, and Morrison details how this makes it difficult for members of the community to recognize the social and political work being performed by visuality. To further document the social power of visualization, she attends closely to the ways her characters, particularly her black female characters, construct their identities in relation to the mass media images they consume. In this way, she considers why black women accept and even choose to identify with images that explicitly exclude them.

Anne Cronin's account of how advertising images work to constitute subjects is helpful in explaining how Morrison's female characters engage mass media. Cronin argues that advertising does not operate by producing a group of images that women draw from in constructing and expressing their sense of self. Instead her work suggests that women are produced performatively as subjects in the moment of engaging images (134–35). Sue Thornham explains that in light of Cronin's work, it seems that "the act of viewing/interpreting these visual signs . . . produces not only knowledge and pleasure, but also the sense of ourselves as knowing and desiring subjects. The advertisements in turn, through their textual strategies, authorize certain forms of understanding and pleasure, certain modes of subjecthood" (48).

Yet Cronin also acknowledges that the ads may offer more complex viewing positions than they initially appear to as well. She suggests that "for certain groups of women it enables a 'trying on' of different femininities and of different models of performing/interpreting which access self-consciousness and reflexivity in a way which runs counter to the notion of 'literal' advertisements as unflexive" (129). However, for less-privileged women, such as the ones at the center of *The Bluest Eye*, these iconic images of female beauty may simply represent an "impossible position" (Thornham 49). As Beverley Skeggs's study of working-class women and femininity suggests, for less-privileged women, such "trying on" is "desperately serious," the product of "a desire not to be shamed but to be legitimated" (87). For these women, to "perform" an ironic or "excessive" femininity would be to place them on the side of a devalued, shameful femininity (Skeggs 115). Thornham points out that "femininity may be a matter of commodification and performance, but for women without access to other modes of self-empowerment—other forms of 'cultural capital'—it also confers legitimacy" (49). Indeed images and genres targeted at women sometimes move between these two positions so that the "images they present are offered simultaneously as the stuff of knowing performance and play, and as an ideal to be approximated through the work of self-regulation and self-management" (Thornham 49).

Interestingly, Morrison depicts the identification with images as "desperately serious" for all her female characters, regardless of their differing class positions. Because of their racial classification, all of them look to identification with images as way to achieve legitimacy rather than a way to play with identity. But nowhere is this clearer than in Morrison's discussion of Pauline and Pecola, whose consumption of mass media she details in the novel. Pauline turns to films in order to escape the harsh realities of her life, and in order to enjoy the films, she imagines herself, in hooks's words, "turned into the white woman portrayed on the screen" (*Black Looks* 121). The influence of this fantasy on her consciousness is evident when she attempts to style her hair like Jean Harlow's. Pauline explains, "I fixed my hair up like I'd seen hers on a magazine . . . It looked just like her. Well, almost just like. Anyway, I sat in that show with my hair done up that way and had a good time" (123). However, Pauline's attempt to legitimize herself via identification with Jean Harlow turns into shame when her front tooth falls out in a piece of candy; she explains, "Look like I just didn't care no more after that. I let my hair go back, plaited it up, and settled down to just being ugly" (123). While the films offer Pauline a temporary way to escape from reality, identifying with them is ultimately a trap, leading her to accept the message that she is ugly.

Pecola's identification with the dominant aesthetic is even more complete than her mother's, and, in her, Morrison demonstrates the full implications of attempting to legitimize oneself via mass media images. Pecola wishes for blue eyes throughout the novel because she realizes that white girls with blue eyes and blond hair are much more highly valued than are dark-skinned black girls. While Pauline consciously chooses to perform the femininity she associates with Hollywood starlets, Pecola desires to actually remake herself from the inside out. She believes that looking at the world through a set of blue eyes will change the way the world appears to her even as it makes her more attractive to others. To this end, she literally seeks to consume the images she identifies with. Early in the novel, her fascination with Shirley Temple leads her to drink excessive amounts of milk out of a Shirley Temple mug simply "to handle and see sweet Shirley's face" (23). Later, Pecola buys Mary Jane candies as a sign of her identification with the image of Mary Jane that appears on the wrapper: "Each yellow wrapper has a picture on it. A picture of little Mary Jane, for whom the candy is named. Smiling white face. Blond hair in gentle disarray, blue eyes looking at her out of a world of clean comfort... To eat the candy is somehow to eat the eyes, eat Mary Jane. Love Mary Jane. Be Mary Jane" (52). While Pecola takes pleasure from consuming these images,[15] they do not lead to the inner or outer transformation she desires. To escape from the abuses she experiences at the hands of her family and community, Pecola finally retreats completely into the fantasy of herself with blue eyes, and her fantasy becomes more real than the experiences of her life. The conclusion of *The Bluest Eye* finds Pecola cut off from reality, discussing her blue eyes with an imaginary friend. Pecola's identity is essentially negated in the conclusion of the novel—her complete identification with the dominant aesthetic requires that reality be unable to intrude on her fantasy of herself transformed into the desirable blue-eyed child. Even in this fantasy world, however, Pecola worries incessantly that her eyes are not blue enough and seeks constant reassurance from her imaginary friend that her eyes are, in fact, the bluest eyes.

Both Pauline and Pecola seek legitimacy via identification with mass media images of femininity, and both choose to "try on" a version of femininity that seems to offer them an alternative to identifying with the shameful femininity to which they have been assigned on the basis of race and class. However, Pecola and Pauline have limited agency, and beyond identifying with these images of femininity, they have few ways to alter their social positioning. As such, their identification with white femininity is a trap; instead of leading them to recognize that all forms of femininity are a performance over which they have a degree of control, this identification leads them to accept that white femininity is more desirable and to despise their own blackness.

Pauline and Pecola are not the only female characters whose viewing of media images is described in *The Bluest Eye*. Morrison also narrates Claudia's perspective on media images and consumption of consumer products, which differs markedly from Pecola and Pauline's. In fact, as a child, Claudia consciously chooses to define herself in opposition to the dominant aesthetic. This is evident when Claudia and her sister Frieda seek to identify flaws with Maureen Peal and privately nickname her "six-finger-dog-tooth-meringue pie" (63) in order to gain a small "triumph" over her. Claudia similarly rejects Shirley Temple, stating her preference for the brunette actress Jane Withers (19). Most significantly, as Inger-Anne Softing notes, "Claudia is the only character in this novel who consciously makes an attempt at deconstructing the ideology of the dominant society" (90) evident in her destruction of the white baby dolls that are given to black girls as "the special, the loving gift" at Christmas (Morrison, *The Bluest Eye* 20). Claudia destroys the white baby dolls she receives as gifts not out of hatred but in order to "see of what it was made, to discover the dearness, to find the beauty, the desirability that had escaped me, but apparently only me" (23).

The fact that Claudia and Pecola are such obviously different viewing subjects has often led critics to regard the characters in dichotomous terms. The same is true for the MacTeer and Breedlove families more generally as well, which are also often posited as opposites of one another. For example, Crystal Lucky refers to the Breedloves as models of "failure" and "tragedy" (26) and to the MacTeers as models of "success" (21) and "victory" (26).[16] While it is clear that Morrison develops a contrast between Claudia and Pecola, I do not think the characters are truly dichotomous, particularly because the opposition between Pecola and Claudia often sets up a number of other oppositions—between white culture (Hollywood images) and black culture (the blues) and between the visual and the aural. And accepting these oppositions (e.g., to conclude that Morrison recommends aurality over visuality and offers it as a more authentic site for black subjectivity and social critique), risks oversimplifying Morrison's complex critique of visuality in the novel and also the implications of her critical strategies for resisting visuality.

Morrison depicts visuality as a complex web that involves classification and separation as well as aesthetics. And this has important implications for the possibilities of resisting visuality. Within the traditional focus on images, the solution to the problem of black female spectatorship becomes interacting with images differently, for example, by substituting positive images of black women for negative ones.[17] Within the expanded view of visuality that Morrison depicts, the solution becomes visualizing events and history differently.

Resisting Visuality

Mirzoeff stresses that visuality is susceptible to resistance. Specifically, he explains that when visualized authority becomes visible itself this represents a crisis in its authority, which is most successful when it masquerades as natural ("Introduction" xxxi). He suggests, then, that individuals and groups can precipitate a crisis in visualized authority by demanding the right to be seen, the right to look, and the right to be seen looking, particularly if they document their looking ("Introduction" xxxiii). I argue that Morrison employs exactly this strategy in *The Bluest Eye* and that examining the text in this way helps to undo the false opposition of Pecola as failed subject and Claudia as successful subject.

In fact, Morrison's demand to be seen crystallizes around Pecola. In Morrison's account, visualizing American history differently means visualizing black girlhood, and this adjusted focus provides a radically different view of postwar American life. By making Pecola the protagonist of her novel, Morrison insists on the right for the most vulnerable and damaged member of society to be seen, and she subsequently places Pecola's narrative front and center. Along with this, she demands that readers see "difficult" subjects such as female menstruation and sexual abuse. Certainly, the focus on Pecola and the realities of girlhood do make the novel difficult for some readers to identify with and perhaps even understand. For example, Toni Cade Bambara has described how her students have difficulty dealing with the novel. Among other things, they fail to appreciate the traumatic aspects of Pecola's first period because this is so rarely discussed in American culture. Bambara observes, "The initiation or rites of passage of the young girl is not one of the darlings of American literature. The coming of age for the young boy is certainly much more the classic case. I wonder if it all means that we don't put a value on our process of womanhood" (247). However, by placing these issues at the center of the novel, Morrison insists on the right for these subjects, central to female lives, to be seen and on her own right to look at these difficult issues.

When asked why she wrote *The Bluest Eye*, Morrison responded, "I was interested in reading a kind of book that I had never read before. I didn't know if such a book existed, but I just never read it in 1964 when I started writing *The Bluest Eye*" ("Complexity" 252). Nancy Larrick's study of 5,206 children's books published between 1962 and 1964 confirms Morrison's sense that books about black childhood were largely missing at that time. Only 349 of the books Larrick examined included even one black child either in the illustrations or in the text. Of the 6.7 percent that do show a black child, all but a small fraction are "set outside the United States or before World War II. Quite clearly, the books used in American schools were primarily by and about white, Anglo-Saxon, middle-class people" (84–85).

In the context of this absence of literature focused on black girls, though Pecola's "failure" is still painful to read about, it is nevertheless a success inasmuch as Morrison forces the reader to really see Pecola as a human subject, terribly abused, by placing her story at the novel's narrative center. Moreover, Michael Awkward and John N. Duvall have also argued that Morrison explicitly confronts Ralph Ellison's inadequate representation of incest in *Invisible Man* (1952) via her depiction of Pecola as well. This is most obvious in her "bringing to the foreground the effects of incest for female victims in direct response to [Ralph] Ellison's refusal to consider them seriously [in *Invisible Man*]" (Awkward 66). Indeed the parallels between Morrison's Breedlove family and Ellison's Trueblood episode in *Invisible Man* highlight her revisionary work. *Invisible Man*, which also foregrounds the racial dimensions of visibility as its title indicates, includes an episode focused on a sharecropper, named Trueblood, who has impregnated his daughter. Ellison's representation of incest "silences the women and constantly makes the father-daughter incest a voyeuristic site for the male gaze" (Duvall 33) as a variety of men, from black school administrators who want to remove Trueblood from the community to Trueblood's white protectors, "wanted to hear about the gal lots of times" (52). Trueblood's daughter, Mattie Lou, has been described by the novelist as of "no compelling significance" in this narrative and is subsequently rendered silent and largely invisible (qtd. in Baker 93). Even more, some critics such as Houston A. Baker have claimed Trueblood as a hero for his resistance to dominant sexual norms. Baker discusses Trueblood as an example of the uncontrollability of phallic energy and holds up Mattie Lou as one of the "bearers of new black life" (185). This interpretation, like Ellison's depiction of Mattie Lou, minimizes her experience as an incest victim, sacrificing her to the larger consideration of the power of black male sexuality. In *The Bluest Eye*, Morrison emphasizes the perspective of the incest victim by placing Pecola's story of abuse by her father Cholly at the center of the novel and suggesting that Pecola's inability to narrate her story for herself—the silence that seemed to make Ellison's incest victim less compelling for him—is a direct result of the trauma she has experienced.

In this way, Morrison demands the right for Pecola, and for all black girls, to be seen, a crucial part of resisting the way history and reality are visualized by dominant authority structures. But Mirzoeff also stresses that to resist visuality successfully one must not attempt to look from within the visual system already in place. Instead, resisting visuality requires one to identify a space outside the authority structure from which to look and to use strategies to capture the moment of looking. While he contends that often images are used to capture the moment, in *The Bluest Eye*, Morrison uses literature to achieve this effect. Though of course, as a fictional, print-based text, there are no real looks and gaze exchanges to be traced in *The Bluest Eye*; a close reading of how Morrison's narrator Claudia negotiates the scopic regime that both depends on and facilitates gazes yields important insights into possible modes of resistance. In this way, *The Bluest Eye* is, above all else, a fervent demand that readers see Morrison—and Claudia—looking and in fact documents that looking to hold the moment in place.[18]

As an unauthorized position from which to look, Morrison turned to the blues, and *The Bluest Eye* represents the literary equivalent of a piece of blues music, a connection Morrison builds on with the title as well. Claudia learns to sing the blues from her mother, who responds to the hardship of her life with singing Saturdays. According to Claudia, "she would sing about hard times, bad times, and somebody-done-gone-and-left-me times. But her voice was so sweet and her singing-eyes so melty I found myself longing for those hard times . . . Misery colored by the greens and blues in my mother's voice took all of the grief out of the words and left me with a conviction that pain was not only endurable, it was sweet" (25–26). Cat Moses explains that "the blues wisdom that fills the house on Claudia's mother's singing Saturdays has fostered [Claudia's] recognition [of the destructive reification of caste and whiteness]" (627–28). August Wilson has observed that the blues provide "a way of processing information about Black life, particularly information about the nobility . . . the beauty . . . and the resiliency of Black life" (*August Wilson*). It is not surprising, then, that Claudia turns to the blues to testify to the power of images, especially their impact on Pecola, and give form to the pain she carries with her over Pecola's multiple betrayals. The blues give Claudia a framework for interpreting her childhood experiences and Pecola's story.

Claudia's use of the blues represents her attempt to identify a critical—unauthorized or formalized—space in the novel. However, this space is not imagined to be the opposite of the dominant aesthetic or in any sense "authentic." In the first place, Claudia herself is not a complete opposite to Pecola. Though she emerges as a critical spectator as an adult, she admits to having worshipped Shirley Temple and prizing her white dolls for a time as an adolescent. Claudia describes her embrace of the dominant aesthetic as inevitable in the course of maturation. Claudia learns to hide her desire to dismember her white baby dolls under the cover of "fraudulent love" (23). It is, as Claudia points out, "a small step to Shirley Temple," who she comes to "worship" over time (23). Claudia's family also, though they contrast sharply to Pecola's, shares some of the same values as the Breedloves and submits, to some extent, to the dominant aesthetic. Thus the MacTeers present their daughters with white baby dolls for Christmas as a highly prized gift, laugh when Mr. Henry refers to Claudia and Frieda as Greta Garbo and Betty Grable, and include a Shirley Temple mug among their possessions.

Moreover, Morrison does not advocate rejecting mass media as a viable strategy for resistance. Instead she draws on the irony that the white media that condemn blackness as ugly are derived in large part from the unacknowledged appropriation of black culture. Kimberly Hébert points out that—while images such as Shirley Temple organize Western culture around whiteness, creating "destructive images of African-descended and other black peoples who share the same space of neighborhood and nation" (193)—Shirley Temple's style originates in appropriations of blackness seen in minstrelsy. Thus Temple offers a "white-faced performance of blackness" (Hébert 190, 193), and her popularity in American culture suggests that American whiteness is itself a performance of blackness. Morrison draws attention to this cultural appropriation by allowing Claudia to view "Temple's performance as a trespass into black culture" (Werrlein 66). In expressing her hatred for Temple, Claudia observes, "I hated Shirley. Not because she was cute, but because she danced with Bojangles, who was *my* friend, *my* uncle, *my* daddy, and who ought to have been soft-shoeing it and chucking with me" (19). Given the roots of media in black traditions, neither Morrison nor Claudia is interested in rejecting media images outright since to do so would be to deny, to some extent, the black traditions on which they are based. Rather they want to reclaim the black roots of white media and, in doing so, expose the appropriation of black traditions. Mrs. MacTeer's blues songs and Claudia's blues novel are located on a continuum along with the white media products; in this novel, there are no white media distinct from black culture, just as there is no American history without black Americans. Morrison squarely locates black individuals, communities, and traditions at the center of American culture and history, suggesting that only through a willed and deliberate blindness do white—or black—Americans fail to recognize this.

Morrison's refusal to set up a false dichotomy between the visual and the aural and between white and black culture distinguishes her vision of a politically engaged black aesthetic from other members of the Black Arts movement. While some in the Black Arts movement argued that the black artist needed to disentangle himself "from those who would submit to subjection without struggle [and] deserve to be enslaved" (Fuller 1813), Morrison offers a much more inclusive perspective. All her characters "submit to subjection" to a greater or lesser extent, but rather than suggesting that they "deserve to be enslaved" as a result, she instead implies that resistance can grow out of becoming aware of the ways in which one is subjected. Along with this, she also does not advocate for rejecting parts of black culture and black traditions that have been co-opted by white consumer culture, such as the blues. In 1968, Maulana Karenga had questioned the validity of the blues for the Black Arts movement, writing, "We will not submit to the resignation of our fathers who lost their money, their women, and their lives and sat around wondering 'what did they do to be so black and blue'" (64). In contrast, Morrison argues for reclaiming black cultural traditions and using these as a way to demonstrate the central "presence" of black Americans in the public sphere.

Furthermore, Morrison implies that the power and hegemony of consumer culture might negate any attempt to build an authentic black aesthetic. She does offer a glimpse of authenticity in the novel but only to demonstrate the difficulty of building a usable aesthetic out of it. In *The Bluest Eye*, Morrison equates authentic black culture with "funkiness," and, indeed funkiness, as Morrison characterizes it, stands in stark contrast to the sanitized Hollywood aesthetic. She describes funkiness by voicing the fears of those black characters who are most closely associated with white culture and intraracism. The "sugar-brown" girls who seek respectability and chase the values of white culture are motivated out of a fear of "the dreadful funkiness of passion, the funkiness of nature, the funkiness of the wide range of human emotions" (83). In other words, funkiness is associated with the authenticity often attributed to nature, sexuality, and emotion, and it should not be surprising that those spheres are most policed and restricted in the inauthentic community of Lorain. The "sugar-brown" girls, for their part, are described as sexually frigid and emotionally vacant, and they cultivate domesticity marked by the display of consumer goods and an outward of appearance of order and respectability. Interestingly, funkiness resists both visual and textual representation in *The Bluest Eye*. Not only do the white media Morrison describes largely exclude funkiness, but Morrison herself refers to it minimally in the novel—as it is "negated" by the "sugar-brown" girls. In this way, Morrison signals that funkiness resists being controlled; it is so excessive that neither text nor image can capture or hold it. The oral tradition, which seems to retain a stronger tie to funkiness, is also subject to co-optation by consumer culture, suggesting that funkiness cannot be fully represented aurally either or it risks losing its critical potential.

Consequently, funkiness resides on the margins of American culture in *The Bluest Eye*, and the novel implies that because racism has infiltrated every level of American society, there is no viable site for an authentic black aesthetic. Indeed nature itself is a compromised space in this novel; the ostensible reason Claudia narrates the story is to consider why the ground was hostile to the marigolds she and her sister planted during the summer of 1941. This is signaled particularly clearly in Morrison's depiction of the man-hating whores, who do have a more authentic relationship to their bodies than do other characters in the novel yet sell those bodies for money.[19] The whores perfectly symbolize the commodification of black culture and the ways in which American consumer culture renders everything—including the concept of authenticity—a product for exchange.

Morrison's depiction of her characters as compromised and implicated also acknowledges that her readers are likewise implicated and compromised. Her allusions to popular culture in fact require readers to draw on their knowledge of these figures. She does not have to explain who Shirley Temple is because, even decades after the peak of her popularity, Temple lives on as one of the images of childhood femininity to which all women are heir. Nevertheless, confronting visuality in this novel does not require one to locate or inhabit some authentic space free from the infiltration of consumerism, racism, and/or sexism. Rather it requires one to identify his or her own critical position for examining the way authority visualizes itself and capture that act of looking in some tangible way, which Claudia (and Morrison) does via the literary text.

The Bluest Eye's Impact on Literature

Morrison's use of literature to actively engage visuality set an important precedent for subsequent women's writing. Thus despite the differences among them, all the texts included in *Confronting Visuality* embrace the notion that resistance is possible even in the absence of authenticity and despite the fact that consumer culture co-opts efforts at resistance. And like Morrison, writers such as Bobbie Ann Mason, Margaret Atwood, Louise Erdrich, Gish Jen, Chitra Banerjee Divakaruni, and Alison Bechdel also seek to bridge divides between high and low culture in their works and to explore the potential of a variety of mediums to effectively reach contemporary audiences, including through media such as film. To reach an audience, as Claudia's narrative makes clear, a writer must understand that audience, and both the community of Lorain and Morrison's contemporary readers are immersed in mass media. Claudia's narrative, and critique, is possible not because she stands apart from the people in her community but because she shares their culture and understands, from experience, their values and desires. This would become a new model for some contemporary women writers—one in which writers enter the trenches with their readers, considering both the allure of visual images and foregrounding complex and multifaceted readings of these images.

2

Transforming Culture and Consciousness in Bobbie Ann Mason's *In Country*

One of the contemporary writers who followed in Morrison's footsteps was Southern writer Bobbie Ann Mason. However, Mason's path to writing about visuality was markedly different from Morrison's. While Morrison's decision to "peck away at the condemning gaze" grew out of her observations about the ideological work images performed in communicating racism and sexism, Mason was prompted to explore the contemporary impact of popular media because she recognized its growing importance in the lives of the people she wanted to write about, people living, for the most part, in rural western Kentucky. She has explained, "the characters in my world don't have the guidance or perspective to know that there might be this other view of television or malls. They're in that world and they like television fine, thank you. And they love the malls, and I don't judge them for it. When they go to the shopping mall . . . they're looking at deliverance from a hard way of life" ("Bobbie Ann Mason's Border States"). Though Mason does not judge her characters, or readers, for being attracted to popular and consumer culture, she does seek to help them develop a critical perspective with which to evaluate the possibilities presented to them by media and consumerism. Moreover, Mason pioneered new literary techniques in order to explore the shaping effect of electronic media on human perception, techniques that seem, even after nearly thirty years, increasingly relevant given the recent turn to issues of cognition within literary studies.[1] Though Mason is best known for leading the "regional renaissance" in American literature in the 1980s, I suggest her work is equally important and deserving of attention for its contribution to women writers' critical engagement with contemporary media.

Author of five novels, five collections of short fiction, a memoir, two works of literary criticism, and a biography of Elvis Presley, Mason has been recognized as a leader of the "regional renaissance" in American literature in the 1980s. Mervyn Rothstein has described how Mason, "along with other writers—fellow Kentuckian Marsha Norman and the West Virginians Jayne Anne Phillips, the late Breece D'J Pancake and, most recently, Pinckney Benedict ... has mapped out a previously neglected literary territory: the North-South border states" (Mason, "Bobbie Ann Mason's Border States"). Mason is also well known for her distinctive literary style, which is minimalist and includes ubiquitous allusions to popular culture.[2] Mason incorporates media images into her fiction via these allusions, paying special attention to television in her early fiction. Though Mason did not publish her first novel until the age of forty, that novel (*In Country*, published in 1985) is still her most commercially and critically successful work. At the time, *In Country* received considerable attention as the first novel to explore the aftermath of the Vietnam War from a young female perspective and use the controversial Vietnam Veterans Memorial in Washington, DC, as a setting.[3] It was also an early literary depiction of post-traumatic stress disorder on Vietnam veterans, a condition only added to the *Diagnostic and Statistical Manual of Mental Disorders* in 1980.[4]

Moreover, for my purposes, it is significant that *In Country* is particularly focused on exploring the power of electronic media to shape perception, including the ways in which images mediate traumatic experiences for individuals and the culture at large. Like Morrison, Mason stresses in interviews that she wanted *In Country* to affect change in readers, specifically by helping them confront their feelings about Vietnam and providing a means of catharsis. Indeed the idea that fiction has important "cultural, mediatory, critical, and possible mourning functions" (Vickroy, *Trauma* 222) has long led writers to explore issues of trauma in their work and develop literary techniques to represent the experience of trauma.[5] In *In Country*, Mason's innovative use of pop culture allusions to depict how these become "deep metaphors," which shape everything from individual perception to the work of mourning, not only suggests that popular culture can complicate mourning but also illustrates how literature can fill what Mason perceives as a gap in contemporary popular culture.

Popular Culture Transforming the South

Flux defines the region about which Mason writes—she depicts western Kentucky becoming less distinct and connected to tradition due to the encroachment of media and consumer culture. In *In Country*, television and shopping malls are changing the ways in which men and women understand their gendered social roles and the possibilities they imagine for themselves as residents of Kentucky. For example, one of the most important decisions that the protagonist of *In Country*, Samantha (Sam) Hughes, makes is *not* to become pregnant as a teen, a decision that distinguishes her from her own mother as well as her best friend, Dawn, who does become pregnant during the course of the novel. Television reveals to Sam a world outside of Hopewell, Kentucky, a world that Sam aspires to see for herself, and she recognizes in looking at her own mother's life that having a child would limit her future possibilities. Mason has described how the transformation of rural communities has positioned residents of these communities "on the threshold of possibility ... Their lives are being changed, and they're very excited by it. They're getting a chance maybe for the first time in their lives to get somewhere and to prove something and to do something" ("Bobbie Ann Mason's Border States"). Consequently, she explains, "Many of my characters are caught up in the myth of progress; from their point of view it means liberation, the promise of a better life" ("Bobbie Ann Mason's Border States"). In terms of the possibilities newly available to women, Mason underscores the positive effects that exposure to media images can produce in her rural characters' lives, as when Sam decides to pursue college instead of marriage. At the same time, Mason does not uncritically celebrate popular culture in *In Country*, and she problematizes the "myth of progress" that her characters sometimes unthinkingly embrace. The transformations media produce are double-edged; along with expanding opportunities, community traditions have been increasingly replaced by mass media and consumer culture. As Robert Brinkmeyer notes, "Having grown up in an age given to suburbs and shopping malls, Mason's characters ... fail to develop a consciousness rooted in history and irony that would add richness to their vision and would allow them to understand better elemental matters of meaning and existence" (24). In place of a vital community history, characters in *In Country* belong to media culture, and their reliance on media images is problematic in the context of the aftermath of the Vietnam War, which has left the community desperately in need of mechanisms and traditions to facilitate healing.

At the center of *In Country* is Sam Hughes, whose father died in the Vietnam War and who has no direct memories of the war herself but embarks on a quest for information about the war in the novel. Sam lives with her uncle Emmett, a Vietnam veteran who suffers from PTSD and possibly from the effects of Agent Orange. Throughout *In Country*, Sam is caught between the imperative to forget the past and move on with life—symbolized most clearly by her mother Irene, who has remarried, moved to Lexington, and has a new baby—and the inability to get past Vietnam—symbolized in the story by Emmett, who has essentially dropped out of American society, refusing to hold a job or develop romantic relationships in favor of watching television. Sam's responsibility is to negotiate these positions, as well as those represented by her grandparents, who lament the passing of what they consider simpler times, and other members of her own generation, such as her friends Dawn and Lonnie, who fail to understand the relevance of Vietnam to their lives and do not imagine a future beyond Hopewell, Kentucky. In doing so, she is in largely uncharted territory. She does not have the community traditions of the past to guide her actions, and she, like all the characters in the novel, is largely reliant on television for information—about everything from the Vietnam War, to political and social debates of the 1980s, to new consumer products, to changing gender relations, and to the role of the South in contemporary culture.

Mason registers the increasing importance of television to working-class families in the 1980s by describing her characters in the act of watching television and negotiating the meaning of televisual messages. Hopewell, Kentucky, seems to be without a movie theater, but Sam's family does pay for cable television, so she has access to televised films and stations such as MTV and HBO, networks breaking from traditional broadcast channels in significant ways at the time.[6] In *In Country*, Sam's and Emmett's daily lives are largely organized around television. Early in the book, Sam recounts the viewing pattern she, her mother, and Emmett once shared: "On Saturday nights, years ago, we used to watch TV. She'd pop popcorn and her and Emmett and me would watch about three hours of comedy shows, one right after the other. First there was *All in the Family*, then *M*A*S*H*, then Mary Tyler Moore, then Bob Newhart, and after that Carol Burnett was on for an hour. It was incredible" (42). This viewing pattern is so well established that Sam uses it to chronicle changes in her family: "But the shows changed, and then when Lorenzo Jones started coming over a couple of years ago he'd talk when we tried to watch television together. He'd talk during the news too and tell his opinion on world affairs so you couldn't hear the news" (42). Sam registers her dislike for her mother's new husband in terms of his viewing habits and points out that a change in someone's television habits signals a change in that person's values and perspective as well.

By placing television at the center of her novel, Mason illustrates that televisual mediation has come to constitute reality by replacing firsthand experience for growing numbers of Americans. Mason echoes postmodern philosophers, in particular Jean Baudrillard, in this way. According to Baudrillard, the relationship between representation and reality has been reversed as a result of electronic media. Baudrillard explains that electronic media constitute a new media reality—a hyperreality—where the real is subordinate to representation: "Abstraction today is no longer that of the map, the double, the mirror or the concept. Simulation is no longer that of a territory, a referential being or a substance without origin or reality: a hyperreal. The territory no longer precedes the map, nor survives it. Henceforth, it is the map that precedes the territory" (2). Electronic media effectively blur the line between map and territory by allowing for the simulation of ideas as encoded in electronic signals. The result is that in contemporary culture, electronic media increasingly constitute reality for their audiences. *In Country* thematizes Baudrillard's description of the map that precedes the territory since television images, even overtly fictional images, make historical events seem real for Sam and for a majority of Americans. Moreover, in *In Country*, Mason uses literature to explore what it might *feel* like to be immersed in the hyperreal, which not only makes her novel relevant to contemporary readers but also adds an important dimension to postmodern theory by exploring the implications of hyperreality for individuals and American culture, particularly in the larger context of trauma.

Mason's depiction of television also clearly links this medium to the spread of consumer culture and the construction of particular kinds of consumers. Scholars such as E. Ann Kaplan and Lisa Lewis have discussed the importance of television, and especially networks such as MTV, in the 1980s and the ways in which MTV targeted, and in doing so constructed, youth audiences of consumers. Writing in 1989, Noam Chomsky explained that the underlying ideology of *all* mass media is the protection and spread of consumer interests (8).

Mason is particularly concerned with the ways in which television co-opts styles of rebellion and modes of resistance and then, ironically, "sells" these to youth audiences who desire to resist mainstream consumer culture. For example, Lewis points out how MTV provided a forum for the emergence of "female adolescence discourse" in the 1980s, one that not only "provided a vehicle for girls to speak about their experiences" but also "expanded the consideration of gender inequality to include adolescence" (224). This message is one that Sam receives clearly in *In Country* as she expresses dissatisfaction with the status quo of gender relations throughout the novel and seeks to identify herself as a "rebel." Yet Sam's attempts to rebel against her culture demonstrate the extent to which media in the service of consumer culture have constructed her vision of the world for her. Sam turns to the counterculture of the 1960s and early 1970s to channel the rebellion that she feels against the norms within which she lives. However, because Sam's access to pop music and the 1960s counterculture in general is primarily through music television, she does not and cannot encounter it the same way that original audiences did. A description of Sam's experience watching MTV highlights the way that the medium shapes the message Sam receives from potentially subversive music:

> Sam sat around all weekend watching MTV. *99 Lutfballons* kept dancing in her head—all those H-bombs going off. *Legs* by ZZ Top. *Panama* by Van Halen. *Flesh for Fantasy* by Billy Idol. So many videos were full of disasters, with everything flying apart, shifting, changing in the blink of an eye. The random images on the screen were swirling, beyond anyone's control; everything was falling, like their fragile house, but Bruce was still dancing in all that darkness, and the heart of rock-and-roll was still beating, in that song by Huey Lewis and the News. Joan Jett, in her shining black leather, was screaming with her band, the Blackhearts. (229–30)

Sam detects an underlying pattern of violence and chaos running through the videos, but this pattern is strangely countered by the fact that MTV exists to play the random images despite the threat of breakdown. In spite of the potentially subversive message of musicians like Bruce Springsteen and Joan Jett, their co-optation by MTV ensures that the message is at best confused and at worst obscured to the point of irrelevance. Although Sam receives part of the message of this music, enough to question traditional gender roles since "everything [is] flying apart, shifting, changing in the blink of an eye," this message is inherently countered and subsumed by the medium so that on MTV "Bruce was *still* dancing in all that darkness, and the heart of rock-and-roll was *still* beating" (230; emphasis added). MTV acts to counter the subversive message, suggesting that, in contrast to the songs, things are under control, the music is still being played, and it is safe to consume.

Consequently, the media Sam consumes, particularly MTV, continually point her toward consumer choices packaged as "rebellious." Because she and her friend Dawn "feel mad at the world," they imagine starring in a rock video wearing "black leather pants and sunglasses with bright pink rims" looking "tough" (104); at Kmart, Sam buys a cat bank that is "kooky and personal, very expressive" (132); "on a wild impulse" at Kroger, she buys "strange food from the gourmet section—cocktail hot dogs, smoked baby oysters, odd-shaped crackers, even a can of smoked octopus" (137); and on her way to Washington, DC, she orders fried clams for dinner "because they are special" (12) and clashing flavors of ice cream—"they seem like a deadly combination, but she feels daring" (14). While some critics argue that Sam's consumer choices demonstrate her "tactical consumer abilities" (doCarmo 594), I suggest that Mason undercuts the reading of Sam's purchases as truly revolutionary actions by narrating Sam's continual desire to consume. Perhaps her most important purchase in the novel is a rebuilt Volkswagen, which she believes will offer her freedom and does facilitate her trip to Washington—but also breaks down on the road and requires expensive repairs, facilitating Sam's use of her mother's credit card. Mason seems suspicious of rebellion that depends on purchasing for expression. While it gives the illusion of action, consumption really only channels one's energy and desire into making choices that ultimately reinforce the power of the status quo and consumer culture.

Thus Mason situates Sam's quest for the truth about Vietnam in an environment in which media images increasingly constitute reality for the public and in which formerly effective countercultural movements have been co-opted by consumer culture. In this way, Mason demonstrates the need for new and uniquely contemporary modes of resistance to mass media. She considers whether viewers like Sam, who have little firsthand experience of the world, can resist mass media, even though they are also reliant on it and have been shaped by it. To do this, she focuses her narrative on Sam, making her perspective the primary narrative point of view. Less central, but still important to illustrate Mason's ideas, are veterans such as Emmett, who do have firsthand experience of the war and the world but whose war trauma prevents them from accessing their knowledge directly and makes them reliant on media as well.

Mediating Vietnam

Mason's decision to focus the novel on Sam, rather than on her uncle Emmett or one of the other Vietnam veterans in the story, distinguishes *In Country* from most others on the subject of Vietnam, firmly situating a young, Southern female in the center of ongoing considerations of Vietnam and mass media.[7] This is also a key difference between the novel and its film adaptation. Although the novel is narrated in the third person, information is limited to Sam's perspective and filtered through her consciousness. The fact that Mason privileges Sam's perspective when she has no direct memories of the war signals Mason's interest in exploring how a historical event passes into the consciousness and memory of generations without firsthand experience of the event, what Marianne Hirsch has termed *postmemory* (22).[8]

In contrast, in the film adaptation of *In Country* released in 1989, director Norman Jewison "largely eliminates Sam's perspective: while much of the story is still hers, it is no longer seen through her eyes" (Lupack 174). Instead the film elevates Emmett's perspective to such an extent that many reviewers of the film expressed confusion as to why Sam receives so much screen time in a film about the veteran experience; reviewer Caryn James's conclusion is typical of these responses: "Mr. Jewison (*Moonstruck* and *A Soldier's Story*) and the scriptwriters, Frank Pierson and Cynthia Cidre, seem so fearful of Emmett and his Vietnam-veteran friends that *In Country* becomes the lopsided story of a young woman's search for her father's memory, a tale that circles back to the war much too late to justify its final emotional pull." Even Mason, who in general has spoken favorably about the film, acknowledges, "I think it may have lost some of the motivation from the story" ("Bobbie Ann Mason: 'I Had to Confront the Subject'" 178). In the film, Emmett's story is as central as Sam's, and, as a result of its focus on Emmett, the film's treatment of memory and historical knowledge is quite different from the novel's. While Sam has no direct memories of her father or the Vietnam War, Emmett does, and, as a result, the film incorporates several flashback scenes representing Emmett's memories. The film takes this a step further as well, including Sam's father as a character and narrating his experiences in Vietnam, including the details of how he was killed. While Sam is never able to discover an account of her father's death in the novel, the film explicitly represents his death. In the novel, Sam must finally content herself with the realization that she "will never know what happened to all these men in the war" (240), but the film makes such knowledge possible, even for those who were not there. As a result of this changed emphasis, Sam's reliance on mass media for information and her continual struggle to find unmediated information about the war drops out of the film.

Yet it is Sam's recognition that the media script of Vietnam to which she has access is inadequate and inauthentic that gives the novel particular relevance to readers, suggesting, as it does, that Vietnam is important for all Americans, regardless of whether or not they have firsthand experience of the war. As Peter Travers put it, the novel "brought the war home to those of us who'd never been there, to those of us who do the forgetting about men like Emmett." Additionally, Sam's quest has relevance beyond only considerations of the Vietnam War. Increasingly, media representations play a crucial role in negotiating historical events for viewers after the fact. And in *In Country*, Sam's identity and vision of the world have been fundamentally shaped by mass media. What Sam knows about the Vietnam War and even what it means to lose a father is the result of information provided largely by television. Thus Sam's father's death is not real to Sam until she witnesses Colonel Blake's death on *M*A*S*H*: "Sam was so shocked she went around stunned for days. She was only a child then, and his death on the program was more real to her than the death of her own father. Even on the repeats, it was unsettling. Each time she saw that episode, it grew clearer that her father had been killed in a war" (25). Similarly, the war is not real to Sam until "one day soon after they got their first color TV set" (51). Seeing a report on the fall of Saigon when she is 8 or 9 years old, Sam is able to identify with the people fleeing from their homes and recognizes that the road along which they walk "resembled the old Hopewell road that twisted through the bottomland toward Paducah. For the first time, Vietnam was an actual place" (51).

However, Sam recognizes that the picture of Vietnam she has received from television is inaccurate. Despite the fact that Sam consumes every media image of Vietnam that is available to her, she still struggles to pin down the smallest details about Vietnam and realizes she has no way to know what Vietnam actually looked like during the war. She recalls, for instance, that "in a made-for-TV movie about the Vietnam War she'd been surprised to see soldiers marching through a field of corn . . . It surprised her that corn grew in Vietnam. She did not know if it was there because Americans had planted it—or had given the Vietnamese the seed and shown them how to plant it—or if in fact corn was ever in Vietnam, since the movie was filmed in Mexico . . . It bothered her that the truth was so hard to envision. Did corn actually grow in Vietnam?" (69–70).[9] While ostensibly giving viewers access to parts of the world they would otherwise never be able to see or experience, television actually obscures, rather than clarifies, important geographical and political differences. Raymond Gozzi points out that "in electronic media, the world is usually described by narrative, or in terms of drama. Drama emphasizes conflict instead of reason. Electronic narrative can often be just one thing after another, with no clear relationships" (24–25). Sam's experience of trying to piece together a coherent narrative about Vietnam from the conflicting media images she has of the place demonstrates the confusion produced as a result of television's efforts to dramatically represent Vietnam.

The situation is even more fraught for Vietnam veterans, who rely on television's mediation as a coping mechanism for their lingering trauma in the war. Few of the veterans in *In Country* can be said to have mastered their wartime experiences. Most of them, like Emmett, exhibit clear signs of post-traumatic stress disorder (PTSD)—including flashbacks, amnesia, headaches, impotence, and difficulty controlling emotions, among others—stemming directly from what they witnessed in Vietnam.[10] However, media images hold the promise of helping individuals master the traumatic event they cannot help but relive and yet despite reliving can never really know. Films and television shows—aired in the form of reruns—continually return to Vietnam, sometimes even rewriting the Vietnam story in an attempt to master the event. Watching *M*A*S*H*, for instance, allows Emmett to remember the pleasant times he spent as a soldier and suggests that the characters' problems, some of which are similar to those experienced by the soldiers in Vietnam, have simple solutions—each episode of the show is neatly tied together during an hour. Emmett uses television's mediation to live with his own painful memories of Vietnam. Other veterans and Vietnam War–era survivors similarly communicate their experiences via the mediation of mass media. In this way, Mason thematizes a central tenant of psychological studies of trauma—as Cathy Caruth has explained, "the most direct *seeing* of a violent event may occur as an absolute inability to *know* it" (91–92; emphasis added).

While media culture gives viewers access to images of the Vietnam War and allows them to repetitively relive the trauma of the war, it does not help them master the war or the losses suffered during it. In fact, Mason suggests that the frequent repetition mirrors the experience of trauma and may actually exacerbate the veterans' attempts to recover from the trauma they experienced. Indeed psychological studies of trauma are based on the observation that traumatized individuals repetitively reenact the traumatic experience in an attempt to "master" it. Sigmund Freud's work with traumatized World War I veterans prompted him to propose that the pleasure principle could operate only after a person's psyche had mastered whatever "excitations" managed to break through the psyche's barrier against stimuli, so therefore the mastery of a traumatic event really was a first condition for the pleasure principle to operate (41). He explained that traumatized individuals repetitively reenact the traumatic event in their unconscious in an effort to understand what caused the trauma in the first place so this experience could be avoided in the future.

This does not mean that the characters intentionally reenact the trauma but that they cannot help but do so. Michael Barry suggests that Mason's characters are actually desperate to avoid acknowledging death and the horrors committed against the Vietnamese, but this avoidance is impossible because "the war has installed itself as the origin and center of the novel's inquiry into history and the self" (147). Consequently, the war draws "all of the symbolic meaning" throughout the novel to itself, and as characters engage and attempt to interpret a variety of natural symbols—including ants, birds, cats, and chickens, as well as popular culture symbols—they are continually pointed back to Vietnam and thoughts of death (Barry, "Black Holes" 159).[11] A good example is Emmett's attempt to use television to distract himself from his memories. Rather than helping him achieve any sense of recovery or mastery over his trauma, Emmett's obsession with watching reruns of *M*A*S*H*, even at the cost of interpersonal relationships or keeping a job, simply points him back to Vietnam and keeps him locked into the reenactment of the initial trauma.

The Power of Visual Metaphors

Furthermore, Mason is clear that simply rejecting mass media is not a viable strategy of resistance because perception itself has been altered so that viewers cannot escape simply by turning off their TVs. Sam's initial impulse is to reject mass media representations of Vietnam as false and seek an authentic account of Vietnam. Throughout the novel, Sam, along with *In Country*'s other characters, obsessively questions whether any given experience or memory is "real," and she seeks to locate a space free from the influence of media culture where she can get the "real" story of Vietnam. Sam realizes that the answers offered by television are too easy and that she can't expect her life to fall into place like a script. Such is the case when she describes the need for Emmett to express his feelings: "It would be good for him to talk about it more, she told Lonnie—the way Dr. Sidney Freedman on *M*A*S*H* got his patients to talk out their anxieties. But she knew very well that on TV, people always had the words to express their feelings, while in real life hardly anyone ever did. On TV, they had script writers" (45). Sam also realizes that Joan Rivers "is made up pretty and blond, but she isn't really that pretty or that blond" (19), and she questions "if Geraldine Ferraro is any different from other politicians—if she's for real or for show" (19). In this way, Sam resists complete submission to mass media messages. According to Cecilia Tichi, representing characters who "[pull] back when summoned to assent" is a way for contemporary writers to sidestep the "commercial summons [of mass media, which] jeopardizes the autonomy and integrity of the writer and the text" (125).

However, despite Sam's skepticism, Mason is clear that even Sam's thought processes have been shaped by mass media, and *In Country*'s depiction of the power of media to influence perceptual processes represents an important contribution to contemporary literature's treatment of mass media. In *In Country*, visual images transform the ways people think and talk about themselves and others. Gozzi has described how electronic media encourage individuals to talk and think about their experiences in the terms of visual processes and images. As Gozzi notes, "electronic media has moved discourse toward metaphor" (3). This move toward metaphor represents a crucial shift in social discourse away from print-based logic, which respects linear, sequential order and is highly abstract, in that marks on a page have only a conventionalized relationship to their referent. In contrast, "electronic media redescribe the world in moving, noisy images. Their symbolism is concrete and iconic" (Gozzi 52). The logic of electronic media favors the use of symbols, and frequently, as is the case in *In Country*, these symbols are taken directly from television and other electronic media. Visual metaphors created from the material of electronic media enable people to conceive of their experiences as "like" the stories and images they've witnessed in the media and to describe cognitive and perceptual processes as "like" the viewing practices required to watch electronic media. As a result, individuals essentially construct their identities in relation to media—conceiving of their actions as performances, their conversations as dialogue, and themselves as actors or, alternatively, as spectators. One obvious result of this transformation is the increasingly common use of the phrases "like television" or "like a movie" to describe life experiences—for example, the phrase "it was like a movie" was repeated almost endlessly by journalists and citizens in the aftermath of September 11, 2001, and again following the devastation of hurricanes Katrina and Sandy in 2005 and 2012, respectively.[12]

In Country details Sam's use of media images to understand her experiences and actions. Sam frequently thinks of her experiences like particular episodes of *M*A*S*H* or her moods like those of television characters. At one point in the novel, Emmett tells Sam, "You missed that *M*A*S*H* where Hot Lips kicks that door down" to which Sam replies "I'm liable to kick a door down" (189). Her thoughts and conversations are full of references to media, many of which function as visual metaphors for Sam as she experiences her life like the plot of a television show or MTV video. Thus Emmett reminds Sam of "James Stewart in *Harvey*, an old movie they had seen on Channel 7" (50), Emmett's rash is like "the mysterious brand 'X' on the back of the mother's neck in a science fiction movie she couldn't recall the name of" (108), Anita's laugh is "like poppin'-fresh dough from the oven" (115), Pete's laugh reminds her of "the way Frank Burns laughed the time he drove a tank into the women's shower" (135), and "it was as though Dawn had been captured by body snatchers" as a result of her pregnancy (155).

Sam's use of visual metaphors does more than give her a framework for understanding her experiences, however. Her use of these metaphors also signals a deeper identification on her part with media images so that the viewing practices associated with electronic media become deep metaphors for her cognitive and perceptual processes. Mason describes clearly how Sam has internalized common camera techniques as metaphors for her perceptual process, most obviously during an encounter between Sam and Tom, the older Vietnam veteran to whom she is attracted. Sam understands her experience with Tom in terms of editing techniques and television themes: "She was aware that something was about to happen, like a familiar scene in a movie, the slow-motion sequence with the couple rolling in the sheets and time passing. She hoped there wouldn't be jump cuts. She didn't want to miss anything" (126). Confronted by a half-naked Tom, Sam experiences a "flashback": "Now she remembered standing in the doorway of the bedroom a couple of minutes before, when he was in the bathroom. She had stood there, staring at his unmade bed, with the quilt crumpled at the foot. She was on rewind. Start again." Finally, she tries "very hard to concentrate. The strip of light under the bathroom door was like a yellow marker pen highlighting the major themes of her life. She was afraid she would throw up. She was aware of the slow-motion moves, the jump cuts, but they seemed to go nowhere" (127). Mason's description of this encounter highlights the ways in which Sam's sexual experience with Tom fails to live up to conventional television romance sequences and also suggests the impossibility of mapping media romance onto the complexities of most sexual relationships. Even more significantly, though, this passage demonstrates the way that camera techniques can provide visual metaphors for human perception and, at the same time, connects this experience to the condition of PTSD. Sam's expectations for the encounter, her realization that something has gone wrong, and even her ability to remember the evening's events later are shaped by the equation of camera techniques to human perception, but the gaps in her memory and recollection of certain moments of the encounter later are also remarkably similar to the symptoms of PTSD experienced by war veterans.

Because her thought processes have been shaped by electronic media, Sam is unable to break free from the influence of media even when she turns her television off. When Sam runs away to Cawood's Pond to "hump the boonies" and thus discover what war was like for her father and uncle, she perceives her action as "fac[ing] facts. This was as close to the jungle as she could get, with only a VW" (210). Sam imagines herself "in country" (210), "walking point" (211), and she asserts "this was real . . . This was what the soldiers had felt every minute" (217). However, when a shaken Emmett finds Sam in the swamp, their conversation reveals the extent to which both are reliant on information from and metaphors created by mass media. Emmett finally opens up to Sam enough to share the source of the trauma he experienced in Vietnam when his patrol was hit by a mine and he pretended to be dead, hiding for hours under his friends' corpses until he was rescued. Sam's disappearance duplicated for him the horror of the event—"It was like being left by myself and my buddies all dead" (225).

During this particularly important moment of the novel, when Emmett finally shares one of his Vietnam experiences with Sam, she attempts to fit several different types of war stories to Emmett's experience in order to understand what he is saying. Realizing that Emmett wants to talk, Sam first thinks of *M*A*S*H*: "She thought he was going to come out with some suppressed memories of events as dramatic as that one that caused Hawkeye to crack up in the final episode of *M*A*S*H*. But nothing came." She even encourages him to "do the way Hawkeye did when he told about that baby on the bus" (222). When Emmett begins telling the story of losing his friends and being stranded among the dead for hours, Sam interjects, "That sounds familiar. I saw something like that in a movie on TV." Emmett insists, "This was completely different. It really happened... That smell—the smell of death—was everywhere all the time. Even when you were eating, it was like you were eating death." Sam again interjects, "I heard somebody in that documentary we saw say that." This time, Emmett agrees: "Well, it was true!" (223).

Sam is pictured here as literally unable to understand Emmett's story unless she can map onto it another story, one that she has watched on television. Sam wants Emmett's account to in some way live up to the pre-formulated stories she has watched on television. Then she is able to fill in the gaps in what Emmett is saying, having immediate access to the emotions, plot, and conclusion of the televised stories. These stories also provide dialogue for discussing the experience, as seems to be the case when Emmett uses the phrase "it was like eating death"—this is a phrase Sam specifically remembers from a documentary she and Emmett saw together, and Mason strongly suggests that Emmett himself borrows the line from the documentary and applies it to his experiences. Even the experiences of an eyewitness are mediated through television, and Emmett and Sam's first and most important conversation about Vietnam is in many ways scripted by the shows they both have watched about Vietnam and war in general. *In Country* demonstrates again and again how Sam attempts to map the visual metaphors she has borrowed from television onto her experiences. In fact, her reliance on visual metaphors is so complete that the novel suggests she has trouble processing new information at all in the absence of such a metaphor.

For instance, when Sam is confronted by war narratives that do not conform to those that have shaped her image of Vietnam, she immediately retreats from them. At the veteran's dance, for example, a veteran's wife describes to Sam how her husband still keeps a collection of Vietnamese ears. For her part, "Sam didn't want to hear about ear collections. She didn't believe Cindy. She hurried away" (123). She reacts similarly upon reading her father's diary from Vietnam, which reveals that her father took pleasure from killing "gooks" (203). Sam is completely unable to process Dwayne's diary, and Mason explains that not even the horror films she has seen have prepared her for his descriptions of rotting corpses: "She had a morbid imagination, but it had always been like a horror movie, not something real. Now everything seemed suddenly so real it enveloped her, like something rotten she had fallen into" (206). Her response is to become physically sick and then retreat back into her fantasy of Vietnam by running away to the local swamp in an effort to imagine herself "in country."

Sinead McDermott points out that what Sam seeks is identification with her father and the veterans, and she cannot identify with them as perpetrators of violence and horror or understand them simultaneously as perpetrators and victims (14–15). This speaks to the difficulty faced by traumatized individuals whose stories might not be coherent to listeners, even willing listeners like Sam, if they don't conform to a story arc or even a preformulated narrative, and it also testifies the extent to which Sam is reliant on the media for her version of the world. She may buck against this reliance and express skepticism about these narratives, but she is never able to break free from them in *In Country* because they have been wired into her perceptual processes.

Visualizing American National Identity: The Memorial and the Monument

Mason demonstrates the difficulties of resisting mass media in contemporary culture by focusing on the power of consumer culture to co-opt countercultural movements and shape individual perception. The obvious strategies one might employ, either borrowing from effective methods of resistance from the past or simply turning off the television, are not politically viable in *In Country*. Yet the lingering effects of trauma make the challenge of confronting history and memory necessary.

However, Mason does not resolve her narrative of trauma and postmemory in the way one might expect. Though she does provide a degree of resolution to her characters' trauma by including a scene of consolation and catharsis at the Vietnam Veterans Memorial, she ultimately deflects their psychological healing in order to emphasize the importance of dealing with trauma on a sociopolitical level. Like Timothy O'Brien and Christa Grewe-Volpp, who identify a danger of too much healing and failure to take responsibility for killing so many Vietnamese, Mason seems to question the extent to which Americans should "recover" from Vietnam and instead gestures at the end of *In Country* toward the need to develop solutions focused less on the personal and more on the sociopolitical.

Concluding with Sam, Emmett, and Sam's paternal grandmother traveling to Washington, DC, to see the Vietnam Veterans Memorial allows Mason to consider how the nation officially visualizes national mourning. Mason has described her own visit to the memorial as the genesis for *In Country*: "I looked at everyone at the Memorial reading for names, parents crying and people bringing flowers and letters. When I saw all those people there, I knew that was my subject, that it was every American's story in some way or another" ("Bobbie Ann Mason's *In Country*" 128).

Indeed Mason narrates a variety of responses that her characters have to the memorial, exploring the significance of Vietnam for three generations of Americans by including Sam, Emmett, and Mamaw in the group that makes the trip to Washington. But significantly, for Mason, the story of the memorial cannot be told without also alluding to the Washington Monument as well, which is visible from and reflected in the memorial. Together, these two official visualizations of American national identity allow Sam to move from her quest to learn "what happened" in Vietnam to consider instead why and how Vietnam happened, questions that push her to critique American politics at the end of the novel and indicate the ongoing political work necessary even after experiencing a degree of catharsis by visiting the memorial.

Visiting the memorial does seem to offer consolation and catharsis to Mason's characters, though Mason implies this may be because they have been primed by media coverage of the memorial to have such an experience there. Though the memorial was designed as "the purest *mise en abyme*" (Ryan 210) and does not offer any explicit commentary on the war, its construction and opening to the public was also covered extensively by the media, and Emmett and Sam seem prompted to make the visit based on hearing news reports about the memorial.[13] The extent to which they truly do see it and interpret it for themselves is debatable, then, because as Michael Barry points out, "it seems that a host of visitors are all finding the same signifier to represent their nightmares" (160), and the meaning of this signifier has been overdetermined by its repetition in the media.[14] For example, Mamaw responds by reciting a well-worn cliché: "That white carnation blooming out of that crack . . . gave me hope. It made me know [Dwayne's] watching over us" (245). Other visitors to the memorial "walk by, talking as though they are on a Sunday picnic, but most are reverent, and some of them are crying" (240). For his part, Emmett finds the names of his friends who died in the war, and the final image of the novel is of Emmett sitting before the wall as his "face bursts into a smile like flames" (245), an image that suggests the possibility that Emmett has experienced enough catharsis to begin the work of personal transformation.[15] Sam also experiences catharsis from viewing the memorial. She cries upon seeing and touching her father's name on the wall, and finding her own name on the wall a few inches below her father's name validates that she is a part of the Vietnam story, rather than being peripheral to it as people have told her throughout the novel (245). Sam also signals the end of her quest to discover what really happened in Vietnam when she concludes that "she will never really know what happened to all these men in the war" (240). However, though some critics have interpreted this statement as signaling Sam's acceptance of historical indeterminacy,[16] I believe this only represents the end of her quest for a single truth about what happened in Vietnam. In fact, she seems to immediately launch off on a new and potentially more productive inquiry into how and why Vietnam happened, and her analysis of the Washington Monument does not gesture toward indeterminacy but instead toward pointed critique of American imperialism.

For Sam, who notices the monument immediately upon entering Washington and finds it dominating the skyline of the city throughout her visit (238), the Washington Monument is a visible expression of American political power and dominance. When Sam sees "the Washington Monument ris[ing] out of the earth, proud and tall," she "remembers Tom's bitter comment about it—a big white prick. She once heard someone say that the U.S.A. goes around fucking the world" (238). She later notices the Washington Monument reflected in the memorial, a moment that highlights for her the connection between American political power and the deaths of American soldiers in Vietnam: "Sam stands in the center of the V, deep in the pit. The V is like the white wings of the shopping mall in Paducah. The Washington Monument is reflected in the center line. If she moves slightly to the left, she sees the monument, and if she moves the other way she sees a reflection of the flag opposite the memorial. Both the monument and the flag seem like arrogant gestures, like the country giving the finger to the dead boys, flung in this hole in the ground" (240). The reflective surface of the memorial, which gives viewers their own reflections to look at, also reflects back to Sam the image of the Washington Monument, which she perceives as particularly arrogant in this context. Both the memorial and the monument serve as visualizations of America, but juxtaposed as they are for Sam in the closing of *In Country*, the image created is jarring, prompting Sam to recognize a connection between American political power and the deaths of American soldiers. If America is guilty of "fucking the world," it is also pictured here as "fucking" its own citizens and soldiers—not only in sending Americans to die in Vietnam for reasons that remain unacknowledged but also for refusing to take responsibility for poisoning its own soldiers with Agent Orange.

In her description of the Washington Monument, Mason depicts American political power as in crisis since Sam, who at 17 years old and with a consciousness shaped by mass media, is able to recognize the visualization of American power for the construction that it is. And this recognition makes critique possible, which Sam proceeds to do by turning to the repertoire of mass media images in her memory and drawing out Christo's "Surrounded Islands." Though she does not know Christo's name or the name of his installation, Sam resists the way American power is visualized by the Washington Monument by suggesting "that guy who put pink plastic around those islands should make a big rubber for the Washington

Monument" (238). Sam alludes here to Christo's environmental installation "Surrounded Islands," something Sam saw on a television program and expressed admiration for earlier in the novel.[17] Though Sam does not have any real context for Christo's project, it provides her with a visual image she turns to throughout the novel to critique consumer and political culture. In her first reference to Christo, Sam explains, "he seemed to mock the idea of fancy wrapping. You could work hard wrapping a package and buy some pretty paper and a nice ribbon and a name tag, but the person would just rip it all up to see what was inside. Packaging was supposed to deceive, Sam thought, but it never really did. Her father came back from the war in a plastic bag. Attractive and efficient. A good disguise" (120). Christo's art helped Sam look at the packaging of consumer products in a new way, and she made an explicit comparison between consumer culture, with its dependence on packaging and plastic, and her father's death in the war, which is disguised as a heroic act so as to hide the connection between marketplace interests and the war. In Washington, Sam again invokes Christo to critique American political power. Her fantasy of the Washington Monument wrapped in a giant condom ironically reverses America's foreign policy of "containment" during the Cold War by suggesting it is the United States that needs to behave responsibly toward its partners, whether these are countries around the world or American citizens. The anxiety that Sam has felt about pregnancy throughout the novel finds fullest expression here, where she asserts the need for America to be contained so as not to forcibly reproduce its ideals and agenda in others.[18]

Significantly, Sam has access to Christo's work only because it invites media attention and because she has seen it on television.[19] In fact, she knows very little about him or his work. Even at the conclusion of the novel, Mason signals that Sam does not ever break free from media culture and indeed likely cannot since her perceptual processes have been shaped by media. It is not surprising that the end of the novel finds Sam continuing to fit media images onto her new experiences in Washington in order to make sense of them. In this novel, there is no way to get outside of media culture in order to critique it because media images are fused with memory and imagination inside the characters' minds. Nevertheless, at the conclusion of *In Country*, Mason at least offers the possibility that Emmett and Sam will be transformed by their trip to Washington and experience enough sense of healing to begin to productively contest the official and mass media visualizations of America's power and participation in Vietnam that surround them. What exactly this contestation will look like is not clear at the end of *In Country*, but what is clear is that mass media images will give it form.

Mason's keen awareness that mass media have irrevocably transformed perception and social discourse attests to the political importance of her use of popular culture allusions and "shopping mall aesthetic" in her fiction. As Mason has explained, popular culture is "very close to people and it reflects what they feel and believe. Certain people denigrate it because it's not high art, but I don't happen to feel that way. I don't want to have an elitist attitude about the culture. It's very real, it means something to a whole lot of people, and I can't ignore that" ("*PW* Interviews" 425). While Mason highlights the work of Christo in *In Country*, I suggest that she also intends the novel itself to explore and represent the possibility for contemporary literature to facilitate healing and critical insight in the contemporary period. She implies that writers and artists themselves must adapt not only to adequately represent experiences of trauma but also to represent the experiences of and communicate to readers whose thinking processes have been shaped by electronic media.

Part II

Witnessing Visual Manipulation

3

"There Were Signs and I Missed Them"

Reading beneath the Image in Margaret Atwood's Speculative Fiction

Like Morrison and Mason, Margaret Atwood attends to the work of media in carrying ideology into everyday life and the role of images in shaping consciousness throughout her writing. However, because Atwood's vision of contemporary society is bleaker than the other writers', the sense of danger associated with issues of visuality is exponentially greater in her work as is the sense of urgency she associates with writing. Indeed in a recent interview, Atwood explains that because the tools to which humans have access have grown very powerful, with unprecedented powers of destruction, the future of humanity depends on whether "we as a species have the emotional maturity and the wisdom to use our powerful tools well" ("Author Interview"). Although she doesn't mention them specifically in the interview, visual technologies represent some of the powerful tools to which Atwood alludes and to which she returns frequently throughout her writing.[1] In particular, Atwood is interested in exploring the irony that the act of seeing can itself be used to blind or distract people from clear political vision. For Atwood, the gravest danger is associated with the *failure* to see, or the *failure* to recognize and respond to others' suffering. Though the failure to see stems in part from the very mechanics of sight and perception, which require a certain amount of blindness and misrecognition in order to function properly, Atwood is especially concerned with the deliberate manipulation of visual processes for political purposes and the possibility for individuals to "turn a blind eye" toward others in need. It is here that Atwood sees the work of the contemporary writer to destabilize complacency so as to unsettle readers enough that they can see the importance of issues ranging from environmental destruction to gender relations.

In interviews and her own fiction, Atwood has described the role she sees for writers: to help readers develop critical awareness. In one of her most gripping, recent portrayals of the writer's role in society, Atwood characterizes the world in the title story to her collection *The Tent* (2006) as "a howling wilderness" in which "many people are howling. Some howl in grief because those they love have died or been killed, others howl in triumph because they have caused the loved ones of their enemies to die or be killed. Some howl to summon help, some howl for revenge, others howl for blood. The noise is deafening" (143–44). And in the midst of this horror-laden scene, Atwood explains, "You're in a tent" that is "made of paper," and your job is to "write on the walls ... Some of the writing has to describe the howling that's going on outside night and day," and "some of the writing has to be about your loved ones and the need you feel to protect them" (144). The writer's job is made more difficult and more urgent by the fact that many misinterpret the howls, taking them for the sounds of "a picnic out there in the wilderness, like a big band, like a hot beach party" (144–45). In this story and elsewhere, Atwood depicts the writer's job as twofold: to recognize and represent the suffering of others and in doing so to help readers recognize the ways in which others are suffering or causing suffering.

In a career that spans the contemporary period—her first book of poetry was published in 1961, and she remains productive to the present—Atwood has worked in a breathtaking number of genres and developed a distinct literary style in her ongoing effort to unsettle her readers.[2] She has published 12 collections of poetry, more than a dozen novels, four short-story collections, three collections of prose poetry and short fiction, seven books of literary and cultural criticism, six children's books, thirty cartoons and comic strips, and several screenplays based on her own works. She has also served as editor for books of Canadian verse as well as a cookbook, she has written several libretti for operas, and she recently wrote the drama adaptation of *The Penelopiad*. Tying together Atwood's body of work is her distinct literary style as well as her ongoing interest in issues of power and "a feminist attitude to how she sees power playing itself out in the world" (Sheckels viii). Atwood has earned a reputation as a master of irony, and her use of what Theodore Sheckels describes as "an unusual combination of formal realism and postmodernism, which has her spinning the illusion of real characters and real situations while playing with narrative voice and with form, often undermining the latter" (viii) makes it difficult for readers to overlook the political dimension of her writing. Her ironic stance, feminist orientation, and the indeterminacy with which she concludes her novels, so that the reader is not reassured at the conclusion that order has been reestablished or that justice will prevail, are intended to rouse readers out of complacency, and reviews of her books frequently indicate that they succeed at that. For example, the 1986 edition of *The Handmaid's Tale* includes excerpts from a number of reviews of the novel, most of which make some connection between the novel's warning and contemporary cultural practices. Thus the *Houston Chronicle* review urged readers to "read it while it's still allowed," while the *Playboy* reviewer suggested, "Read this book—then contribute to your favorite liberal cause."

Though many of Atwood's works focus on the ethical and political dimensions of visual representation and sometimes even center on protagonists who are visual artists, the dangers of visual manipulation are made particularly apparent in her speculative fiction, in which Atwood traces ideas and practices already present in contemporary culture to their logical conclusions. Atwood has employed this genre sparingly, in *The Handmaid's Tale* (1985) and in the MaddAddam trilogy (published between 2003 and 2013).[3] She defines speculative fiction as "an extrapolation of life . . . a slight twist on the society we have now," distinguishing it from science fiction, which Atwood identifies with "Martians and space travel to other planets, and things like that" ("An Interview with Margaret Atwood on Her Novel"). And visuality emerges as a particular point of concern in Atwood's speculative novels. This chapter will compare Atwood's treatment of visuality in *The Handmaid's Tale* and *Oryx and Crake*, novels that were published almost twenty years apart and reveal how Atwood's perspective on visuality has evolved over time amid changing conditions of visuality.

The Handmaid's Tale and *Oryx and Crake* bridge a period during which global media were profoundly transformed. As the problem of the image evolves from a problem concerning the manipulation of the signifier for political ends in *The Handmaid's Tale* to the complete domination of the signifier and loss of the referent in *Oryx and Crake*, the stakes of visual representation increase as well. Atwood registers these changes by setting her speculative novels in the United States, the center of global image production. Though Atwood is a Canadian writer and most of her works are located in Canadian settings, all her speculative novels are set in the United States. Sheckels has discussed how Atwood uses Americans in her novels to represent the destructive extremes of Western culture. In *Surfacing* (1972), for example, when the narrator comes to view her friends negatively, she thinks of them as American, though they are in fact Canadian. Atwood's US settings are strongly inflected by her Canadian perspective. She perceives of the "extremes" of US visual practices as threatening not only US citizens but also people around the world, and she makes it possible to recognize how greatly global media are shaped by the culture and politics of the United States.

The Evolving Problem of the Image in *The Handmaid's Tale* and *Oryx and Crake*

In *The Handmaid's Tale*, Atwood explicitly questions why people so often cooperate with totalitarian regimes and how they come to accept life under these regimes. *The Handmaid's Tale* takes place in the Republic of Gilead, a totalitarian regime that has evolved from contemporary US culture. In Gilead, a crisis in sterility has prompted a small but well-organized group to install a monotheocratic government. In the resulting society, women are strictly controlled. They are unable to have jobs or earn money and are assigned to various classes: among them, the chaste, childless Wives; the housekeeping Marthas; and the Handmaids, a group of women capable of reproducing but considered morally inferior.[4] The purpose of this structure is to combat falling population rates and ensure that people who raise children are morally fit to do so. Thus Handmaids are impregnated by their Commanders, and when they give birth, their children are taken away and raised by Wives. *The Handmaid's Tale* is told in the first person by Offred, a Handmaid who recalls the past and recounts the evolution of Gilead from contemporary American culture. Offred makes her record in order to understand her own actions and so others can learn from what she experienced, and an important part of her story is recounting how she overcame the metaphorical and literal "blindness" that initially prevented her from recognizing Gilead's ulterior motives as the regime assumed control.

Written and published in the early 1980s, *The Handmaid's Tale* responds to the growing political and social conservatism of the United States during the Reagan era and Atwood's experiences traveling in Afghanistan and Iran during the late 1970s as women's freedoms were being stripped from them.[5] Celia Florén observes that the novel draws "attention to the fragility of western women's newly gained social conquests, reminding them that they are recent and can easily be lost. It is a question of arousing awareness and solidarity, at a moment when in some parts of the world, particularly in some Arab countries, we see how women's role is dangerously regressing" (262). At the same time, Maroula Joannou maintains that the novel has a distinctly US setting: "The customs and observances of the theocracy are those associated with the American New Right, with Jerry Falwell's Moral Majority, and the charismatic American evangelists" (145). Atwood has explained that she couldn't make the novel work in a Canadian setting: "It is not a Canadian sort of thing to do. Canadians might do it after the

States did it, in some sort of watered-down version. Our television evangelists are more paltry than yours. The States are more extreme in everything" (qtd. in Joannou 145). Certainly, the setting serves Atwood's critical focus on issues of vision since the United States has long served as the hub of Western image production and has often been accused of using images to extend political and social influence to nations around the world.

The issue of global media emerges even more clearly in *Oryx and Crake*, in which Atwood explores the role that images play in desensitizing the viewing public and further cementing social and political hierarchies. The novel is also set in the United States, and Atwood again uses the States to represent the most extreme excesses with regard to politics and culture.[6]

The protagonist of *Oryx and Crake* calls himself Snowman, though he is known through most of the book as Jimmy,[7] and he believes himself to be the only human survivor of a worldwide cataclysm that he comes to realize was engineered by his best friend, Crake. Snowman lives on a beach with a group of genetically engineered humans he refers to as the "Children of Crake." Designed without a sense of good or evil, the Children of Crake are completely unable to understand Snowman or his experiences. As a result of his isolation, Snowman spends a great deal of time reflecting on his past, mourning the loss of his enigmatic lover Oryx and his friend Crake, trying to piece together what led Crake to take the actions he did, and pondering his own "blindness." Like Offred, he makes a record primarily to sort through the information he has in order to better understand it. Unlike Offred, however, Snowman believes that as the sole survivor of his culture, his narrative comes too late to help anyone to learn, change, or do things differently.[8]

Through Snowman's reconstruction of his past, readers learn that Crake used his position as a leading researcher at a top biotech company to imbed a deadly virus, known as the JUVE virus, into a pill intended to enhance sexual performance and prevent the spread of sexually transmitted diseases. Simultaneously engaged on a second project to perfect genetic modification of humans, Crake used this project to design a completely new kind of human, one capable of living in harmony with the natural world. Although Snowman remains unclear as to Crake's exact motives even at the conclusion of the novel, his main motive seems to be his desire to affect lasting social change. Crake cannot see any other way of challenging the power of the leading multinational corporations, preventing the further destruction of the earth, and combating the tendency of human beings toward selfishness and greed. Moreover, Crake has internalized the dehumanized worldview to which he has been constantly exposed since childhood. Consequently, he takes the drastic action of attempting to start over. Crake sees himself as a God figure, which is evident in his desire to recreate the Garden of Eden, a desire that requires the eradication of flawed human beings and the creation of a new type of human designed without the knowledge of good and evil. Yet Crake refuses to take responsibility for the Children of Crake beyond their design, leaving only Snowman to protect them after he chooses death for himself and Oryx. In all his actions, Crake embodies a suicidal-homicidal will that cannot be bargained with at any level. He never discusses his plan with any other person, and only Oryx seems to suspect his intentions. The scale of his action only serves to underline the absoluteness of his decision and his belief that it is right.

The Limits of Vision: "Usual Seeing"

In both novels, Atwood explores the limits of sight and the political implications of those limits by employing narrators who are originally blind to the important events happening around them and who use the process of narrating their stories to grow in awareness about what really happened and how they overlooked important details. This narrative strategy allows readers to gain insight along with the narrators and go beyond what James Elkins has referred to as "the wall of usual seeing" (*The Object* 56). According to Elkins, "it is difficult to break through the wall of usual seeing and begin to discover how many other things there are to see. It requires practice and special information—you have to know what you're looking for—and it also requires energy, since it involves special concentration" (*The Object* 56).

Elkins's concept of "usual seeing" emphasizes the link between blindness and sight. In fact, physiological studies of the eye demonstrate that the mechanism of seeing requires a degree of blindness in order to operate correctly. Although the relationship between seeing and perception is still not completely understood, it is clear that the eye functions largely as a "complex processing unit to detect change, form, and features, and which selectively prepares data that the brain must then interpret" (Barry, *Visual Intelligence* 33). Movement and change are significant to the eye; Ann Barry explains that "because all external data is essentially chaotic and ambiguous, the eye—as an extension of the brain that interfaces directly with the environment—works to detect change and no-change, and to create meaningful sense out of the rush of stimuli from the external world" (37). Most significant is that in its effort to create meaning out of the information received, the eye "selectively" privileges some information, while it remains blind to other information. From his work with newly sighted people, Oliver Sacks concludes, "when we open our eyes each morning, it is upon a world we have spent a lifetime *learning* to see. We are not given the world: we make our world through incessant experience, categorization, memory, reconnection" (114). In fact, when an eye is not trained to selectively order information to present to the brain, a person is, in Barry's words, "experientially blind"; everything runs together in a meaningless blur of color and motion; these people can "see but not perceive in a visual mode" (39). It seems, then, that a certain amount of "blindness" is required in order for people to see, and most individuals are adept at processing the information their eyes receive in such a way as to function in the world and communicate with others, albeit with a certain degree of error inherent in this system.

Though sight paradoxically requires blindness, at times, the information that people are blind to is motivated by self-interest or political naiveté. Again, in his discussion of "usual seeing," Elkins points out, "we are all guilty of not seeing, and I think most of us don't see most of the time" (*The Object* 57). Elkins's use of the word "guilt" resonates in *The Handmaid's Tale* and *Oryx and Crake*, where not seeing or giving in to "usual seeing" contributes to oppressive and destructive social systems. Offred comes to recognize that a great deal of her former blindness resulted from a deliberate act of "ignoring" what she didn't want to acknowledge, and she claims "ignoring isn't the same as ignorance, you have to work at it" (74). Jimmy similarly blames his ignorance for making him blind, but he also realizes that his ignorance was "not willed, exactly" but "structured": "He'd grown up in walled spaces, and then he had become one. He had shut things out" (184). In both cases, Offred and Jimmy suggest that they chose blindness as a response to events and inconvenient issues; as a result, they simply didn't see what they didn't want to see and remained inactive.

Because of their blindness, Offred and Jimmy do not see or understand what is happening until it is too late to take action to stop it. For example, Offred ignores Gilead's takeover until open resistance is no longer possible. Her naiveté becomes evident when her more politically aware friend Moira warns Offred to "look out. . . . Here it comes,"[9] and Offred responds "here what comes?" (225). In *Oryx and Crake*, Jimmy is also blind to Crake's actions until it is too late to stop him, and he remains blind to Crake's motives even at the conclusion of the book. In reconstructing the events that led to the extermination of humankind, Jimmy recognizes numerous ways in which Crake signaled his intentions to him, though without ever explicitly confiding his plan. Jimmy concludes the following: "There were signs and I missed them" (320). Whenever Crake alludes to any part of his plan, Jimmy "shuts out" the information and turns the conversation to more pleasant topics.

Manipulating Vision: Surveillance and Spectacle

In addition to exploring the physiological and psychological limitations of sight, Atwood also uses her speculative novels to delineate the dangers posed by the deliberate manipulation of vision. She focuses primarily on the roles surveillance and spectacle play in shaping individuals to suit the will of the dominant regime. In *The Handmaid's Tale*, Gilead's leaders use their expertise in market research to create an appearance of peace and order that functions to convince those within and outside of Gilead not only that everything is under control in Gilead but also that there is no use to resisting. This appearance of control and stability is ultimately designed to maintain the status quo and disguise the fact that the ruling body of men, the Commanders, are sterile. It is illegal to say that a Commander is sterile, and Gilead's official visual record suggests that as a group they are not sterile since the children who have been stolen from "inappropriate" parents are raised by Commanders and their Wives as their own and become incorporated into their family photographs. In contrast, Gilead seeks to destroy photographic (and other) evidence of the Handmaids' existence; thus Offred's family photo album is destroyed, and all official documents naming her or other Handmaids are burned. As a result, Offred realizes that "from the point of view of future history [. . .] we'll be invisible" (295). In reality, of course, Gilead has deliberately falsified its own visual record. Not only are the children depicted in Gilead's family photographs stolen, but Handmaids routinely have sex with men other than their Commanders (especially their doctors) in an attempt to become pregnant and avoid punishment for "failing" to reproduce. Thus even the children that seem born of Handmaid-Commander unions rarely bear a genetic relationship to their "fathers." Nevertheless, the success of Gilead's visual manipulation is evident in Offred's reaction to hearing from her doctor that most Commanders are sterile: "I almost gasp: he's said a forbidden word. *Sterile*. There is no such thing as a sterile man anymore, not officially. There are only women who are fruitful and women who are barren, that's the law" (79). Although Offred seems to know intuitively that the Commanders are sterile, her shock at hearing the doctor voice this truth demonstrates how easily people can accept as a social fact even what they know is a lie. Because this particular lie is enforced by law, Offred has accepted it to some extent—after all, Handmaids bear the legal responsibility for "failing" to reproduce, the punishment for which is hard labor and then death.

Atwood's depiction of Gilead's use of visuality as a way to control its population thematizes Michel Foucault's analysis of surveillance and spectacle. In *Discipline and Punish*, Foucault explains that during the course of the eighteenth century, the "spectacle of the scaffold" (32) gave way to a system of surveillance due to the reorganization of power and the emergence of new technologies of discipline and conceptions of personhood. While the spectacle of the scaffold relied on the public execution (and sometimes torture) of criminals to restore and maintain a hierarchical social order that had been challenged by a criminal act, the society of surveillance constructs "docile bodies" by subjecting individuals to constant, invisible observation so that individuals eventually internalize discipline and effectively police themselves. For Foucault, Jeremy Bentham's Panopticon best exemplifies the particular form of institution capable of observing and molding bodies. The Panopticon is a prison designed to maximize visibility. Not only are prisoners constantly visible and kept in check by the gaze of the prison guards, but the prison guards themselves are visible to and policed by their supervisors. Foucault suggests that the principles of surveillance and social control inherent in the Panopticon can be more generally applied to all facets of society grounded on spoken or unspoken laws. Panopticism operates silently and effectively because of its hierarchical, continuous, and functional nature. Once a system of rules is in place, all members of society can work to maintain those rules simply by observing others' behavior. Everyone is employed in this work, and it operates independently of an organized head, a fact that "enables the disciplinary power to be both absolutely indiscreet . . . and absolutely 'discreet,' for it functions permanently and largely in silence" (Foucault 177).

In *The Handmaid's Tale*, Gilead combines both types of control in order to dominate its citizenry; it is a panoptic society that resurrects the spectacle of the scaffold.[10] Gilead's panopticism is evident in that individuals police each other and internalize the constrictions placed on them although the leadership of the regime is largely invisible.[11] Additionally, police spies are called "the Eyes," and it is impossible to tell who is an Eye since they are planted at every level of society. Offred's life is monitored in numerous other ways as well. Guards posted at towers monitor her movements out of doors; her shopping partner Ofglen is "my spy, as I am hers" (26); her room is frequently searched, and other members of the household monitor her activities in the house. Gilead even extends surveillance to the body's interior as all Handmaids undergo mandatory gynecological exams each month. Offred's costume, her prescribed speech and relationships, and even her name work to limit her individuality and allow for easy policing of her actions.

As well as creating a nation of "docile bodies" that will submit to and work for the regime (Foucault 136), Gilead also resurrects the public and ceremonial system of punishment that Foucault associates with premodern culture. Men and women in Gilead are required to attend and participate in dramatic public hearings and executions, and afterward, the bodies of those executed are displayed theatrically on "the Wall," their faces hidden behind bags and a sign hung around their necks indicating the "official" reason for their execution. Though Gilead forbids or limits many kinds of looking, the regime encourages people to look at the bodies on the Wall. Offred observes, "We're supposed to look: this is what they are there for, hanging on the Wall. Sometimes they'll be there for days, until there's a new batch, so as many people as possible will have the chance to see them" (42). Through these spectacular displays, Gilead enforces "historical amnesia," what Fredric Jameson describes as "the disappearance of a sense of history, the way in which our entire contemporary social system has little by little begun to lose its capacity to retain its own past, has begun to live in a perpetual present and in a perpetual change that obliterates traditions of the kind which all earlier social formations have had in one way or another to preserve" (125). Gilead enforces historical amnesia by employing "superficial and sensately intensified, short lived, and repeatable" (Rogin, "Make My Day" 507) spectacles that cement individuals in the present, inscribing them in the roles allowed by Gilead and with no acknowledgement that society was ever or could ever be organized differently. Gilead's success in enforcing amnesia is evident in Offred's continual struggle to retain memories of her former life throughout the novel, and she realizes that because the next generation of Handmaids "will have no memories of any other way," they will accept life in Gilead as normal (151).

Additionally, Gilead uses public executions to foster identification between the audience and the regime. According to Foucault, in the society of the spectacle, an audience was essential to public executions in order to witness the restoration of the social order. In this paradigm, the executioner represented the monarch during the execution. However, Gilead forces the audience to play the part of executioner and, in doing so, represent the regime. Offred recounts her participation in the public execution of two people in *The Handmaid's Tale*. The first woman is hanged, and Offred and the other Handmaids are required to show "unity with the Salvagers and my consent, and my complicity in the death of this woman" (355) by grasping the rope that initiates the hanging. During the second execution, the Handmaids are literally set loose on a condemned prisoner they are told has raped a pregnant Handmaid. Participation in these executions is mandatory, and the executions are effective both as a means of inculcating Gilead's system of punishment into "spectators" and as a way of identifying those whose allegiance to Gilead is incomplete. Thus Gilead again weaves surveillance into its practice of spectacle, demonstrating the combined power of these forms of control.

The world of *Oryx and Crake* is also characterized by spectacle, and, as in *The Handmaid's Tale*, the mechanism of power is diffuse. However,

Atwood's evolving perspective on visuality is evident in her depiction of spectacle in *Oryx and Crake*, which has more in common with Guy Debord's theory of spectacle than with Foucault's. Though both theorists consider spectacle as a form of social control, Foucault equates spectacle with public punishment and ultimately concludes that in modern societies, public punishment has given way to internalized discipline, while Debord contends that spectacle is on the rise in contemporary culture. Debord theorizes that "the spectacle is not a collection of images, but a social relation among people, mediated by images" (7). This relationship is characterized by a new mass uniformity of thought and action that simultaneously isolates individuals from one another even as images and individuals become more mobile than ever before. Moreover, in Debord's society of the spectacle, only what appears exists, and the mass media have considerable control over what appears to the majority of the public.

This is precisely the situation described in *Oryx and Crake* as media, government, and multinational corporations have become entirely integrated and work together to provide constant entertainment to a public that is increasingly isolated within company-run Compounds. Jimmy (Snowman) and Crake grow up within the walls of one of these Compounds, which combine features of industry parks and gated communities in that all the employees of a given company work and live together. Because they are kept relatively isolated in the Compound, Jimmy and Crake learn about the outside world primarily through television and the Internet. As a result of Crake's skill with the computer, the boys have access to incredibly violent and licentious images, even as adolescents. During one afternoon, the boys might watch "open heart surgery in live time," "the Noodie News," "animal snuff sites," "live coverage of executions in Asia," "various supposed thieves having their hands cut off and adulterers and lipstick-wearers being stoned to death by angry crowds," "electrocutions and lethal injections," "an assisted suicide site," or all manner of child and adult pornography (82–84). In his reliance on mass media for information about the world, Jimmy is very similar to Sam in *In Country*, and there is evidence that his consciousness has been shaped by mass media just as Sam's was.

Though images and visual spectacles are employed in different ways in *The Handmaid's Tale* and *Oryx and Crake*, at the core of both Atwood's speculative novels, the problem of the image is quite similar: because of the limits of human seeing, individuals are blind to much of what happens around them, and visual processes are manipulated to keep the population docile. What is radically different between the two novels, however, is the possibility for critical spectatorship. Although Atwood is not entirely optimistic about the possibility of resistance in either novel, she posits a type of visual literacy in *The Handmaid's Tale*, while within the world of *Oryx and Crake*, she refuses to describe a source of resistance. The only hope she offers in the latter novel is that the events about which she writes have not taken place; thus her contemporary readers have some time to create an alternative future.

"Reading Beneath" as Visual Literacy in *The Handmaid's Tale*

In both novels, the possibility of resistance is correlated to visual literacy. Characters are able to develop empathy and use language to resist hierarchical social codes and effect positive change only after they have begun to question who has produced the texts around them and to what end.

In *The Handmaid's Tale*, Offred signals her resistance to the forces that seek to suppress her own (and other) accounts of oppression by expressing a desire to exchange stories with others if given the chance (344). The repeated line "I compose myself" throughout *The Handmaid's Tale* emphasizes that Offred maintains her identity through making her record (Laflen 95). Telling her story requires Offred to see differently from the way she is authorized to see, and in order to see differently, Offred must first break out of her former pattern of "usual seeing" to become aware of the ways in which her own patterns of seeing keep her blind to other realities. The first time she becomes aware of how her own visual processes are a trap for her thinking comes as she looks at bodies on the Wall with her shopping partner Ofglen (Laflen 97). Offred attempts to come up with a satisfactory way of thinking about the men's bodies hanging from hooks on the Wall. She thinks, "It's the bags over the heads that are the worst, worse than the faces themselves would be. It makes the men like dolls on which the faces have not yet been painted; like scarecrows, which in a way is what they are, since they are meant to scare. Or as if their heads are sacks, stuffed with some undifferentiated material, like flour or dough . . . The heads are zeros . . . The heads are the heads of snowmen, with the coal eyes and the carrot noses fallen out. The heads are melting" (43). When she notices blood seeping through one of the bags, she compares the blood to "a child's idea of a smile" (43), and later she observes, "the red of the smile is the same as the red of the tulips in Serena Joy's garden, towards the base of the flowers where they are beginning to heal" (44). These analogies help Offred distance herself from the men's murdered bodies and in many ways prevent her from seeing the bodies. The analogies ultimately do not suffice, however, and Offred cannot sustain the image of the men as snowmen or the blood as a tulip or smile. It is unusual to see blood on the white bags, and it disrupts Offred's usual seeing of the bodies and forces her to evaluate the analogies. She asserts, "These are not snowmen after all" (44):

> The red [of the blood] is the same [as the tulips] but there is no connection. The tulips are not tulips of blood, the red smiles are not flowers, neither thing makes a comment on the other. The tulip is not a reason for disbelief in the hanged man, or vice versa. Each thing is valid and really there. It is through a field of such valid objects that I must pick my way, every day and in every way. I put a lot of effort into making such distinctions. I need to make them. I need to be very clear, in my own mind. (44–45)

The Handmaid's Tale recounts two effects of Offred's decision to see clearly. First, she comes to recognize numerous ways in which women resist the Gilead regime; most importantly, she learns of the existence of an underground resistance as a result. Second, Offred recognizes that the visual is vulnerable to manipulation, and she uses this knowledge to manipulate the way she appears to others. As she becomes involved in separate intrigues with Serena Joy, the Commander, Nick, and Ofglen, Offred's ability to avoid drawing attention to herself is crucial to her survival. Offred suggests that manipulating one's appearance in this way becomes a form of language in and of itself—a body language that allows individuals to speak to one another without violating prohibitions on speech.

Atwood terms Offred's ability to see differently "reading beneath," and she offers this as a model of visual literacy in the novel (Laflen 83). "Reading beneath" requires Offred to recognize how Gilead's visual culture supports the regime's underlying ideology. In recalling her initial reaction to Gilead's takeover, Offred remembers tuning into television for guidance. Reassured by the message from television, "Keep calm . . . Everything is under control," Offred does nothing to resist the regime and at one point actually feels grateful that someone is in control, since, as she explains, "it was obvious you couldn't be too careful" (225). After Offred begins to see differently, she no longer uncritically accepts the messages she receives from television. Instead she looks for evidence in the types of stories that are reported, as well as those that aren't reported, as to developments in Gilead's war and the progress of the resistance movement. Despite knowing that the media are complicit in spreading Gilead's ideological message, Offred still watches television news when she has the chance, acknowledging that "it could be faked. But I watch anyway, hoping to be able to read beneath it" (105). Offred's ability to "read beneath" Gilead's ideology prompts her to narrate her own experience, using the genre and conventions of eyewitness testimony to expose Gilead's visual manipulations for the lies they are (Laflen 99). In interviews, Atwood has asserted the importance of eyewitness testimony, explaining, "It's obvious now that everything passes through a filter. Doesn't mean it's not true in some sense. It just means that nobody can claim to have the absolute, whole, objective, total, complete truth. The truth is composite, and that's a cheering thought. It mitigates tendencies toward autocracy" ("An Interview 1983" 232). In *The Handmaid's Tale*, Gilead provides a frightening example of an autocratic society that brokers no tolerance for information that does not accord with its version of reality. In response, Offred does not substitute her own reality for Gilead's—instead Offred highlights the inconsistencies within her own narrative and continually reminds the reader that her narrative is a reconstruction, which necessarily involves interpretation and editorializing. This approach is consistent with Atwood's belief in the importance of recognizing that truth itself is often a matter of context that is best approached by allowing for as many perspectives on any issue as possible.

Proliferating Images in *Oryx and Crake*

Oryx and Crake is also narrated as an eyewitness account, but in contrast to Offred, Jimmy has no illusion that his record will reach an audience. Since there are no readers left, he writes only for himself. Yet Jimmy's isolation predates the catastrophe that leaves him the sole bearer of his culture's language and knowledge because of the condition of literacy in his culture. Though Jimmy does not develop into a critical spectator until it is too late, he is characterized as a lover of literature from his youth. His appreciation for words in a society that privileges images isolates him throughout his life, but it also helps Jimmy preserve his humanity and makes him suitable, in Crake's view, to be a caretaker for the Crakers.

In Jimmy's world, literature shares a spot on the endangered species list along with numerous plant and animal species and is relegated to libraries, which resemble mausoleums in the novel. People like Jimmy are hired to keep watch over literature, to make sure that colorful turns of phrase and important texts are not lost, but, in the novel, literature is culturally irrelevant. Not surprisingly, without a vibrant body of literature, the population of *Oryx and Crake* has lost a key avenue for reflection and critical thought, and the digital forms that have replaced literature do not inspire the same level of critical awareness.

Atwood's growing pessimism about the possibility of resisting visual manipulation stems from the evolution of media during the twenty years following the publication of *The Handmaid's Tale*. Put differently, the ways in which visual images are manipulated and used in *Oryx and Crake* were not technologically possible during the 1980s when *The Handmaid's Tale* was published.

In the years following the publication of *The Handmaid's Tale*, cultural and technological developments expanded the reach of visual culture in new ways. In *Practices of Looking*, Marita Sturken and Lisa Cartwright explain that "the media landscape of the late-twentieth century and early-twenty-first centuries has changed with the rise of a worldwide communication infrastructure and multinational corporations, the decline of the central power of the sovereign nation-state, and the resulting emergence of new forms of local and global cultures" (315). Though many of these changes were under way in the early 1980s when *The Handmaid's Tale* was published, they undeniably accelerated in the late 1980s and throughout the 1990s with the development of fiber-optic networks and digital compression that signaled, in Frances Cairncross's words, "the death of distance" (xi). As a result, distance is no longer an obstacle to the global distribution of images, a fact that has created new markets for information, products, and services. Simultaneously, the 1990s saw the consolidation of media on an unprecedented scale. As one example, the 1996 merger of Disney, Capital Cities, and ABC brought together "five film production companies; four magazines; a book publishing company; a hockey team; a utility company; multiple TV channels; eight newspapers; and a radio network with 3,500 affiliates" (Sturken and Cartwright 318). As Sturken and Cartwright conclude, "a single corporation thus has an enormous hold over global visual culture" (318).

The implications of the globalization and centralization of media are still unclear and are hotly contested by scholars. Proponents of global visual culture frequently discuss it as the fruition of Marshall McLuhan's vision of a media-based "global village," whereby people around the world enjoy a previously impossible connectivity and kinship due to the reach of media across geographical and political boundaries. In *The Death of Distance*, Cairncross employs this sort of celebratory rhetoric when discussing the potential benefits of global communications networks: "Free to explore different points of view, on the Internet or on the thousands of television and radio channels that will eventually be available, people will become less susceptible to propaganda from politicians who seek to stir up conflicts. Bonded together by the invisible strands of global communications, humanity may find that peace and prosperity are fostered by the death of distance" (279). In contrast, critics such as Herbert Schiller and James Ledbetter challenge the nature of the "freedom" and "bonds" facilitated by global media. They equate the globalization of media with the practice of colonialism, arguing that digital media serve the interests of multinational corporations by allowing them to expand their markets globally in ways that reinforce inequality within nations and between so-called First and Third World nations. Moreover, they point to the unidirectional flow of images as evidence, drawing on the fact that although the flow of images from the United States and Europe has increased dramatically into the Third World, images from the Third World (at least those created apart from the First World) still struggle for visibility in First World markets.

Atwood shares this latter perspective and responds to proponents of global visual culture by describing a "global village" in *Oryx and Crake* that draws little distinction between images of prisoners being executed in Asia, child pornography, and political speeches. As images with significant political and social messages are held up alongside (and ultimately appear to the public indistinguishable from) the most trivial and debased images, viewers lose the ability to distinguish between images that are important and those that are banal. The images to which Jimmy and Crake are exposed as children and adults do not foster empathy or critical awareness; rather, as she describes Jimmy and Crake in the act of watching these images, Atwood makes clear that they suffer from such extreme information overload that they have become emotionally numb. While Crake "didn't seem to be affected by anything he saw, one way or the other, except when he thought [the image] was funny," after hours spent surfing the Internet, Jimmy feels "as if he'd been to an orgy, one at which he'd had no control at all over what had happened to him. What had been done to him" (86–87).

In addition to information overload, the difficulty of distinguishing images of real events and people from those that are digitally altered prevents Jimmy and Crake from accepting the authenticity of any images they see. The ability to digitally alter images is another significant change to media culture following the publication of *The Handmaid's Tale*. According to William Mitchell, the late 1980s and early 1990s saw an "accelerating crisis of the image" (17) as digital technologies made capturing and processing images widely accessible. This crisis stems from the fact that photographs, regarded since their inception as "incontrovertible proof that a given thing happened" (Sontag 5), depend on a supposed correspondence with reality for credibility.[12] The ability to manipulate and alter images with digital technologies has created a situation in which "the connection of images to solid substance has become tenuous. The currency of the great bank of nature has left the gold standard: images are no longer guaranteed as visual truth—or even as signifiers with stable meaning and value—and we endlessly print more of them" (Mitchell, *Reconfigured Eye* 57). Digital imaging technologies allow editors to easily and seamlessly combine image fragments from different sources and change the appearance of images.[13]

As a result of the digital alteration of images, viewers have been forced to accept that the photographic signifier does not necessarily correspond to any referent. In other words, they must assume instead that all images are inauthentic. As Andy Grundberg speculates in a 1990 column for *The New York Times*, "even if news photographers and editors resist the temptations of electronic manipulation, as they are likely to do, the credibility of all reproduced images will be diminished by a climate of reduced expectations. In short, photographs will not seem as real as they once did" (29). In *Oryx and Crake*, the impossibility of determining the authenticity of images is politically dangerous. Crake glibly assures Jimmy that the "bloodfests" supposedly broadcast live from Asia or the Middle East are "probably taking place on a back lot somewhere in California, with a bunch of extras rounded up off the streets" (82). He similarly explains that the incidents of violence that characterize legal, real-time coverage of executions are "bogus": "He said the men were paid to do it, or their families were. The sponsors required them to put on a good show because otherwise people would get bored and turn off" (83). Jimmy even questions the legitimacy of a video of his own mother's execution that he is shown by security agents: "What if the whole thing was fake? It could even have been digital, at least the shots, the spurts of blood, the falling down. Maybe his mother was still alive, maybe she was even still at large" (259). In contrast to Offred's strategy of "reading beneath" the manipulated images produced by the Gilead regime, there is no similar possibility for reading beneath visual images in *Oryx and Crake*. Crake and Jimmy approach images only with a skeptical cynicism whereby the boys pick apart their technical construction without considering who has created the images or for what purpose. Rather than critical understanding, Crake and Jimmy's approach leads to cynicism, and this cynicism is ultimately dangerous, leading Jimmy to accept the status quo and Crake to believe that there is no other way to effect change than through murder and death.

There is hope in *Oryx and Crake* that comes from the continuing appeal of art, the power of which is evident in Jimmy's life. Even in its degraded form, Jimmy finds meaning and beauty in art, and the quite different reactions that Jimmy and Crake have to art signal the major difference between them. While Crake dismisses art as a way for otherwise inadequate males to attract women—it is "a stab at getting laid" and nothing else to him (168)—Jimmy finds even degraded art powerful and rich. He recalls an Internet program he enjoyed as a teen called "At Home with Anna K.," a "self-styled installation artist with big boobs who'd wired up her apartment so that every moment of her life was sent out live to millions of voyeurs." It seems that this program opens up a possibility for critical spectatorship and resistance for Jimmy. Anna K. introduces Jimmy to Shakespeare: "taking all the parts, while sitting on the can with her retro-look bell-bottom jeans around her ankles" (84). Though Jimmy acknowledges that Anna K.

is "a terrible ham," he feels "grateful to her because she'd been a doorway of sorts. Think what he might not have known if it hadn't been for her. Think of the words. *Sere*, for instance. *Incarnadine*" (84–85).

Moreover, Atwood links art appreciation to one's humanity in the novel, suggesting that Jimmy retains a core of humanity that Crake has lost. The difference between them is best captured by their responses to Oryx, whom they originally encounter in the form of an image on a child pornography website and later develop relationships with in real life. As adolescents, Jimmy and Crake visit a "global sex-trotting site," where they both notice a particularly striking little girl who actually gazes into the camera, making Jimmy and Crake feel as though she is watching them watch her. This is a pivotal moment for both boys. By calling into quesestion the "reality" of the images they consume, Oryx's look represents a moment when the boys might adopt a critical perspective on images. That the boys recognize the look as unusual is evident in their responses to it. Crake is immediately motivated to freeze and print a copy of her look, and he gives the print copy to Jimmy and, unknown to Jimmy, keeps a digital copy for himself. Only in this exchange does Jimmy consider the humanity of the person he is watching. Whereas "none of those little girls had ever seemed real to Jimmy—they'd always struck him as digital clones" (91), when Oryx looks into the camera, "for the first time he'd felt that what they'd been doing was wrong. Before, it had always been entertainment, or else far beyond his control, but now he felt culpable" (91).

In this one case, global visual culture does facilitate human connection. Jimmy comes to perceive of his feelings toward the image as love, and, except for Crake, she remains the only other person Jimmy does love throughout the novel. Crake is also captivated by the image and uses it to locate an adult Oryx later in his life. Both he and Jimmy transfer the bond they felt with her image to the living woman. For Jimmy, the bond he experiences with Oryx's image and later with Oryx is an ethical bond. It motivates him initially to question the morality of viewing pornography, a question that troubles him even more after meeting Oryx. As an adult, Jimmy "remembered himself watching. How could he have done that to her?" (92). Jimmy hides his copy of Oryx's image, and throughout his life, that image reminds him of human vulnerability; thus he strives to protect and cherish Oryx when he meets her in an attempt to make amends for what he perceives as his violation of her as a child. In contrast, Crake is driven to possess Oryx in the flesh just as he has possessed her image for so many years. Oryx's look signifies differently for Jimmy and Crake and attests to the power of interpretation, which can be highly individual even when two people regard the same image.

While Jimmy manages to retain a measure of humanity despite the dehumanized world in which he lives and remains capable of feeling love and valuing art and other forms of human expression considered culturally irrelevant, Crake is truly the product of his society and demonstrates why it is so dangerous for a society to support a visual culture that devalues life. Although Crake glibly dismisses the images he sees as fake, he nevertheless accepts the dehumanized vision of the world they convey. As a result, Crake adopts a perspective on other people that views them as ciphers to be dealt with and not human beings that can be reasoned with or who have dignity in their own right. Even Oryx and Jimmy, the two people to whom he is closest in the novel, serve this function for him. He kills Oryx as the culmination of his plan and uses Jimmy to ensure the survival of the Children of Crake. While Crake's actions are extreme and do not represent the inevitable result of being exposed to graphically violent images, as Atwood shows through her characterization of Jimmy, Crake's actions nevertheless help demonstrate the stakes of visual representation, which does not take place in a cultural vacuum and can motivate individuals to take sometimes unintended actions.

Atwood's Warning in Context

Atwood's attempt in *Oryx and Crake* to explicate those conditions that convince people that murder and death are not only viable solutions but also perhaps the only solutions to social problems means that *Oryx and Crake* resonates strongly in an era characterized by acts of global terrorism, and Atwood has acknowledged the events of September 11, 2001, and the subsequent anthrax attacks as contexts for the novel. Although she began working on the novel months prior to the events of September 11, in an essay on *Oryx and Crake*, she explains that the attacks gave a special urgency to the message she wished to convey in the novel: "I stopped writing for a number of weeks. It's deeply unsettling when you're writing about a fictional catastrophe and then a real one happens. I thought maybe I should turn to gardening books—something more cheerful. But then I started writing again, because what use would gardening books be in a world without gardens, and without books? And that was the vision that was preoccupying me" ("Writing"). Atwood's assertion that a fictional work like *Oryx and Crake* is even more important after the 2001 attacks testifies to her belief that literature can effect social change and provide personal revelation as it fosters critical literacy. Though Jimmy's insights come too late to prevent Crake's actions, his belated critical spectatorship may help readers achieve a more critical and alert attitude despite, or possibly even because of, his failure. Thus Atwood sends Jimmy's warnings out to her contemporary readers to demonstrate the urgent need for critical literacy in the early twenty-first century, something she regards as one of the only possible correctives to adopting the extreme and destructive perspectives that threaten the future of humanity.

Atwood's depiction of literature as an "antidote" to media culture in *The Handmaid's Tale* and *Oryx and Crake* does distinguish her representation of text/image relations sharply from those more hopeful depictions in Morrison's and Mason's texts. And her implication that literature is "endangered" by media images could be misunderstood as her support for the notion that word and image are dichotomous and mutually opposed. However, taken in the larger context of Atwood's career—a career that has included work as a visual artist and has seen the adaption of her work into film and performance—it is clear that Atwood's warnings in her speculative novels are to be taken in the context of regimes that seek to detach the visual from the textual and manipulate the limitations of sight itself in order to forestall critical thinking and political engagement.[14] It is significant that Atwood drew heavily on the Third Reich's use of visual propaganda and spectacle in crafting Gilead and that her depiction of Crake's act of genocide mirrors recent acts of terrorism designed to "perform" violence and murder on a grand scale for an audience of media spectators. I take her point to be less that images threaten text and more that readers should be very wary of those who try to empty out the context and content of either image or text and manipulate the limitations of vision for political ends. Interpreted this way, Atwood's depiction of visuality represents more of an evolution of those concerns expressed by Morrison and Mason, as she engages important strands of contemporary theory such as those articulated by Foucault and Debord rather than a radical departure from these other contemporary women writers.

4

The Politics of Vanishing

Bearing Witness to the Wounded Family in Louise Erdrich's *Shadow Tag*

Like Margaret Atwood, Louise Erdrich has expressed concern over the future of humanity. Her concern stems from the fact that "our planet, which at best estimate might support 2 billion modest lifestyles, will see our population jump to 7 billion in just two years" ("Dartmouth"). In her 2009 Dartmouth commencement address, she put it bluntly: "We're in a nosedive unless we can change as a species." Erdrich's writing attests to her belief that change is possible and that literature has a role to play in facilitating the kind of change she believes is necessary. She has explained that, "although fiction alone may lack the power to head our government leaders off the course of destruction, it affects us as individuals and can spur us to treat the earth . . . as we would our own mothers and fathers" ("Where I Ought to Be" 50). However, the source of change for Erdrich is markedly different than for the other writers included in *Confronting Visuality* because, as a writer of mixed German American and Ojibwe descent,[1] Erdrich offers a perspective that reflects her experiences with both cultures. She has described herself as "on the edge" (*Conversations* 111), and David Stirrup asserts that "written from this place, Erdrich's representations of marginality cannot help but hold some power, whether it resides in transforming infrastructures or in offering transformative potential to those who recognise themselves or their predicaments in her characters" (15).

Author of 14 novels, four volumes of poetry, a short story collection, two books of nonfiction, five children's books, and a textbook on writing, Erdrich has been among a group of mixed-blood native writers to forge a new literary tradition out of the materials of Native American culture and storytelling but using genres and forms provided by Euro-American culture. Though this work has proven controversial,[2] Erdrich's sense that humanity is in a "nosedive" makes it urgent. She exhorts, "No matter what we believe, no matter what our political convictions, ethnicities or religious faiths, we have to get together and steer this thing. We must stop fighting endless wars and act to heal and love this world" ("Dartmouth"). And to do so, she recommends pursuit of the Ojibwe good life, or *mino bimaadiziwin*, as offering the possibility for positive change. In her Dartmouth address, Erdrich described *mino bimaadiziwin* as "Knowledge with courage. Knowledge with fortitude. Knowledge with generosity and kindness" and "devotion to the world," and she contrasts it to "dead knowledge," warning "beware of knowledge without love."

Debra Madsen has identified *mino bimaadiziwin* as Erdrich's "core concern" throughout her writing (11), and at stake in Erdrich's writing is whether *mino bimaadiziwin* is viable in the contemporary world and what particular strategies of what Gerald Vizenor has described as survivance, or "continuation through time of a tribal world view" (Madsen 11), make it possible.[3] In considering these questions, Erdrich naturally engages the ethics and politics of visual representation because visuality is tied up with the issues of power and knowledge that are central to Erdrich's writing. Often in Erdrich's writing, visuality is associated with the type of "dead knowledge" that she describes as inimical to the good life. For example, in the poem "Dear John Wayne" (1984), she recounts the experience of a group of young Native American men who cheer along with everyone else as John Wayne slaughters Indians in a Western, and in *Love Medicine* (1984), Nector Kashpaw abandons his successful acting and modeling career when he finds that the only role available to him is of the dying Indian.

Though Erdrich has at times seemed to link visuality itself to dead knowledge, in 2010 she published her most sustained examination of visuality to date with her novel *Shadow Tag*. And in this novel, Erdrich makes clear that her problem is not with visuality per se but with a specific type of visuality: specularity. Specularity, or speculation, refers to a particular model of vision and knowledge associated with "a totalized visual field" (Gallagher 5). Martin Jay explains that speculation derives from one strain of Greek ocularcentrism (*Downcast Eyes* 28–29): "That strain we might call the argument for specular sameness" (*Downcast Eyes* 31). In her study of women's writing focused on the world wars, Jean Gallagher explains that women writers of the early twentieth century often associated specularity with "the workings of militarism (and its extreme extension in fascism) and its attempts to create a unified national subject that will repress or erase any disrupting traces of difference—ideological, sexual, or racial" (6). This chapter focuses on Erdrich's examination of specularity, which is similar to the writers Gallagher discusses but considers the role of specularity in American self-definition specifically. Erdrich associates the construction of a unified American subject with the historic and ongoing subordination of women and Native Americans in an effort to "repress or erase any disrupting traces of difference." Moreover, she suggests that European and Euro-American artistic traditions, especially portraiture, have helped normalize a specular mode of looking as vision itself. Therefore, I propose that in *Shadow Tag*, Erdrich works to pry apart specularity from vision and recommends a more ethical model for looking.

The Myth of Vanishing: Visuality and Native American Cultural Presence

Erdrich's interest in visuality springs naturally out of her focus on issues of Native American sovereignty and cultural presence and reflects the unique ways in which visuality functions in regard to Native American culture. In contrast to other ethnic groups in the United States, for Native Americans, visuality is tied up with ongoing issues of Native American nationalism and sovereignty. Richard Rodriguez has observed that "America is an idea to which natives are inimical. The Indian represented permanence and continuity to Americans who were determined to call this country new. Indians must be ghosts" (4). As Rodriguez contends, American national presence can be seen as predicated on a native absence, and iconography has long served as an important site for promoting stereotypes of Native Americans as stoic and as historically "vanishing." In portraits, photographs, television shows, and films, Euro-American culture predictably replicates the image of Native Americans in the process of being exterminated, and though some of these representations may present the destruction as tragic, they share a sense of inevitability and finality. Moreover, representations of Native Americans as vanishing have tangible effects on contemporary Native American individuals and communities. As Madsen explains, "The myth of the 'Vanishing American' places Native communities in relation to 'untamed wilderness,' the disappearance of which with the closing of the frontier suggests that no 'real' Native currently exist" (119). And if no "real" natives exist, then ongoing social justice efforts, in regard to land claims or treaty rights, among Indian cultures make little sense. Consequently, as Gina Valentino contends, "Nationalism in Native American discourse means something very different from nationalism in Asian American, African American, and Chicana/o discourses. Nationalism in those other contexts is primarily a cultural matter . . . Native nationalism by contrast has always been tied to sovereignty and is not simply a unifying metaphor; it points to a legal discourse that animates the field" (123).

In *Shadow Tag*, the notion that contemporary Indians are not "real" Indians due to the closing of the frontier plagues Erdrich's twenty-first-century Native American characters because "tribal enrollment issues and government treaty-right benefits, which extend even to eventual college preference" are tied up with blood quantum (13). This issue directly affects the couple at the center of novel, Gil and Irene, because Gil is only "one-quarter" Indian and "his tribal roots—the wrong fractions of Klamath and Cree and Montana Chippewa—weren't recognized" (13). As a result, "he had no casino per cap and had to live by his art" (13). Gil's anxieties over being excluded from official recognition as a Native American and being denied any economic advantage as a result are further exacerbated by the fact that his artistic career has nonetheless been limited in some ways by his ethnicity: "He had not made the big leap. He was known as an American Indian artist, or a native American artist, or a tribal artist, or a Cree artist or a mixed-blood artist or a Metis or Chippewa artist, or sometimes an artist of the American West, even though he lived in Minneapolis" (37–38). Gil's tenuous status causes him considerable anxiety, which he projects onto his relationship with his wife Irene, a mixed-blood woman with Ojibwe and Dakota origins (92). By possessing the body of a native woman, Gil attempts to compensate for what he perceives as his own inadequacy. In previous works, Erdrich has highlighted contemporary disputes over land as these relate to Native American sovereignty,[4] and land claims enter *Shadow Tag* as well since Gil identifies his exclusion from land claims as the raison d'être for his art. However, in *Shadow Tag*, Erdrich explores contemporary issues of nationalism even more clearly in relation to the body of the "Native woman," and in doing so, she points out how an emphasis on family blood claims necessarily links Native American nationalism to patriarchy in a problematic way.[5] Gil takes as evidence of Irene's love her willingness to have children: "Native women of whatever blood quantum are extremely discriminating about the men they have their children with ... Having children was the big thing" (13). Through his art, Gil seeks to further possess Irene, depicting her as a woman that other men desire and thereby constructing himself as the "owner" of a desirable object.

Therefore, one of the most tangible effects of the vanishing myth on characters in *Shadow Tag* is to push them into acceptance of Anglo gender norms, a move that fundamentally shapes the ways they relate to one another as well as the larger community. Julie Tharp maintains that "assimilation into a patriarchal, capitalist culture has shifted the social fabric from one of nurturance and flexibility ... to one of ownership and rigidity" (126). For example, traditional Ojibwe culture treated the end of a marriage very differently and much more casually than does Euro-American culture: a spouse had only to "set the other's belongings on the ground outside the lodge to indicate divorce," a practice that reflected the larger notion that "it was accepted as natural and normal in the course of life to move on to a new life or identity" (Tharp 126).[6] The shift toward Anglo gender norms is reflected in *Shadow Tag* as Irene and Gil struggle in a marriage that is effectively over yet cannot end due to feelings of possessiveness and jealousy.

With its, at times, "claustrophobic" focus on Gil and Irene's marriage, *Shadow Tag* differs to some extent from Erdrich's previous works, as early reviewers were quick to note.[7] Indeed the novel is one of only a few not located in the fictional world she has created in and around Argus, North Dakota. Also, it does not employ her characteristic strategy of narrating the stories of multiple generations of a family or tribe, instead focusing on the five members of a postindustrial nuclear family living in Minneapolis, Minnesota. However, as an extension of Erdrich's critique of visuality, *Shadow Tag* puts issues of visual representation at the center of her text by focusing on the power dynamics between a male artist and his female model who is also his wife. In doing so, the novel provides a detailed examination of the specular mode of looking and considers a variety of ways to resist specularity, and it ultimately promotes ethical witnessing as integral to achieving *mino bimaadiziwin*.

The Specular Economy of *Shadow Tag*

Though the characters in *Shadow Tag* inhabit a contemporary landscape in which they are surrounded by media including television and the Internet, Erdrich explores issues of visuality in this novel primarily through her depiction of Gil, the artist figure, and his relationship to Irene, his model and wife. As a painter, Gil has become famous, and financially secure, painting Irene as an ever-changing series of native womanhood: "She had allowed him to paint her on all fours, looking beaten once, another time snarling like a dog and bleeding, menstruating. In other paintings she was a goddess, breasts tipped with golden fire. Or a creature from the Eden of this continent, covered with moss and leaves. He's done a series of landscapes . . . in which she appeared raped, dismembered, dying of smallpox in graphic medical detail. She had appeared under sheaves of radiance, or emerging from the clay of rough ravines" (30).

A self-taught painter, Gil is obsessed with mastering artistic techniques in order to find and depict the "Truth" about Irene via his portraits of her. Jane Hedley explains that "portraits encourage us to suppose that we can find 'the mind's reflection in the face'" (29), a belief that Gil holds and that drives his work. At the same time, although Gil understands that "her portrayals immediately evoked problems of exploitation, the indigenous body, the devouring momentum of history" (11), he refuses to acknowledge the political or ethical dimensions of his paintings. Instead he approaches the issue of representation only in terms of technical challenge and aesthetic tradition. The fact that Gil paints "Indians" is incidental to him: "He painted Indians when he painted his wife because he couldn't help it" (37). Gil's artistic goal is to capture his wife's image so as to possess it, and he counts it as a success when each of his children, in turn, "called out to the mother on the canvas, and cried when she didn't answer" (37). It embarrasses him when critics interpret his paintings in the context of Native American representations, and he resents being classified as "an American Indian artist" (37–38). He claims that "he had used [Irene's] humiliation as something larger" but not, as one critic suggests, to depict the "*iconic suffering of a people*," which Gil finds "chokingly reductive" (36). Instead Irene's humiliation serves the larger purpose of challenging Gil artistically.

Erdrich spends considerable time in *Shadow Tag* presenting Gil's own perspective on his work and the ways in which he romanticizes his artistic relationship with Irene: "If his brush were merely the eyelash of a cat and he had one canvas to work on for the rest of his life, it would be a painting of Irene" (12). Despite his "not always . . . gentle" depictions of Irene, Gil interprets the portraits as "an act of fascinated love" (36). However, Erdrich also calls Gil's perspective into question, using a variety of narrative strategies to encourage the reader to interpret his work as only one manifestation of a specular mode of looking that is dominant in Western art.

Erdrich aligns Gil with specularity most clearly by using the trope of reflection throughout *Shadow Tag*. Critical definitions of specularity invariably employ the metaphor of a mirror to describe a totalized visual field: "a Mirror reflecting only itself with no remainder" (Jay, *Downcast Eyes* 31–32) or the eye "seeing itself in an infinite reflection" (Jay, "Scopic Regimes" 64). According to Rodolphe Gasche, "The mirroring that constitutes speculative thought articulates the diverse, and the contradictions that exist between its elements, in such a way as to exhibit the totality of which this diversity is a part. Speculation, then, is the movement that constitutes the most complete unity, the ultimate foundation of all possible diversity, opposition, and contradiction" (44). Furthermore, Luce Irigaray has argued that the visual and epistemological tradition of speculation is founded on sexual difference. As Gallagher explains, "women, or cultural constructions of women as 'woman,' have been imagined as the medium, the mirror that reflects the male gaze seeking its own reflection" (6). According to this theory, "woman" can only exist within this closed visual circuit in Western philosophy, which is "incapable of representing femininity/woman other than as the negative of its *own* reflection" (Moi 132).

In *Shadow Tag*, Gil articulates this connection when he describes his motives for painting Irene: "It was a way of getting at the essential other, the unknown essence" (36). Irene comes to realize, "Gil wanted me in relation to another man's desire ... It was why he magnified my sexuality in the paintings. It was why he teased the viewer with my image. He was competitive. He needed to possess something other men wanted" (184), and she employs the image of a mirror to explain how this excludes her entirely: "He fell on the mirror every night and made love to his own image every day, every night, the image he had created of a woman desired by other men" (184).

This scenario is often imagined in terms of entrapment and constraint: women "are imprisoned in a male specular economy in which they are always commodities" (Jay, *Downcast Eyes* 533). Gil attempts to capture Irene within his portraits of her and even believes that he has achieved "mastery" over her image, as when he thinks "he'd progressed to a technical level that allowed him an almost limitless authority" (11). He therefore blames technical challenges that he encounters on Irene: "His paintings were hiding from him because Irene was hiding something" (9).

Erdrich also wants the reader to see that specularity is not unique to Gil but in fact has been naturalized in Western culture through the work of many, seemingly dissimilar, artists. In this way, she seeks to change the way readers view artistic representations of women and ethnic Others and help them recognize how portraiture, in particular, colludes in processes of objectification and stereotyping. Consequently, *Shadow Tag* is rich in ekphrastic descriptions of and allusions to portraits, both those produced by Gil as well as many other artists.

Through ekphrastic descriptions, Erdrich explores aspects of Native American and female representation and connects diverse artists and artistic traditions. Erdrich employs both actual and notional ekphrasis throughout *Shadow Tag*.[8] She uses "actual" ekphrasis to describe paintings by George Catlin, Rembrandt, and Bonnard and "notional" ekphrasis to describe Gil's paintings of Irene. Though the artworks Erdrich describes vary widely in subject matter, period, and style, through her ekphrastic descriptions, Erdrich connects the works in terms of how they depict gendered or racialized Others. For example, her ekphrastic descriptions of Rembrandt's *Lucretia* and Gil's own depiction of Irene as Lucretia emphasize how both artists aestheticize female suffering and self-destruction and ignore or erase the quite different historical and cultural contexts in which Lucretia is driven to suicide and Irene is driven to alcoholism. The Lucretia Gil views in Minneapolis "has already committed the violence to herself and still clutches the stained knife. Her dressing gown is soaked with blood, the gossamer clings hauntingly to her skin, her spirit dissolves her features in a muted blaze, violently alive even as she drains of life" (54), whereas in Gil's painting of Irene as Lucretia, "Irene was clothed like the Lucretia, in blood and rust. Her right hand also gripped a cord slender as the life that was left in her. But instead of a knife in Irene's other hand, Gil had painted a bottle" (55).

Additionally, Erdrich uses ekphrasis to describe how Gil attempts to organize domestic life in a way reminiscent of visual art. Ekphrastic writing relies on figurative techniques such as metaphor, color imagery, and simile to develop word pictures, and Erdrich describes how Gil interacts with his family using language that establishes a direct parallel to his own artistic process. For example, when Gil prepares dinner for the family, his focus is more on the aesthetics of the meal than anything else: "Gil surveyed the organized table. Very satisfying. Green plates, yellow napkins. The cheese soufflé. Crusty baguette. A fresh salad of baby spinach, toasted walnut, pears. A bottle of chilled white" (14). Similarly, it is the aesthetics of his marriage to Irene that most concern him; when Irene insists that the relationship is in trouble, Gil replies, "I think we're beautiful" (96). And Irene realizes that from the outside, her marriage to Gil does appear perfect, "an iconic marriage" (90).

The technique of ekphrasis is well suited to Erdrich's project of examining the specular basis of Western art because, as W. J. T. Mitchell argues in *Picture Theory*, ekphrasis helps writers and readers confront and think about otherness, and he explains that "the alien visual object" can "reveal its distance from the speaker (and the reader)" in the register of cultural or historical difference, in terms of "alienation between the human and its own commodities," and in many other ways as well (181). Yet the one that Mitchell primarily focuses on is sexual difference. Mitchell notes that "the treatment of the ekphrastic image as a female other is commonplace in the genre" (168). Though scholars such as Joanne Diehl, among others, have pointed out that this argument rests on overlooking the long tradition of women's ekphrastic writing, Diehl also contends that this tradition means that women who use ekphrasis work within the "deeply gendered" tradition of ekphrasis, and it becomes an interesting technique through which women have engaged issues of gender and visuality in critically resistant ways (43). For her part, Erdrich uses ekphrasis to expose patterns of power and value in dominant Western art and in doing so, suggests that it can be revised and rewritten. Similarly, she refuses to "master" the images she describes by advancing a particular perspective on them but instead multiplies points of view, unfixing authority and making the specular basis of Western art more visible.

Erdrich also includes numerous allusions to artists, including Velázquez, Hopper, Wyeth, Picasso, de Kooning, Kitaj, John Currin, Rauschenberg, and George Morrison, among others. Erdrich's allusions emphasize the predatory quality behind Western portraiture. Gil suggests that his own obsession with Irene is "like Velázquez, like Degas creeping up on a prostitute in her bath" (12). Similarly, Picasso is characterized as "limitless and devouring" (36). However, allusions to George Catlin are particularly prevalent throughout *Shadow Tag* because Irene is writing her dissertation on Catlin's nineteenth-century paintings of Native Americans, and allusions to Catlin bring the predatory quality of portraiture into full focus because the Native Americans he painted objected to his work on the basis that he was "stealing" from them (7). Although Gil laughingly dismisses these concerns as ignorant, Irene similarly uses the rhetoric of harm and theft to characterize her relationship with Gil, establishing a clear connection between Gil and Catlin in doing so.

In another parallel to Gil, Erdrich also emphasizes the great love that Catlin professed to feel toward his Native American subjects. Although, as Irene explains, they "broke his health, broke his heart. Stole the comforts of his life" (135), Catlin was driven to capture their images before they disappeared entirely, a fate he saw as tragic but inevitable. In doing so, however, Catlin played an important role in contributing to the myth of the vanishing Indian despite the fact that he lamented rather than celebrated the destruction of Indian cultures and rejected the discourse of progress that framed most nineteenth-century discussions of Indian removal and Western expansion. John Hausdoerffer explains that by portraying "the catastrophe as inevitable, as outside choice, as natural," Catlin enacts "the very discourse and logic of domination characteristic of the power he intended to challenge" (144). In his *Letters and Notes on the Manners, Customs, and Conditions of North American Indians*, Catlin describes his purpose for painting Native Americans: "I have flown to their rescue—not of their lives or of their race (for they are *doomed* and must perish), but to the rescue of their looks and their modes, at which the acquisitive world may hurl their poison and every besom of destruction, and trample them down and crush them to death; yet, phoenix-like, they may rise from the 'stain on a painter's palette,' and live again upon canvas, and stand forth for centuries yet to come, the living monuments of a noble race" (16). Hausdoerffer points out that "Catlin does not set out to prevent the destruction of societies, the exploitation of environments, or the massacre of individuals" (147). Instead he wanted to prevent "the vaporization of any *record* of 'natural' Indian societies or beautiful Indian landscapes that whites may study for enlightenment or enjoy for pleasure" (147). In this way, Hausdoerffer contends that Catlin was actually quite similar to President Andrew Jackson since both argued that "genocide was a destined fact of nature; both strengthened a discourse that eliminated the choice of social and environmental justice for native peoples, strengthening power over them" (148).

By stressing the extent to which artists from Rembrandt to Catlin to Gil are driven by a desire to possess and consume gendered and racialized Others via imagery, Erdrich aligns them with the Ojibwe figure of the windigo, a connection that underscores the danger of specular looking. A windigo is an "Ojibwe figure of excessive consumption, predatory sexual appetites and greed" (Tharp 131), and this figure features with increasing prominence in Erdrich's writing. According to Tharp, "although the original windigo denotes only an 'ice spirit of awful hunger,'" Erdrich has come to use the windigo to represent "male-dominant, urban, material, non-Ojibwe life" (118).[9] Erdrich signals that Gil is a windigo figure by his desire to consume Irene via her image, which causes him to act out violently against even his own children because he is jealous of their claim to Irene's time and affection. His feelings emphasize the connection to consumption: "Irene's distance aroused in Gil a desolate craving" (11).

Furthermore, Erdrich suggests that Gil has actually chosen to release a windigo into his family out of what he sees as artistic necessity. He believes that conflict with Irene actually drives his best artistic work: "He'd become aware that the worse things were between them, the better his work came out. It did not yet occur to him to wonder whether his suspicions about Irene were also a method of pushing her away from him, so that he could feel her absence, and in turn feel an aching desire out of which he could make his art" (81).

Ultimately, Gil is also a casualty of his having unleashed a windigo in his life. After Irene changes the terms of their relationship by presenting Gil with divorce papers, he undergoes a physical transformation. Irene notes that "He did not look like the man he was last year, nor like the man she had married. He did not look like anyone she had ever seen before" (242). When she explains that he can move back into the house but that their relationship can no longer include sex or painting, "He looked puzzled, and thought she was absurdly out of touch for thinking those things could interest him now. When he'd stopped drinking, he'd stopped eating, and when he'd stopped eating, he'd stopped wanting anything" (242). In the end, Gil is depicted as himself consumed by the same forces through which he attempted to consume Irene. Erdrich's warning about the dangers of specularity is clear here: though speculation may seem to offer back to the presumably white male viewer a reassuring reflection of himself, it is also liable to consume the male viewer in the process.

Deception as Resistance

While Gil is an irredeemable loss in *Shadow Tag*, Irene also fails to survive the novel, and in this way, Erdrich critiques the strategies that Irene employs in response to Gil. Despite her own failures, however, Irene offers an important counternarrative to oppose Gil's romantic interpretation of his work. Gil's masterpieces incite physical revulsion in Irene, and what he interprets as a sign of his love, she understands as a sign of his narcissism. "I'm just food" (91), she tells one of Gil's fans who marvels at their relationship. In this way, Irene, though not an easy character to identify with herself, brings to the fore a dissenting perspective that undermines the authority of Gil's interpretation of his work. Irene also provides an important way for Erdrich to test possible strategies to resist the specular mode of looking.

Irene is at once a participant in and victim of the specular economy detailed in *Shadow Tag*. A casual academic who struggles with the self-discipline required to finish her PhD in history, Irene is described as possessing a "brilliant" scholarly mind (7), and she produces complex analyses of her relationship with Gil and of his paintings of her based on her historical research. She realizes, for example, that "her name was now a cipher joined to a simulacra. And the portraits were everywhere. By remaining still, in one position or another, for her husband, she had released a double into the world. It was impossible, now, to withdraw that reflection. Gil owned it. He had stepped on her shadow" (39). Despite her analytical abilities, however, Irene is almost completely unable to move from analysis to action.

Irene experiences Gil's single-minded gaze as oppressive, and she seeks to "shed the weight of his eyes" throughout *Shadow Tag* (21). Sometimes she literally tries to hide from his gaze by leaving the house or escaping to the bathroom or her office. More often, she hides the truth from Gil, as when she falsifies historical records to communicate with him. Most importantly, she keeps a false diary she knows he is reading, in which she casts doubt over the facts of their relationship and his paternity of their children.

Irene's responses to Gil are characterized by the "enigmatic inaccessibility" that some French philosophers, including Nietzsche, Derrida, and Irigaray, have discussed as providing women with a possible way to resist "full incorporation into the specular economy of phallogocentric culture" (Jay, *Downcast Eyes* 527). Throughout *Shadow Tag*, Erdrich relies on the imagery of water, in particular, to symbolize Irene's inaccessibility. Thus when Gil describes Irene's increasing emotional distance, "it was as if she weren't really there, but watching him from underwater" (10). Irene seeks frequent solace from Gil's demands in the bathtub where she can "gradually soothe the ache of self-awareness" (21), Irene and her daughter, Riel, ice-skate on the frozen lake outside their home, and Irene is described as a powerful swimmer. For both Nietzsche and Irigaray, water became a potent symbol for women, a "fluid medium that both frightened and attracted Nietzsche" (Jay, *Downcast Eyes* 527), which Irigaray discusses in terms of its power to disrupt "rigidity of both frozen forms and mirrors. It is a place which I wouldn't call the opposite but different, in relation to the sun" (qtd. in Jay, *Downcast Eyes* 527). However, if water is associated with the positive ability to resist specularity in French philosophy, there is a more "sinister role played by water" (Noori 91) in Ojibwe mythology, a role important throughout Erdrich's fiction. Despite the fact that Irene's own name invokes a song about drowning, she blithely answers her daughter's anxious question, "Could you save me if I fell in?" with "I could save anyone" (101), though this proves sadly untrue in the novel's climax, when Irene loses her own life while attempting to rescue a suicidal Gil.

Irene's diaries further signify her "enigmatic inaccessibility" in *Shadow Tag*, and her keeping a false diary is one of the most tangible ways she resists Gil. In this, Irene is also aligned with French theorists such as Derrida, who "pitted *écriture* against style" (Jay, *Downcast Eyes* 527), suggesting that "if style were a man (much as the penis, according to Freud, is the 'normal prototype of fetishes'), then writing would be a woman" (Derrida 57). And for Irigaray, as well as other French theorists such as Kristeva and Cixous, the issue of the relationship between woman and writing (or language, in general) was central. While the concept of *écriture féminine* or a unique woman's language is complex and still subject to considerable debate, the important point, as Jay observes, is that "these various claims for a special women's relationship to language were frequently couched in antiocular terms, often pitting the temporal rhythms of the body against the mortifying spatialization of the eye" (*Downcast Eyes* 528). Moreover, running throughout Irigaray's writing is the idea that "rather than aspiring to the condition of men, seeking to emulate their search for theoretical, speculative, and evidential truth and eidetic essences, women ... should positively embrace their identification with precisely what defeats such a quest: the dissimulating veil that 'hides' the truth" (Jay, *Downcast Eyes* 526–27).

Irene clearly embraces the "dissimulating veil" by using her diary to deceive Gil. In her "red" diary, Irene falsifies their history together and questions Gil's paternity of their children, illustrating, in doing so, that she understands that Gil is motivated by his feelings of inferiority based on his blood quantum. However, while Irene intends that her "blue diary" is her "real" diary in which she honestly reflects on the lies recorded in her "red" diary, Erdrich indicates that both diaries are really false inasmuch as Irene omits details she does not wish to acknowledge even in her "true" diary. In this way, Irene deceives herself just as she deceives Gil. Most importantly, she has "walled off" an affair she actually did have, and "she did not ever, or almost ever, go behind that wall" (105). Here Irene is pictured veiling the facts of her life even from herself. Similarly, she refuses to look at Gil's paintings of her because she believes "it was best not to look too long at the paintings" or "her portrayals would stick in her mind" (30). Irene's goal seems to be to not give mental assent to those aspects of her life of which she is ashamed.

However, the difficulty of this self-deception drives Irene to alcoholism, which facilitates the process of forgetting, and ultimately seems to compromise her memory. Irene is pictured as literally unable to hold a thought as when she attempts to discuss the human right to privacy with Gil. When Gil interprets the issue in light of policies such as the Patriot Act that loosen restrictions on wiretapping, Irene interjects, "Can you stop talking political shit? I didn't mean privacy as in civil rights, I meant between humans in an emotional sense" and argues, "When you take away that person's privacy you can control that person" (33). However, this insight is met with silence from Gil, and the novel describes how "Irene's thoughts *flickered away*" (33; emphasis added). As she changes the conversation to other topics, her point is lost on Gil and herself. Even worse, Irene seems to have largely forgotten her early teaching in Ojibwe culture and language due to this same process of self-enforced amnesia (129) and therefore largely fails to pass on her cultural knowledge to her children. Unlike Gil, who was raised by his white mother and never knew his Native American father, Irene was raised by a single mother active in the American Indian Movement. She was "carted to every AIM event" (35), and Riel even has memories of attending powwows prior to her grandmother's death. However, as Irene hides more and more of herself from Gil, her family, and herself, she seems to lose not only her connection to Ojibwe culture but even her memory of it.

In the end, Irene's deceptive practices keep her locked in a power struggle with Gil that prevents either of them from moving on together or alone. Consequently, she drowns while trying to save Gil from drowning. Riel concludes, "She died because she could not let go of him" (250). Just as Gil's unleashing of the windigo ultimately destroys him, Irene ultimately succeeds best at deceiving herself.

The Importance of Ethical Witnessing

Shadow Tag serves as a cautionary tale by focusing on Gil and Irene's ultimate inability to achieve *mino bimaadiziwin*, and, in doing so, it demonstrates the problems of not only the specular mode of looking but also the use of deception as a strategy to combat speculation. The novel also offers a strong contrast to these destructive practices via the character of the couple's daughter Riel, who is revealed in the conclusion to be the omniscient narrator of the novel. Riel's "knowledge of compassion" allows her to avoid the extremes adopted by Gil and Irene and illustrates that Erdrich's critique is not focused on vision itself, since Riel's story is based on "bearing witness" to what she observed as a child as well as her careful readings of her family's artifacts. Riel is a witness to the final months of her parents' lives. In *Shadow Tag*, which she submits as her master's thesis as "a writer in a creative writing program" (251), she testifies to what she observed as an 11 year old, using her memories to reconstruct the narrative of her parents' final months, in addition to interviews with their therapist and friends and, most importantly, the artifacts they have both left behind: her father's paintings and her mother's diaries. She explains that in the novel, she has "put it all together . . . filled in certain events and connections" (251), and indeed her purpose for writing seems to be to reconcile all the disparate materials she has inherited in order to understand why her parents could not survive their marriage.

Erdrich's choice of Riel to narrate *Shadow Tag* is significant because of all the members of her family, Riel retains the strongest connection to her Ojibwe heritage. Riel, the middle child and only daughter (named after the Metis patriot to whom Gil's family is distantly related), senses that something is amiss and begins preparing herself to survive a terrorist attack that seems inevitable to her. Riel realizes that her Native American heritage might be the best defense she has against the dangers she perceives. Becoming acutely aware of herself as "an Indian, an American Indian, a native person," she determines to "plan out how to survive a terrorist attack, using the skills of her ancestors" (60). Riel begins creating detailed memory charts to identify useful patterns in her own life and from history, reading voraciously about Native American practices and survival strategies and stockpiling survival supplies. It is no surprise, then, that Riel leads her brothers to revolt against Gil's physical abuse and ultimately succeeds in taking away the power he has over them. Riel sets about methodically to take away Gil's power, realizing that "if she observed her father closely enough, she would figure out how to get the better of him" (62). She first recognizes that she can intimidate him by drawing attention to his physical mistreatment, and later, when the children ask to shelter an abandoned cat and Gil refuses, "Riel, who would normally have folded obediently or stiffened under her father's touch, turned on him in a cool fury and shoved him with all her strength" (209). While Gil struggles to his feet, Riel wraps the cat in a scarf, and "although no one else in the family had seen Riel push her father, they all sensed immediately that Gil's opinion was now of no concern" (210).

Even as a child, Riel recognizes the danger that Gil poses to the family and adopts an active, resistant stance based on strategies she gleans from Irene's research materials and her own research at the middle-school library. Her success at resistance even at the age of 11 is an indictment of Irene, who not only fails to respond productively to the threat posed by Gil but also refuses to even fully recognize this threat.

Riel's connection to her heritage is further strengthened after her parents' deaths, when she finds herself in a large, extended Native American family, adopted, along with Florian and Stoney, by Irene's half sister May and her partner, Bobbi. This large family helps Riel understand that "old-time Indians are us, still going to sundances, ceremonies, talking in the old language and even using the old skills if we feel like it, not making a big deal" (248–49).

Though reviewers were tempted to read a parallel between Erdrich and Irene due to the fact that both were part of an "iconic marriage" that ultimately failed amid charges of abuse and finally resulted in suicide,[10] Riel's narrative strategies make her more of a direct parallel to Erdrich. Indeed what Riel describes as a strategy of "putting it all together," Erdrich has referred to in interviews as "incorporation," and she has described "incorporation" as absorbing alien elements into a traditional framework. Erdrich has recounted how her grandfather practiced incorporation in his storytelling as he narrated the geography of the reservation. Pointing to the low hills, he would identify features of the land, each receiving the name of the animal it resembled. He "even incorporated the highways into the shapes because some of them got their tails cut off" ("Whatever Is Really Yours" 80, 79). According to Brogan, "Incorporation takes the new into the old, changing both, creating an entity different from either that is nevertheless experienced as continuous with the past" (34). Erdrich suggests that her grandfather's ability to incorporate the highway as a new, anomalous element into the traditional framework speaks to the "resilience" of the Turtle Mountain Band of Chippewa and is "one of the strengths of Indian culture": "you pick and choose and keep and discard" ("Whatever Is Really Yours" 79). Her grandfather's verbal revisions supply Erdrich with a model for the way tradition is continually reshaped and thus survives. As Brogran explains, "What threatens to 'cut off' elements of tribal tradition is accepted, and becomes survivable, through a kind of imaginative accommodation" (35). Though Erdrich has modeled this storytelling technique in various ways throughout her fiction, she offers *Shadow Tag* as an example of a novel-length work of incorporation.

The process of incorporation is effective at resisting the predatory, controlling urges behind speculation. Incorporation prevents Riel from attempting to master the story of her parents' marriage and instead offers a way that the material artifacts of Riel's family—the paintings and the diaries—inform one another, offering a more complete picture than either one could alone. Moreover, through the techniques of ekphrasis and allusion, Riel/Erdrich puts the story of Irene and Gil's marriage alongside a wide variety of museum and domestic objects, historical and media accounts, illustrating the wider significance of Gil and Irene's conflict as well. Thus "put[ting] it all together" allows Riel to narrow in on the power dynamics of her parents' relationship while also demonstrating a way to ethically witness the suffering of others, even when it is rendered beautiful.

In this way, Erdrich posits the type of ethical witnessing that Riel practices as not only an effective but a necessary corrective to specular looking. Throughout Erdrich's writing, a recurring issue is whether people can learn to see the absence of traditional Native American culture as politically significant—since this absence testifies to the near genocide of America's indigenous people—and can learn to recognize the continuing existence of Native Americans despite their cultural invisibility. As one of her characters observes of Ojibwe land lost to timber interests, "The place will be haunted I suppose, but no one will have ears sharp enough to hear the low voices, or the *vision clear to see* their still shadows" (*Tracks* 31; emphasis added). Similar to how Atwood describes her role as writer as helping readers to recognize that the "howling" in the wilderness signifies suffering rather than joy, Erdrich links her vocation as writer to bearing witness to the destruction of traditional native cultures and the subsequent cultural invisibility of Native Americans. She has said,

> I think all Native Americans living today probably look back and think, "How, out of the millions and millions of people who were here in the beginning, the very few who survived into the 1920s, and the people who are alive today with some sense of their own tradition, how did it get to be me, and why?" And I think that quest and that impossibility really drives us in a lot of ways. It's central to the work, and so we go about telling these stories, we feel compelled. We're, in a way, survivors, of that tradition; there aren't a lot of people who are going to tell these stories, or who are going to look at the world in this particular way. (Erdrich and Dorris 98–99)

Erdrich's description of her role as writer emphasizes that she wants not only to bear witness to the historic genocide of Native Americans but also to explore the extent that tradition can be usable for contemporary Native Americans as well.

Riel is the culmination of Erdrich's consideration of visuality, gender, and nationalism in *Shadow Tag*, and her critical abilities offer a model for readers. Riel resists the urge to offer any kind of totalizing narrative about her parents by writing a multivoiced text in which they both speak; she similarly refuses to turn a blind eye to those aspects of her parents' lives and relationship that are unflattering and painful; instead she honestly examines them to discover any insight she can. And the fact that Riel chooses creative writing as the medium through which to best "put it all together" implies real importance for Erdrich's own textual strategies. In Erdrich's view, in the twenty-first century, it is a young, mixed-blood, urban female who is best able to carry on the traditions that will help Native Americans, and all readers, survive and thrive in the face of ongoing legal and social disenfranchisement.

Part III

Spectatorship in an Expanded Field of Vision

5

Against Visual Objectivity in Gish Jen's "Birthmates" and Chitra Banerjee Divakaruni's "The Ultrasound"

Images objectifying and fetishizing the external female body in mainstream media are so common that writers like Morrison, Mason, Atwood, and Erdrich can rely on readers' familiarity with these images when engaging issues of visual representation in their texts. However, increasingly, writers can also assume that readers will be familiar with images of the interior female body as these have become ubiquitous in medicine as well as in advertising, television, and film. In the contemporary period, the development of visual technologies that promise to "transparently" represent the interior body has not only revolutionized the practice of medicine but also created new issues with which feminist scholars and writers have had to grapple about the ways women's bodies become visible via these technologies and how medical images are deployed in medicine and the larger culture.[1]

Critical scholarship has long recognized a variety of ways that imaging technologies, ranging from x-ray, to mammogram, to laparoscopy, reproduce gender inequalities.[2] But no medical imaging technology has been more greatly inflected by the politics of gender—and race—than fetal imaging. For example, recent legislation in 24 US states mandating ultrasounds for women considering abortion illustrates the connections between gender, race, and imaging as women seeking abortions—who are disproportionately women of color, low income, and have the least access to imaging as part of prenatal care[3]—are now required to view fetal ultrasounds as part of first-trimester abortion despite the fact that an ultrasound is not considered medically necessary for first-trimester abortions and adds to the cost of the procedure (Guttmacher Institute, "Requirements").

As the Guttmacher Institute report on this legislation concludes, it seems to represent an attempt "to personify the fetus and dissuade a woman from obtaining an abortion."[4]

However, the assumption that viewing a fetal ultrasound image will automatically translate into the acceptance of fetal personhood directly conflicts with data out of areas of India and China where fetal ultrasound has been linked to sex-selective abortions and is increasingly banned in prenatal care as a result (Mallik; Guihau; Plafker 1233). Rather than personify the fetus and dissuade women from abortion, in the context of patriarchal Indian and Chinese cultures where males are much more highly valued than females, the availability of ultrasound images has led to skyrocketing abortion rates, to the extent that male/female gender ratios have been noticeably skewed (Last; "Illegal Gender Selection"; "Preventing Gender-Based Sex Selection"). That the same images could be perceived in the United States to prevent abortion and in China and India to encourage abortion illustrates that, as Lisa Mitchell observes in *Baby's First Picture*, "although [fetal] ultrasound is perceived to be a 'window,' it is a 'window' through which different groups see different things" (7).

Indeed fetal images are informed by political, commercial, medical, and domestic contexts, and any given spectator might see these images in a number of ways depending on how he or she is positioned within these contexts. Even in a US context, it is difficult to predict how an expectant woman will see and interpret her ultrasound images because her viewing will be informed by whether or not the pregnancy is desired, what she thinks about the issues of abortion and fetal personhood, her feelings about medical intervention in pregnancy, and her age, race, class, nationality, and religion. It is not even uncommon for a specific viewer to adopt multiple, sometimes conflicting, viewpoints from which to see and interpret fetal images. The issues of spectatorship that have been implicit in all the texts included in *Confronting Visuality* thus become explicit, and in fact urgent, in works that focus on fetal imaging.

This chapter focuses on two short stories, both published in 1995, that place the difficulty of interpreting fetal images at their imaginative centers. In "Birthmates" and "The Ultrasound," Gish Jen and Chitra Banerjee Divakaruni focus on Asian American characters who are marginalized in the United States because of their ethnicity and consequently have difficulty adopting any one of the dominant discourses on fetal imaging. As the characters attempt to identify with various authoritative perspectives on fetal images and yet ultimately find that each perspective is limited despite its claim to authority, the characters gain awareness of themselves as readers and of some of the difficult problems of interpreting visual images. Ultimately, Jen and Divakaruni question whether a single, authoritative perspective on fetal imaging is possible and suggest that the only hope of objectivity comes from recognizing the existence of multiple, partial, and contradictory viewing positions.

Visuality in Asian American Culture

Jen and Divakaruni represent a group of contemporary Asian American writers who consider issues of visuality as a way of exploring the paradoxical position that Asian Americans have long held in the American visual economy. On the one hand, Asians are often referred to as a "visible minority," a label suggesting that the markers of Asian identity are primarily visible. As Eleanor Ty points out, it is the "visible hieroglyphs imprinted on our eyes, our black hair, our noses, our face, and our bodies . . . along with our yellow or brown colour" that "mark us indelibly as other, as Oriental, as exotic, subservient, mysterious, deviant, or threatening" (3–4). On the other hand, American media and culture have historically constructed America in bipolar terms, as white or black. Consequently, in Gary Okihiro's words, "whites render Asians, American Indians, and Latinos invisible, ignoring the gradations and complexities of the full spectrum between the racial poles" (75). This invisibility serves to erase the differences between Asian American groups—ways in which Korean Americans differ from Filipino Americans and Chinese Americans, for instance. Timothy Fong concludes that Asian Americans are "visible only in such stereotypes as 'perpetual foreigners,' 'overachievers,' and the 'model minority'" and are invisible "due to widespread ignorance of their distinct histories and contemporary experiences" (3).

Consequently, though important differences distinguish the Chinese American couple about which Jen writes from the Indian American families that are the focus of Divakaruni's story, the politics of the visible represent a point of common concern and a subject worthy of literary treatment for both authors. The politics of the visible refer to the fact that for Asian Americans, remaining invisible signals social and political disenfranchisement, while becoming visible, even within literature, runs the risk of representing ethnic difference in such a way as to "[fall] prey to Western scopophilic fantasies" (Ty, *Politics of the Visible* 10). For Asian American writers, the challenge is to resist stereotypes while still representing the everyday acts that constitute the self. Jen and Divakaruni's solution to this problem is to put the focus on the "trap" that is the visible—to expose the limitations not only of visual knowledge but also of claims to be able to objectively and authoritatively interpret visual information. Because ethnic difference complicates the characters' identification with any one of the supposedly objective discourses on fetal imaging in "Birthmates" and "The Ultrasound," the characters develop partial perspectives that are clearly tied to their embodied experiences as gendered, racialized individuals. Moreover, Jen and Divakaruni suggest that these partial perspectives might offer a way to achieve objective vision. In this, they advocate what Donna Haraway has called "situated knowledge," or knowledge that recognizes the extent to which it is embodied and constructed. In terms of vision, Haraway explains that "only partial perspective promises objective vision" (190). Jen and Divakaruni promote the value of situated knowledge by illustrating the limitations of three contrasting but culturally authoritative and dominant discourses on fetal images: documentary discourse (associated with anti-abortion politics and the mass media), diagnostic discourse (the position of the medical community), and skeptical discourse (the feminist response to fetal imaging).

Contrasting Perspectives on Fetal Imaging

The fetal ultrasound image is a familiar enough staple of American iconography that most viewers immediately recognize the fetal silhouette, "with its enlarged head and finlike arm, suspended in its balloon of amniotic fluid" (Petchesky 268). Fetal images are more widely accessible to the public than are other types of medical images and have become ubiquitous in mass media and anti-abortion propaganda. Additionally, in recent decades, fetal ultrasounds have become a "rite of passage" for expectant women—at least those with insurance—despite their questionable medical value and the possible risks associated with them (Leary). However, though fetal images have become ubiquitous, they still pose considerable interpretive difficulties, difficulties that are generally not acknowledged within the most common discourses on fetal imaging.

Likely the most pervasive perspective on fetal imaging is associated with anti-abortion politics and the mass media. This discourse is manifested in the numerous public uses that have been made of fetal images. While anti-abortion groups continue to depend heavily on these images in their materials, using them on protest signs, roadside billboards, and in other literature, fetal images have also been central to commercial campaigns by AT&T, Volvo, Honda, and Huggies, and in television programs and films. Though mass media representations of fetal imaging construct "pleasurable consumer linkages with products and services" (Mehaffy 178) while anti-abortion representations tend to link the images to "narrative[s] of violence and death" (182), Marilyn Mehaffy notes that the two types of representations are strikingly similar. Both construct the fetus as "a speaking, thinking subject and cinematic family member" (Mehaffy 178), and, at the same time, they present the fetus as the single image of pregnancy, largely erasing the maternal body and disembodying pregnant women by suggesting that the fetus is completely independent of the context of a maternal body.

Moreover, medical imaging technologies and mass media technologies have long enjoyed a symbiotic relationship, one that cultural historian José van Dijck explains operates on three levels: (1) "their technological developments tend to go hand in hand, meaning that innovations in one domain usually benefit technical advancements in the other domain"; (2) the media provide new ways to distribute "interior-body imagery among the public at large [that] has undoubtedly contributed to a rising public interest in medical issues"; and (3) "medical and media technologies converge in their production of visual spectacle—displaying the inside of the human body" (9–10). The symbiotic relationship between media and medical imaging technologies has significant implications for the kinds of stories that the mass media can and do tell about medical imaging. Viewers are always held at a "camera-eye's distance" in mass media representations of medical imaging. In terms of narrative, this means that even when viewers share the perspective of the imaging camera and purportedly penetrate the human body, viewers share what Ella Shohat refers to as the perspective of the "traveling image maker" (260)—never the one who is imaged. Viewers almost always identify with the perspective of either the physician or the camera itself rather than with the person whose body is being imaged.

In order to construct the fetus as a person using ultrasound technologies, mass media representations invoke documentary access to fetal bodies, and the coherence of these representations depends on the viewer accepting the images as realistic and accurate, despite the fact that "neither the moving sonographic image nor its still photograph constitutes a 'picture' in the familiar realist sense, but rather a digitally-replicated image of deferred sound" (Mehaffy 180–81). Medical images in general do not employ the kinds of details that characterize photographs. Instead medical images fall into the category of "quasi-objects" because "the image and the information circulate and, through technology, mutually support each other to produce assent among trained observers" (Crawford 74). Medical images are attributed with realism because expert readers agree that these images accurately represent the body at work and are more precise than other methods of representation. The documentary discourse on fetal imaging depends on faith in the authenticity of medical images to claim that the fetus is fully and recognizably human.

While the documentary discourse on medical imaging does promote a biomedical view of the interior body, it also diverges from the second dominant discourse on imaging, which is a strictly medical perspective. The medical community's diagnostic discourse on fetal imaging contests the notion that an ultrasound provides documentary access to fetal bodies. For medical professionals, fetal images serve as diagnostic tools, and the medical community has been adamant that medical interpretation should accompany fetal imaging (US Food and Drug Administration). Diagnostic discourse suggests that the visual information about pregnancy garnered through imaging is unmatched by any other type of information available. Thus medical interpretation of fetal images has taken precedence over women's lived experiences of pregnancy. The kinds of sensory data, such as cravings for certain foods or repulsions to certain smells or tastes, that women traditionally relied on for information about pregnancy is dismissed as unreliable and unnecessary given the ability of physicians to use technology to "[strip] away the walls of the abdomen and uterus and [look] into the womb" (Beck 21).

Doctors use fetal ultrasounds to identify a number of genetic and/or developmental disorders with the fetus, ranging from life-threatening conditions such as anencephaly, to socially stigmatized conditions such as dwarfism and cleft palate. Images can also confirm multiple fetuses and, in high-risk pregnancies, help determine the placement of the fetus and the placenta. Most commonly, though, fetal ultrasounds are prescribed in order to determine gestational age. Although a 1984 report by the joint National Institutes of Health/Food and Drug Administration panel recommended against "routine use . . . to view . . . or obtain a picture of the fetus," it approved of use of the technology to "estimate gestational age," and therefore ultrasounds have become routine (qtd. in Petchesky 273). The medical community has guarded its privileged perspective on imaging by opposing attempts to remove imaging from medical contexts (US Food and Drug Administration). Although some ultrasounds do take place in commercial "photo studios" equipped with 3-D ultrasound machines and with names like "Fetal Fotos," the vast majority of ultrasounds continue to be created and interpreted by medical experts, and despite widespread familiarity with ultrasound images, most people are unable to read these images for themselves apart from a medical interpreter.

In contrast to both the documentary and diagnostic discourses, the skeptical, or feminist, discourse on fetal images denies that these images are realistic or provide particularly valuable knowledge of pregnancy. Feminists have tended to reject fetal images outright due to the widespread use of these images to support the concept of fetal personhood. In doing so, they follow the logic that "we can give primary consideration to women or to fetuses, but not to both" (Michaels 113). According to the skeptical view, only pregnant women can say anything definitive on the subject of their pregnancies; therefore it is only their perspective on fetal images that could possibly matter. The fetus, for all intents, remains "a blob of protoplasm" in the feminist view (Michaels 117), and attempts to make the fetus visible are equated with attempts to make the fetus a person. Consequently, the idea that fetal images pose a danger to women is repeated over and over in feminist literature. From Ann Oakley's 1984 assertion that "as the 'iron curtain' of the mother has been swept aside revealing the womb and its contents in their full glory, it has become no longer necessary to consult mothers about their attitudes" (183), to Carol Stabile's 1998 echo: "In order for the embryo/fetus to emerge as autonomous—as a person, patient, or individual in its own right—all traces of a female body . . . must disappear" (172), feminist scholars have traditionally critiqued fetal imaging. In place of the visual knowledge of pregnancy offered by imaging, feminists emphasize women's haptic experiences of pregnancy, arguing that pregnant women, not doctors or other spectators of fetal images, have privileged access to information about pregnancy.

Though the three dominant discourses on fetal imaging seem to share little common ground, they do share similar aims. Each of them claims to view and interpret fetal images from a uniquely authoritative and privileged position. The pro-life and mass media discourse suggests that these images document fetal personhood for all viewers, while the medical community argues that trained experts alone are equipped to interpret these images, and feminist discourse dismisses the visual information provided by imaging to emphasize women's embodied experiences. By claiming a privileged, authoritative position on fetal images, each of the discourses advances a particular ideological position toward the fetus, a position that reflects underlying assumptions not only about fetal and female personhood but also about power and who is best equipped to make important decisions about who counts as a person and what status is accorded to various types of people. In this sense, each discourse is ultimately less about what the fetal image really does or does not show and more about "who will control the vast material resources of the U.S." (Berlant, "America" 97). Thus the fetus made visible through imaging becomes a cipher through which groups can argue with one another about issues that transcend even the abortion debate.

Fetal Imaging and the Politics of the Visible in "Birthmates" and "The Ultrasound"

In "Birthmates" and "The Ultrasound," the protagonists have difficulty identifying with any one of the dominant discourses on fetal images due to their marginal status within American culture. Published in *Ploughshares* in 1995, and later selected by John Updike for inclusion in *Best American Short Stories 1995*, Gish Jen's "Birthmates" highlights the perspective of a father toward pregnancy and ultrasound. Art Woo is a 38-year-old divorced computer salesman who sells a technology (the minicomputer) quickly becoming obsolete. Though Art is an American citizen, he faces racist speech and even violence due to his ethnicity. Art's boss, for example, strikes him in the face with a tennis racket during a heated conversation about the future of minicomputers. "*Don't talk to me about fault, bottom line it's you Japs who are responsible for this whole fucking mess*," he comments before attacking Art (114). Furthermore, Jen suggests that Art has internalized this negative self-image and sees himself through the lens of the dominant culture. Consequently, he assumes an attitude of "understanding" with regard to his boss's behavior and even accepts the insulting apology his boss offers following the attack: "Art shouldn't take what he said personally, in fact he knew Art was not a Jap, but a Chink" (114). Art also regards the small raise he is subsequently offered as a sign of his "victory" in the matter.

"Birthmates" takes place during a business conference, during which Art finds himself housed in a welfare hotel and is thwarted in his attempt to find a new job. Art's professional failure prompts him to reflect on his failed marriage to Lisa. Lisa divorced Art as a result of his inability to grieve along with her when, after many months of fertility treatments and two miscarriages, Lisa's pregnancy was medically terminated at four-and-a-half months because the fetus was afflicted with brittle bone disease. Lisa and Art are at odds over how to define and therefore grieve their loss. Lisa mourns the loss of her "baby," while Art refuses to grieve for "just a baby-to-be" (118). Jen was prompted to write the story as a result of her own experience terminating a much-desired pregnancy, but she has distanced herself from both Lisa's and Art's perspectives: "In my mind, I'm not on the side of either one of these characters. I think that she has a viewpoint and he has a viewpoint. She hasn't had to grapple with some of the hard realities he's had to deal with. It's not as though I see her as right. I see her as having learned to retain some of the humanity, but also as naive in some ways" ("Gish Jen"). Instead of using her story to advocate for a "correct" position, Jen considers how spectators shape the meaning of fetal images and are shaped by fetal images.

Like "Birthmates," "The Ultrasound" puts emphasis on conflicts that emerge between and within characters about how to interpret fetal images. Published in 1995, in a collection titled *Arranged Marriage* that earned Divakaruni a 1996 American Book Award, "The Ultrasound" is narrated in the first person by Anju, a newly married Indian woman who has moved to the United States with her husband and is expecting her first baby. The story is part of an emerging body of Indo-American literature, which as Laurie Leach points out, "is relatively new and small compared to other American ethnic groups and literatures" (197). According to Leach, Indo-American literature is concerned primarily with the experiences of the first generation of Indian immigrants to the United States, and this is true of "The Ultrasound," which focuses on Anju and her husband, Sunil, who are Indian born but, living in southern California, strive to assimilate into American culture. In contrast to Art's perspective, Anju's view of America is idealized for most of the story. For Anju, America represents freedom from the dominating patriarchy she associates with India, and she and Sunil seek to assimilate into American culture most obviously by modeling American marriages, which they equate with the professional development of both partners. To this end, Sunil encourages Anju to attend college and supports her financially and emotionally toward this goal, and Anju recognizes that because of this freedom to pursue a career, "I have it better than most of the girls I grew up with" (214).

When "The Ultrasound" begins, Anju is planning a special telephone call to her cousin Runu, who lives in the rural provinces of India with her in-laws and is due to give birth within a few days of Anju. Anju eagerly anticipates comparing the results of their amniocenteses during the phone call. Anju's amniocentesis reveals that her male fetus does not carry the genetic defects that run in Anju's family. But Runu is carrying a girl, and because of this, her family decides that she should have an abortion. While Sunil suggests that perhaps Runu should be obedient and have the abortion, Anju is motivated by the memory of her own ultrasound to encourage Runu to run away.

As Anju seeks a way to help Runu, she develops a more complex understanding of the United States, recognizing that, for her, the American rhetoric of individual liberty is at odds with economic and social imperatives that render her essentially dependent on Sunil. Anju comes to realize that she is disadvantaged as a woman and an immigrant in the United States, and as she looks for a way to assert her own authority as an individual, she attempts to use her pregnancy to renegotiate her American identity.

Because their identities are tenuous and marginalized, Art and Anju's seeing of the fetal images is complicated. Other characters in the stories interpret the fetal images based on their particular views of personhood and fetal subjectivity, some of which put emphasis on fetal health, some on gender, and some on the mother's embodied experience. But Art and Anju, positioned on the margins of each of these groups, have difficulty identifying with any one perspective. And because the perspectives offer radically different explanations about what it means to be a person and who is best equipped to interpret the images, the characters also have difficulty reconciling the positions. Instead the stories show them cycling through the dominant discourses on imaging and finding each one, in turn, to be limited.

At stake in both stories is what it means to be a person and to have a legal and social identity. Ideas about what it means to be a person are informed by culture but also have a deeply individual dimension as well. Thus though it has been common to distinguish a Western concept of selfhood, which emphasizes "the autonomous *individual*" from "the more 'relational' or 'sociocentric' self found in [non-Western] cultures" (Mitchell, *Baby's First Picture* 12), more recent work within the field of anthropology suggests that "concepts of the self, and of social action based upon those concepts, are constituted differently among different collectivities within particular societies" (Mitchell, *Baby's First Picture* 13). In addition to culture, characteristics such as gender, ethnicity, disability, religion, and age determine how individuals experience themselves and others as "persons" (Mitchell, *Baby's First Picture* 13). The protagonists of "Birthmates" and "The Ultrasound" are positioned at the intersection of several competing "collectivities," and therefore their own concepts of personhood are quite complicated and appear fluid throughout the stories.

Prior to imaging, Art and Anju interpret the fetus as a nonperson, and they, along with their partners, initially privilege the diagnostic discourse on imaging. This reflects the reality that medicine provides the context in which most fetal images are created, viewed, and interpreted. In "Birthmates," Art and Lisa have a long history of infertility and miscarriages, so Art has already emotionally distanced himself from the pregnancy even before viewing the fetal image. For him, pregnancy is not a natural process; having already required medical assistance to become pregnant, he welcomes medical management, and the fetal image is just one more diagnostic test to pass on the way to parenthood. Lisa's perspective on the image is a bit more complicated than Art's; however, she also desires the diagnostic reassurance that the pregnancy is progressing well.

In "The Ultrasound," Anju and her husband Sunil also initially view their fetal image as a diagnostic tool. Looming over Anju's pregnancy is the threat of genetic deformity because Anju's family has a history of genetic disorders. She remembers "the drooling boy with albino eyes who used to be kept hidden in a small room in the dark and crumbly Calcutta mansion where another aunt lived" (209). In the waiting room, Anju contemplates, "What will I—we—do if . . . ? But my mind, freezing on that thought, refuses to proceed further" (215). Although Anju contends that she isn't sure what she and Sunil will do if something is wrong with their pregnancy, the clear implication is that they will abort any fetus diagnosed with a genetic disorder. Thus Anju refuses to think about the fetus as a baby until after the diagnosis. Her perspective is altered when the doctor declares the fetus free from deformity. At that point, Anju allows herself to experience a bond with the fetal image and even names the fetus.

Following the medical interpretation of the fetal images in "Birthmates" and "The Ultrasound," the stories diverge widely, reflecting the very different diagnoses rendered. Art and Lisa's fetus is diagnosed with brittle bone disease, while Anju and Sunil's fetus is diagnosed as healthy and male. However, in both stories, medical interpretation continues to focus the gaze of viewers, anchoring them into particular viewing contexts.

Interpretive Conflict in "Birthmates"

In "Birthmates," amniocentesis provides the anchoring text for the image, and Art initially privileges and reads the ultrasound image through the lens of the amniocentesis. Like the ultrasound, the amniocentesis is a representation of the fetus, only a numeric rather than a visual representation. It measures chemical balance and chromosomal levels, presenting these in a numeric breakdown that requires the interpretation of medical professionals, just as the ultrasound does. However, the two representations vary dramatically because the fetal image gives visible form to the fetal body. The concept of personhood is strongly linked to one's body, and Jenny Hockey and Janet Draper have explained that one reason fetal imaging is so closely connected to fetal personhood is because imaging provides the fetus with a social identity as spectators project their desires onto the body represented by imaging (49). The same is not true of amniocentesis. In fact, in "Birthmates," Art's privileging of the amniocentesis prevents his bonding with the fetal image. As a result, his position is like that of the doctor who uses both amniocentesis and fetal ultrasound as a diagnostic tool. Consequently, once disorder is diagnosed, Art welcomes the chance to take preventative measures—in this case, aborting the fetus. Although he cannot see the presence of brittle bone disease in the image, his knowledge that it is present prevents him from being able to interpret the image in any other way. In contrast, Lisa reads the ultrasound image in the context of her entire experience of pregnancy. She already thinks of the fetus as her baby before the ultrasound—she explains to Art that her body knows the baby—and the ultrasound merely provides a visual focal point onto which she can project her desires and fantasies. The amniocentesis does not shake this bond even though she agrees to an abortion to terminate the pregnancy.

Following the abortion, Art's and Lisa's radically different perspectives cause them to clash. Art, parroting the doctor, pragmatically insists to Lisa that brittle bone disease is "a genetic abnormality such as could happen to anyone" and that the fetus was "not a baby, just a baby-to-be," and he "steeled himself for another attempt" at pregnancy (118). His contention that "they knew they could get pregnant, and, what's more, sustain the pregnancy. That was progress" (118), illustrates the extent to which he has adopted a diagnostic perspective—he is even encouraged by the fact that this time they were able to get pregnant, ignoring the loss of the fetus altogether. In contrast, after the abortion, Lisa attends a grief support group and upsets Art by referring to the fetus as "her baby" (118). She defends her grief to Art by insisting that "he didn't understand, couldn't possibly understand, it was something you understood with your body, and it was not his body but hers that knew the baby, loved the baby, lost the baby" (118).

By focusing on the conflict between Lisa and Art, Jen highlights the indeterminacy of visual knowledge. Both characters initially approach the image from the diagnostic perspective; however, conflict ensues because this perspective proves too limited, unable to account for Lisa's haptic knowledge of pregnancy. At the same time, Lisa's haptic experience excludes Art, further marginalizing him. Though Art is drawn to the medical perspective on imaging from the outset, he seems driven to identify with the doctor's perspective and oppose Lisa's perspective because of the way his gender and ethnicity complicate his ability to see the fetus in context. As a male, Art has little access to the pregnancy other than through the image. Draper's longitudinal study of expectant fathers found that for men, viewing an ultrasound of the fetus facilitated a "body-mediated moment" where the expectant man began to negotiate "his transition to fatherhood" using "the woman's body to gain or mediate access to the fetal body" ("It's the First" 566). Without these kinds of moments, men tend to feel distanced and removed from the pregnancy (Draper, "It's the First" 568). Thus it is not surprising that Art's rejection of Lisa's perspective on the pregnancy is essentially a rejection of her haptic experience. By adopting the medical perspective, he attempts to assert his own ability to know the fetus in a way that is as authoritative as Lisa's. What's more, because of his ethnicity, Art's standing in American culture, especially business culture, is marginalized. Realizing this, Art tries throughout the story to align himself with medical discourse as a strong masculine and rhetorical position from which to solidify his identity and his opinions.

Although Art clings to his identification with the doctor throughout the story, this identification is ultimately broken when Art learns through a series of misfortunes that adopting the perspective of the dominant culture has not altered the way he appears and is consequently treated by that culture. As Art reflects on the multiple losses he has experienced, these crystallize for him in the fetal ultrasound image. He remembers how perfect the fetus appeared in the image and is able to recapture some of the wonder he felt briefly before the results of the amniocentesis altered his perspective on the image. As he remembers the ultrasound, Art is driven to reach out to Lisa. Even though it is "years too late," he wants to tell Lisa that "*Yes,* that *was a baby, it would have been a baby*" (125). With this conclusion, Jen demonstrates the appeal of the documentary discourse on fetal images. Despite Art's preference for the numeric, it is ultimately the image with which he is left; it offers him evidence that at some point in the past, he had something "real," or at least the representation of something real, in his life. In the absence of any other fulfilling relationship, Art can recall and finally bond with the fetal image, which remains static and cannot be taken away from him. By asserting that the image offers a realistic representation of the fetal body, Art also asserts his own right to interpret the image without relying on the doctor's or Lisa's mediation. Though Art moves closer to Lisa's position at the conclusion of the story and is even prompted to reach out to her as a result, he continues to deny Lisa's haptic experience of pregnancy because he has adopted the logic of fetal personhood. He has changed his opinion about the image but doesn't question the underlying logic of the autonomous fetus.

In this way, Jen reveals the limitations of each of the three dominant discourses on imaging. Interestingly, her story represents an alternative to them as well. By placing emphasis on the necessarily partial and contradictory nature of viewing images, Jen illustrates that only this kind of viewing position could possibly yield objective vision. As long as Art or Lisa tries to adopt only one authoritative position, they fall into the trap of mistaking an embodied, partial perspective for one that is total and objective. And they remain blind to important information in and about the fetal image as a result. Real objectivity in Jen's story comes from recognizing that Lisa does have access to knowledge about the pregnancy that Art does not have access to, but that the visual knowledge gained through imaging is also important and does not necessarily have to mean denying Lisa's haptic experience. Though neither character embraces this kind of vision in the story, Jen nevertheless uses their conflict to warn readers to be wary of discourses that claim the ability to interpret visual information objectively.

Pregnancy as a Public Event in "The Ultrasound"

While "Birthmates" focuses on the conflict between expectant parents over how to interpret their ultrasound image, in "The Ultrasound," imaging transforms pregnancy into a public event, open to the interpretation of a wide range of spectators. Draper contends that the effect of privileging visual knowledge of the fetus has been to equalize the "respective positions" of spectators as "knowers of the baby" ("It Was" 782), and the private, formerly invisible activity taking place within a woman's womb becomes a very public drama due to the advent of fetal ultrasound. Conflict results as characters privilege a variety of perspectives in interpreting the images and as different forms of knowledge essentially compete for dominance.

Conflict between characters in "The Ultrasound" arises due to disagreement over what constitutes a "quality baby." As in "Birthmates," fetal health is an important consideration for characters in "The Ultrasound"; however, these characters are equally concerned about the sex of the fetus. In this way, "The Ultrasound" adds the dimension of cultural context to the issue of interpreting fetal images. In "The Ultrasound," the identification of Anju's fetus as "boy" and Runu's fetus as "girl" serves as the anchoring text, placing the ultrasound images into the context of patriarchal cultures, whether Indian or American, wherein male babies are considered more valuable than female babies.

"The Ultrasound" thus explores the use of ultrasound and amniocentesis to determine sex and genetic disorder for the purpose of screening out less desirable babies. While the medical community considers the identification of a fetus's sex a secondary issue during imaging, what is considered a quality baby depends on the historical and cultural context. The fact that selective sex abortions are on the rise around the world and have already skewed the average numbers of boys and girls born yearly in some parts of the world (Mallik; Guihau; Plafker 1233) attests to the importance that many families and cultures place on sex. Though both Anju and Sunil express commitment to American values by insisting that the sex is insignificant to them, to Runu and Ramesh in India, the fetus's sex is as important as its health. "The Ultrasound" takes place in this context of the cultural preference for boys over girls, which is particularly strong in India and China, and subsequently, Runu's mother-in-law declares that "it's not fitting that the eldest child of the Bhattacharjee household should be a female" (224) and insists that Runu have an abortion.

In "The Ultrasound," conflicting interpretations of fetal images expose cultural prejudices and complicate the politics of abortion. Though Anju is not opposed to abortion in principle and doesn't even object to the use of imaging as a mechanism to screen for a "quality" baby—she undergoes amniocentesis to screen for genetic defects—she does oppose abortion as a mechanism for screening on the basis of sex. Like Art, Anju seeks an authoritative stance from which to interpret the images and to bolster her support for Runu's pregnancy. However, she cannot employ medical discourse to speak authoritatively about the image because Runu's family has already rejected the authority of the medical diagnosis of the fetus as healthy. Consequently, she adopts both feminist rhetoric and the documentary discourse on fetal imaging, attempting to reconcile these quite different perspectives.

Anju turns to feminist rhetoric to assert Runu's right to self-determination and encourage Runu to run away from her in-laws, suggesting that Runu get a job to support herself and her daughter. Yet Anju's use of feminist rhetoric is starkly at odds with her own choices throughout the story, a contradiction that Sunil capitalizes on to counter Anju's feminist arguments. Though Anju wants her marriage to be an equal partnership, she acknowledges that she is a "good girl" who even allowed her mother to arrange a traditional marriage for her (206). Most significantly, Anju still experiences considerable pressure to produce a "quality" baby—a pressure that Petchesky argues has intensified as a result of prenatal testing and that Divakaruni suggests is particularly strong for Indian women (Petchesky 282). Anju explains that in India she has heard stories of "women chastised, even beaten, because they couldn't have children. Women whose husbands stopped loving them because they'd reneged on the unspoken wedding contract. Women from whose faces people averted their eyes because they were bad luck" (217). Anju continually distances herself from this reality by insisting that her life is blessed since her pregnancy came "easily—almost unasked, like grace" (216) and her Americanized husband would put no such pressure on her to reproduce. But Anju's attitude of fear as she awaits the results of her ultrasound and amniocentesis suggests that she experiences the pressure to produce a quality baby as keenly as other Indian women do and prompts her to attempt to reconcile Indian and American values. Though she is permitted more freedom in her marriage than is Runu, Anju is not the liberated woman that she claims to be, and, as a result, Sunil easily dismisses her arguments based on feminist principles. Early in the story, he responds to Anju's feminist rhetoric with the retort, "You need a reality check . . . Then perhaps you'd be a bit more grateful" (218).

Anju's feminist perspective is undercut most seriously by her acceptance of the documentary discourse on fetal imaging. Though Anju discusses her fetus in only the most abstract terms for most of the story, upon learning that he is free of genetic defects, she becomes convinced of his essential personhood and even begins referring to him by the name she has chosen. She recalls her ultrasound: "At first he is a vague shape on the screen. Then as the image is enlarged I see the delicate shape of his perfect fishbone spine, the small bump of his sex. He waves his arms and legs in a graceful underwater dance, though as yet I don't feel any of it" (229). Anju insists, "The ultrasound had changed everything, made my baby, my Anand, real in a way that nothing else had. I know it must have been the same for Runu" (229). Anju thus attributes her desire to help Runu directly to her experiencing ultrasound imaging and becoming convinced of the concept of fetal personhood. Though Anju is the only character in "The Ultrasound" to support Runu's wish to carry the baby to term, her support is ultimately not based on respect for Runu's right to control her own body. While all the other characters in the story continue to interpret the fetal images through the lens of cultural expectations concerning health and gender, Anju comes to believe that fetuses deserve the rights and protections of other individuals after seeing her own fetus presented as an autonomous individual during the ultrasound.

That Anju uses the documentary perspective on fetal images to simultaneously undercut and support a feminist position demonstrates the difficulty of reconciling these dominant discourses on imaging. As in "Birthmates," Divakaruni illustrates that the documentary perspective, with its connection to fetal personhood, so effectively erases the female body that it is virtually impossible to use it to advance a feminist agenda. At the same time, Anju, like Art, finds the fetal image compelling, and she cannot just dismiss it as irrelevant.

Though Anju is unable to reconcile the contradictory discourses on medical imaging, this interpretive difficulty does help her gain awareness of her own marginal position as a female immigrant in the United States. She finds that there are limits to her freedom due to her economic dependence on Sunil; she realizes that when she asks Sunil about "sponsoring Runu, maybe getting her a student visa," he will "fight it at first, give me a hundred reasons why we can't do it. Why we shouldn't" (230). In the end, Anju chooses to use her own cultural capital to help Runu. She determines to capitalize on the prejudice for male fetuses by using hers as a bargaining tool to gain power and assist Runu. Carrying a highly prized male baby, Anju believes she is in a position to "fight back. Already I'm learning how. I'll use what I have to—my pregnancy, even. It's worth it—for Runu and, yes, myself" (230). In contrast to her initially naïve and optimistic view of life and marriage in the United States, by the conclusion of the story, Anju's new critical awareness motivates her to fight patriarchy in both India and the United States.

In the end, Anju is a relatively successful model of the kind of embodied vision that Jen, Divakaruni, and Haraway advocate. Her perspective is always partial and contradictory as she attempts to reconcile feminist and documentary perspectives. This is certainly no easy task since, as feminist scholars agree, imaging makes the fetus visible by erasing the pregnant body. Nevertheless, if imaging has rendered the pregnant body invisible, feminists also often seek to bring the pregnant woman back into focus by erasing the fetal image in a way that doesn't correspond to women's lived experiences of pregnancy. As Divakaruni illustrates the danger of erasing the pregnant body and privileging visual knowledge of the fetus and simultaneously attends to the meaning that fetal images have for individuals and families, the result is a view of contemporary pregnancy as a complex negotiation of identities and spectatorial roles.

Productive Interpretive Dissonance

In both "Birthmates" and "The Ultrasound," the critical potential associated with fetal imaging comes not from the fetal images themselves but through the interpretive dissonance caused by difficulties in seeing the fetal images in context. Simply put, these stories complicate claims of objectivity. Because images and spectators help define one another, there is no basis for objective vision. As a result of their difficulties finding an objective position from which to view the images, Art and Anju are forced to adopt multiple, often diametrically opposed positions. Thus Art at times employs the diagnostic perspective and at other times asserts his own ability to interpret the fetal image. Anju tries to reconcile a feminist viewing of the fetal image with the rhetoric of fetal rights. These are not perspectives that naturally cohere, and despite the characters' attempts to reconcile them, their efforts are at best partial. Nevertheless, these contradictory, partial perspectives can provide an ethical foundation for the characters' actions, supporting Donna Haraway's notion that a "split and contradictory self" is the only self capable of achieving the objectivity of partial perspective (193).

That the characters achieve this partial perspective largely because they are situated as Asian Americans seems particularly significant. Though the stories do not specifically challenge visual misrepresentations of Asian Americans, the insistence on partial perspective as a means to objectivity implicitly calls into question those ways of knowing Asian Americans that privilege visual knowledge over other forms of knowledge, since what is erased are cultural particularities that distinguish groups, histories, and individuals. Thus these stories are important interventions into the politics of visuality not only with regard to fetal images but also with regard to visual representation as a whole, and they represent how women's writing is keeping pace with technological developments and contributing to ongoing critical dialogues about the role of particular visual technologies in society.

6

Queering Spectatorship in Alison Bechdel's *Fun Home*

While the previous chapters of *Confronting Visuality* have focused on how women's writing in traditional literary forms such as novels and short stories has evolved in conjunction with visual technologies and practices, one of the most important developments in contemporary American women's writing has been the coming-of-age of graphic narratives that depict visual relations in entirely new ways.[1] Graphic narratives in fact foreground issues of representation and gender by portraying women as both viewing subjects and objects. In doing so, these texts prompt readers to think about how women are positioned within looking relations in particular social contexts and historical periods. Nevertheless, until very recently, graphic narrative was considered largely the domain of male writers. It was not until the publication of Alison Bechdel's graphic memoir *Fun Home* in 2006 that critical and commercial attention began to focus on American women's graphic narratives.[2] This chapter focuses on *Fun Home*, arguing that Bechdel expands the range of women's writing about visuality significantly by focusing attention on how we frame events and come to see them through the material artifacts of family, and on how issues of sexuality inflect visual relations.

Fun Home, subtitled "A Family Tragicomic," is intensely personal, narrating Bechdel's coming out as a lesbian and also providing a postmortem coming-out narrative for her father, a closeted homosexual who committed suicide shortly after Bechdel came out to her family. Bechdel's own coming out to her family was complicated when it prompted the revelation of her father's hidden sexual identity. These multiple revelations focused on sexuality, followed so closely by her father's death, leave Bechdel questioning everything she knows about him, her family, and ultimately herself. In *Fun Home*, Bechdel rereads and reimagines key moments of her life and family documents through the lens of the knowledge she has an adult. She uses her memoir to reconsider her memories and investigate her family archive of documents, considering how it is that she didn't recognize her father's sexuality prior to her mother's revelation of it, how this explains particular parts of her childhood that she didn't understand while growing up, and looking for evidence of suicide. At the same time, Bechdel is herself a "character" in *Fun Home*, and via the graphic narrative form, Bechdel is able to contrast her adult knowledge of her father's homosexuality and eventual death to her autobiographical avatar Alison's[3] ignorance. In this way, *Fun Home* foregrounds what Eve Kosofsky Sedgwick has referred to as "the epistemology of the closet," the question of who knows what about whom regarding matters of sexuality.

Prior to *Fun Home*, Bechdel was best known as the creator of *Dykes to Watch Out For*, a serial comic strip that has been published in many papers and collected in anthologies such as *The Essential Dykes to Watch Out For* (2008). Since the publication of *Fun Home*, Bechdel has published a second graphic memoir focused on the reception to *Fun Home* and her relationship with her mother titled *Are You My Mother?* (2012). While Bechdel's work in *Dykes to Watch Out For* and *Are You My Mother?* shares with *Fun Home* a commitment to challenging stereotypes about lesbians and depicting the real, lived experiences of lesbian characters, *Fun Home* represents an important departure point for both Bechdel and American literature, demonstrating the possibilities for and reach of contemporary literature more generally. Not only was the book's publication by Houghton Mifflin the first time a mainstream press had published a feminist graphic narrative, but the book was also a bestseller and was selected by *Time* as book of the year for 2006. *Fun Home* has also, as Hillary Chute notes, "put productive pressure on the academy" by "expand[ing] what 'literature' is" (*Graphic Women* 178).

Certainly, graphic narratives have been reshaping literary studies in the new millennium. The publication of a special issue of *Modern Fiction Studies* in 2006 on the subject of "Graphic Narrative," edited by Chute and Marianne DeKoven, serves in some ways as a signal of the official recognition of graphic narratives as an important "part of an expanding literary field, absorbing and redirecting the ideological, formal, and creative energies of contemporary fiction" (Chute and DeKoven 768).[4] Though Chute and DeKoven acknowledge in their introduction to the special issue that the medium of comics "has always contended with much denigration," they assert that "it is no longer necessary to prove the worthiness and literary potential of the medium" (768) and take as a foregone conclusion that long-form works like Art Spiegelman's *Maus* (1991) have "demonstrated clearly how moving and impressive comics can be" (768). The task now, they explain, is "to explore what the form can tell us about the project of narrative representation itself. What can we gain from works that are, in their very structure and grammar, cross-discursive: composed in words and images, written *and* drawn?" (768).

However, until the publication of *Fun Home*, the status of American *women's* graphic narratives was much less certain. In fact, until very recently, graphic narratives were thought to be the province of male writers. As an example, a 2004 *New York Times Magazine* cover story on graphic narratives referred to female authors only in passing and asserted, "The graphic novel is a man's world, by and large" (McGrath 24, 30). The publication of Satrapi's *Persepolis* in 2003 drew attention to women's participation in comics, but not until the publication of *Fun Home* in 2006 did American women's graphic novels come into their own. The word "groundbreaking" frequently appears in critical assessments of *Fun Home*, and critics have considered how *Fun Home* builds on and breaks ground within the contexts of earlier women's graphic novels and the larger genre of memoir.[5] Within comics theory, *Fun Home* necessitates new models that account for the gendered and sexualized content that Bechdel includes,[6] while within literary studies, *Fun Home* has challenged scholars to develop critical models and a vocabulary to use in discussing graphic narrative.[7] In addition, the strategies Bechdel pioneers for depicting visual relations represent a crucial evolution of women's writing about visuality, demonstrating the critical possibilities when a writer can depict the exchange of gazes visually in a literary work. In *Fun Home*, Bechdel not only illustrates the inherently queer nature of spectatorship but also uses the form of the graphic narrative to position the reader as a type of queer spectator. I argue that in doing so Bechdel seeks to unsettle not only a heteronormative perspective but also a homonormative perspective and to transcend divisions between straight and gay individuals as well as between gay men and lesbian women. Moreover, Bechdel positions the reader as part of a queer model of desire by developing visual strategies to connect the reader's literal body and gaze to Bechdel's own throughout the narrative.

"To Think, and Imagine, and See Differently"

Understanding and analyzing the ways in which Bechdel sets out to queer spectatorship in *Fun Home* does require some introduction to the narrative possibilities of comics, as well as the ways in which Bechdel has innovated within those possibilities. On the one hand, Bechdel makes use of a set of tools that other female writers have used in graphic narratives. Writers are able to depict looking relations in different ways in graphic narratives than in either texts or films and to involve the reader in new ways as well. For my purposes, it is particularly significant that readers of graphic narratives can observe the interplay of the gaze in a way not possible in text alone, as characters look or do not look at one another and even gaze out at the reader at times or use other strategies that evoke the reader as observer. And in contrast to film, graphic narratives require a much greater degree of reader involvement to make meaning. In fact, according to Scott McCloud, "No other artform gives so much to its audience while asking so much from them as well" (92) due to the fact that readers are required to perform "closure" to make meaning out of discreet panels. McCloud explains that closure involves "observing the parts but perceiving the whole" (63), and closure is essential to comics since readers are required to help create the meaning "between" the panels of a comic—in the gutter—and even within panels that often include only partial information. As a result of closure, McCloud suggests that the audience for comics is "a willing and conscious collaborator and closure is the agent of change, time and motion" (65).

The power of closure to involve readers in graphic narratives means that the medium of graphic narrative is particularly well equipped to help readers think critically about important issues. For example, in his introduction to Joe Sacco's graphic narrative *Palestine*, Edward Said explained, "I felt that comics freed me to think and imagine and see differently" (ii). It is not surprising, then, that feminist artists have recognized the potential for this medium to help readers think differently about issues of gender and to intervene in visuality. For some feminist artists, this has taken the form of challenging traditional notions of feminine beauty (such as in Aline Kominsky-Crumb's and Lynda Barry's works); for others, it has meant challenging the supposed "to-be-looked-at-ness" of women, as Phoebe Gloeckner does in her graphic memoir *A Child's Life* (1998) by having her autobiographical avatar, Minnie, gaze directly out of the panel at the reader. Although Gloeckner depicts child sexual abuse in her narrative, Minnie at times gazes directly at the reader with a look of challenge. By gazing at the reader, invoking the presence of a reader, Gloeckner challenges the reader's voyeuristic impulse and imbues her avatar with a sense of agency. Even as she is being sexually abused in the panel, Minnie's gaze reaches out to readers, implicating them as participants in her abuse by watching it and reminding the reader that Gloeckner, as artist, is in control of the narrative. For Bechdel, intervening in looking relations takes the form of using the process of "closure" to build identification between the reader and Bechdel's own queer looking position as well as experimenting with the multiple diegetic levels provided by the graphic narrative form.

Fun Home pioneers new narrative techniques to depict and consider looking relations on multiple diegetic levels. Robyn Warhol explains that the narrative of *Fun Home* functions on at least three levels: the first verbal level of "the extradiegetic voice-over narration, printed in a font that looks like free hand capital letters, always filling borderless horizontal boxes that run above the panels of the cartoon" (5), the second verbal level of the "intradiegetic dialogue, representations of words spoken inside the narrative world, encircled in word balloons and set in the same font as the voice-over" (5), and the third pictorial level, where "we find a cascade of reproduced pictures and maps copied from books; original maps drawn by Bechdel; copies of handwritten and typed letters, notes, and diary pages; hand-inked copies of photographs; and drawings of books whose titles are clearly legible on the bindings" (5). Warhol further observes that "each of these classes of images gestures in the direction of different diegetic levels, multiplying the worlds invoked by the narrative structure of *Fun Home*" (5). In its use of these different levels of narration as well as other features of graphic narratives, *Fun Home* breaks ground in representing visuality and spectatorship even within the medium of graphic narratives, greatly contributing to the critical examination of visuality that has emerged in contemporary American women's writing.

Unsettling Sight(s)

In *Fun Home*, Bechdel exposes the queer base on which traditional models of spectatorship have always rested. Queer, as a critical concept, encompasses the nonfixity of gender expression and the nonfixity of both straight and gay sexuality. As Richard Dyer explains, the contemporary formulation of queer functions in sharp contrast to its past; it signifies a fluidity of identity where, historically, queer represented an "exclusive and fixed sexuality" (4). To be queer now, then, means to be untethered from "conventional" codes of behavior. Michele Aaron contends that "at its most expansive and utopian, queer contests (hetero- and homo-)normality" ("New Queer Cinema" 5). Queer, in this sense, presents "the resistance to, primarily, the normative codes of gender and sexual expression—that masculine men sleep with feminine women—but also to the restrictive potential of gay and lesbian sexuality—that only men sleep with men, and women sleep with women" (Aaron, "New Queer Cinema" 5).

Spectatorship rests on a queer base because of the role of cross identification in visual pleasure, a concept originally developed to account for the way that film spectators identify with characters unlike themselves. This work grew out of efforts to delineate the role of the female spectator within the male visual economy outlined by Laura Mulvey. Most famously, Mary Ann Doane asserted that the female spectator on-screen and off-screen (i.e., in the audience) is forced to identify with the male gaze in a transvestite manner; otherwise, she is left to identify masochistically with the objectified female. More recently, critics have further discussed the complexities of cross identification, whereby spectators identify with the perspectives of characters unlike themselves. Anne Friedberg claims that one of the major pleasures of cinema is oppositional identification: "Isn't cinema spectatorship pleasurable because new identities can be 'worn' and then discarded?" (65). Similarly, Rhona J. Berenstein claims that spectators can enjoy identifying against themselves as much as they enjoy identifying with a character that closely corresponds to them. This work on cross identification highlights how unfixed the identities of spectators can be, particularly with regard to gender and sexual identity. Cross gender or cross sexuality identification can provide an opportunity for spectators to develop empathy for those who differ from themselves, but even if empathy does not occur, the very possibility of cross identification undercuts the notion that gender and sexuality identity are fixed, blurring boundaries between identity categories often regarded as immutable.

Bechdel employs a number of strategies to consider the queer nature of looking relations in *Fun Home*, but she begins by unhooking the sexuality of looking from its heteronormative roots. In particular, *Fun Home* focuses on how people—characters in the story as well as implied readers—look at bodies, with particular emphasis, as Julia Watson has observed, on "the necrotic and the erotic" (35). Drawings of bodies being embalmed or displayed at the family's "fun home" contrast to "erotic bodies in action, in scenes of her father's and her own sexual encounters" (Watson 35). With her focus on bodies, Bechdel also considers how bodies become visually legible—read as evidence about how someone died, about a person's sexuality, and so on—and these issues are linked as well to how society attaches value to particular types of bodies.

Importantly, Bechdel specifically does not invoke a heterosexual male spectator for the bodies in *Fun Home*, and she actually undercuts that viewing position in several ways. In fact, though she acknowledges the social power generally accorded to heterosexual male spectators, she ultimately renders the conventional male gaze laughable and ridiculous. Alison briefly experiences the force of an objectifying male gaze as a child when her father inexplicably asks her to hold on to a "dirty" photo of a pinup girl during a camping trip (111). When Alison looks at the image, thinking "it looked clean enough to me" (111), she is disgusted and experiences a feeling of intense personal identification with the woman depicted, an identification that leaves her feeling "as if I'd been stripped naked myself, inexplicably shamed, like Adam and Eve" (112). This shame even prompts her to disavow her gender throughout the camping trip. Her reaction contrasts strongly to her brothers', who leer at the image, mock the woman's breasts, and tease Alison about it (112, 115). Bechdel's depiction of the male gaze in this scene emphasizes its objectifying power, its link to scopophilia and voyeurism, and the ability of visual objectifications of women to demean all women.

However, at a later age, Alison again confronts the objectifying male gaze at the home of her friend, Beth Gryglewicz, and finds its power diminished. Teenage Alison and her brothers stay with the Gryglewiczes so their mother, Helen, can work on her master's thesis. The Gryglewiczes, both of whom have PhDs, have decorated their house with erotic, nude paintings of the female Dr. Gryglewicz. In contrast to the pinup girl, these images are entirely comic and not at all threatening to Alison. No one even glances at the painting in the scene; not even Alison's brothers seem to find it interesting in the least. Bechdel draws attention to the painting with a humorous, extradiegetic comment: "One of Dr. Gryglewicz's many interesting paintings of Dr. Gryglewicz" (160). Bechdel includes the painting as a form of comic relief; she mocks the Gryglewiczes' liberal open-mindedness—depicting female sexuality visually in their home and requiring the children to refer to them both as Dr. Gryglewicz—which contrasts to their inherent conservatism as a married couple who share the same last name. She also plays on the fact that teenage Alison, pretending to be a police officer, yells "spread 'em" to her friends and brothers while standing in front of the painting of Dr. Gryglewicz doing just that. Here the male gaze is rendered ridiculous and comical and not at all threatening to Alison.

That the male gaze is not the important erotic site in the book is also evident in that dead, white male bodies become objects of the (queer) gaze throughout *Fun Home*. Through her father's work as a funeral director, Alison has many opportunities to view dead bodies as a child. And her father actually draws her attention to these bodies at times, usually when the cadaver is that of a young, seemingly healthy person as opposed to the "usual traffic of desiccated old people" (44). In a particularly important scene, her father, Bruce, asks for Alison's assistance while working on a nude male cadaver whose chest cavity is split open. Alison finds both "the strange pile of his genitals" and the cavity in his chest shocking (44), and Bechdel questions why her father wanted her to see this sight, suggesting he might have wanted to elicit an emotional reaction from her that he can no longer produce himself. This scene dramatically shifts the power dynamics away from the privileged male spectator and toward a pair of queer spectators, one of whom is a young girl. The fact that the man has a "dark red cave" in his chest reworks the traditional, Freudian concept of women as castrated men, whose absent penis is frightening for men to perceive; here it is the male body associated with a frightening, shocking absence, despite the manifest presence of his male genitals. Bechdel relocates Freud's lack from the genitals to the man's chest cavity, and Bechdel remembers that this is "what really got my attention" (44). Throughout *Fun Home*, Bechdel focuses on moments when Alison comes to see things differently or recognizes a reality she did not know existed. In this scene, with the "gaping cadaver" (44), Bechdel highlights how a shocking sight changes Alison's perspective on male dominance. Alison literally sees a lack at the very core of masculinity. This sight not only prefigures her to witness her own father's death, as Chute has discussed, but also signifies a larger shift from the privileged, evaluative male gaze to the critical, queer, female gaze.

In a book focused on "necrotic and erotic" bodies, the "gaping cadaver" is one of the most "unsettling sights" Bechdel records, though it is not the only one. In fact, *Fun Home* in general testifies to the productivity of disrupting vision via the experience of witnessing unexpected, even disturbing things. For example, Alison's viewing of the pinup girl, though it upsets her, also makes visible structures of female oppression. More important are those "sights" that unsettle a heteronormative perspective, such as the open and visible expression of homosexuality. In fact, Bechdel uses the phrase "unsettling sight" specifically to refer to such a visible expression. In narrating her coming-out story, Bechdel identifies a moment early in her childhood when Alison intuitively recognized the "unsettling sight" of a bull dyke in a restaurant when she was "4 or 5" with "a surge of joy" (119). In a four-panel sequence, Bechdel depicts Alison's recognition of the dyke. Throughout the panel, Alison is depicted wide-eyed, openly staring at the woman for the most part. Bruce immediately "recognized her too" and makes a connection between the woman and Alison, asking, "Is *that* what you want to look like?" (119). Although Alison answers "no" since she perceives that the woman's lack of femininity is offensive to her father, she continues to stare at the woman, even looking back toward the restaurant after she and her father leave, and she recounts that "the image of the truck-driving bulldyke sustained me through the years" and contrasts this to her father "as it perhaps haunted my father" (119). Seeing the woman unsettles Alison and her father differently; while she offers Alison a model of female identity distinct from the femininity her father imposes on her, Bruce perceives her openness as a threat to his shame and hiding.

Bechdel further unsettles a heteronormative perspective by locating lesbian desire as the central erotic site in the text, which she does by depicting Alison's sexual initiation with her college girlfriend, Joan. This relationship signals the transition of Alison's lesbianism from theory to practice and demonstrates Bechdel's commitment to what Valerie Rohy has described as an "ethic of full disclosure" as a "remedy for repression" (353). Judith Kegan Gardiner contends that the "desired happy ending in [*Dykes* and *Fun Home*] is coming out, a personal triumph that requires at least some resonance in a specific social setting and historical period" (200). As such, Alison's sexual relationship with Joan is in many ways the culmination of her coming-out narrative, and Bechdel's extradiegetic narration compares Alison's sexual initiation to "Odysseus" acting in "true heroic fashion" (214). Even though, as Gardiner points out, Alison's coming out is "shadowed by Alison's continuing guilt in the belief that her coming out contributed to her father's death" and therefore is "subordinated to the tragic mode" (200), the graphic depictions of sex between Alison and Joan stand in stark contrast to the mystery and confusion cast over sexual matters in Alison's family and by the larger culture as she was growing up.

Alison comes to recognize over time that language itself is inadequate to express important concepts with relation to gender and sexuality. Even the dictionary, which Alison turns to again and again to define the important terms that are unsaid and undefined in her home, turns out to be unstable and unreliable. Although reading the definition of "lesbian" confirms for Alison that she is indeed a lesbian, she later finds that the "mammoth Webster's" omits from its definition of "queer" any association with homosexuality, and the definition of "father" proves to be equally vague: "One who has fathered a child" (197). Over and over again, language fails or characters are silent on important questions about sexuality. In her own diary, Alison comes to refer to menstruation and masturbation as "ning," a signifier devoid of any referent and therefore suitable code for any reference to gender and sexuality. Warhol explains that the medium of comics helps solve "the problem for Bechdel of the slipperiness of the signifier . . . in a text like *Fun Home* there's no need for language to carry the whole weight of the visual—the physicality of things, of the body, is unnarratable in words, so the drawings stand in . . . as signs pointing to the gap in signification" (10). This is certainly true in the depiction of Alison and Joan's sexual relationship, in which the pictures work together with the extradiegetic allusions to Homer's *Odyssey* to make lesbianism visible and locate romance in a female world that resists the masculine/feminine and butch/femme clichés.

Significantly, *Fun Home* seeks to unsettle not only a heteronormative gaze but also a homonormative gaze, signaling, once again, Bechdel's interest in a distinctly queer model of looking relations. Aaron has discussed how the notion of queer is as unsettling of some of the givens of homosexual identity as it is of heterosexual identity. In particular, a queer perspective often seeks to transcend divisions between gay men and lesbian women, differences that reflect their very different social histories and circumstances. By aligning Alison's gaze to Bruce's in *Fun Home*, Bechdel offers a profoundly queer model of desire.

Though Alison and Bruce are deeply divided in their reactions to femininity, they are nevertheless linked by a deep affinity of desires, which Bechdel describes as a "slender demilitarized zone: our shared reverence for masculine beauty" (99). Although their desire is directed differently—Alison wishes to be masculine herself, while her father is attracted to masculine beauty in others—Bechdel nevertheless, repeatedly, shows how aligned their gazes are. Early in the narrative, for example, as the family stands up at mass while the altar boys exit the church, Bruce casts a sidelong glance at the boys, while Alison openly watches them (see Figure 6.1). In contrast, one of her brothers stands with eyes closed, and the other stares at the ceiling, while her mother, wearing a haggard expression, stares straight ahead. In this panel, Bechdel aligns Alison with her father even as she illustrates that what Bruce partakes in furtively, Alison will be openly curious about. Later when describing their shared love of masculine beauty, Bechdel depicts the two gazing at an ad in *Esquire*. Both ignore the female figure in the ad (Bechdel includes only her face and arm in the panel) and focus in on the muscular male model. When Alison directs her father to look at the ad, telling him "you should get a suit with a vest," Bechdel depicts the two gazing at the ad in exactly the same way, as Bruce responds, "Nice. I should" (99).

By linking Alison's gaze so strongly to her father's, Bechdel "proposes a more fluid understanding of identification and desire, in which seeming oppositions are revealed to have always been convergent" (Watson 42). Nor are Bruce and Alison singled out as irregular due to their connection to a fluidity of desire. For example, Alison's, presumably heterosexual, brother

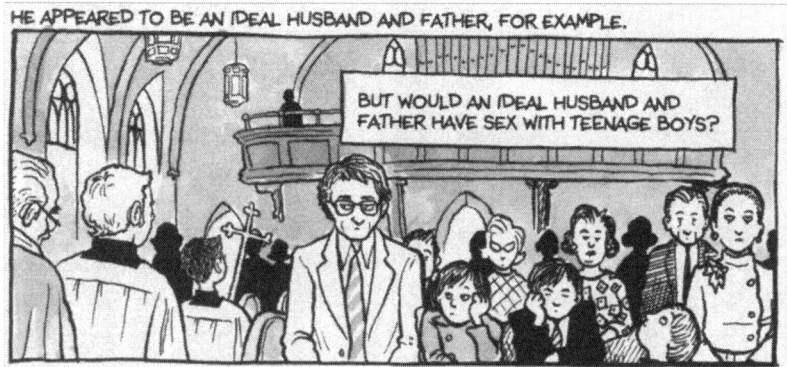

Figure 6.1 Panel from page 17 of *Fun Home: A Family Tragicomic* by Alison Bechdel Copyright © 2006 by Alison Bechdel. Reprinted by permission of Houghton Mifflin Harcourt. All rights reserved.

pretends to be a gay flight attendant, waving his arms theatrically and asking "Coffee, tea, or me?," while Alison and her other brother play at being an airline pilot and hijacker. Later Alison and her, also presumably heterosexual, friend Beth dress up in men's suits and pretend to be con men and life insurance salesmen. Bechdel suggests that sexuality is a spectrum, one that is fluid and changing, and in this way, the text avoids "rigid categories, ready answers, or the supposition of singular responsibility" (Aaron, "New Queer Spectator" 192). As Gardiner has pointed out, Bechdel ultimately critiques Bruce more for being a cold and distant father rather than a closeted homosexual (191).

Bechdel also positions the reader as part of this queer model of desire, developing visual strategies to connect the reader's literal body and gaze to Bechdel's own. In the middle of *Fun Home*, Bechdel includes a single two-page panel in which she reproduces a photograph that she found after her father's death depicting the family's yard work assistant/babysitter Roy lying on a bed wearing only underwear (see Figure 6.2).

This image, one of the most frequently discussed in criticism of *Fun Home*, is significant for a number of reasons. Not only is it placed at

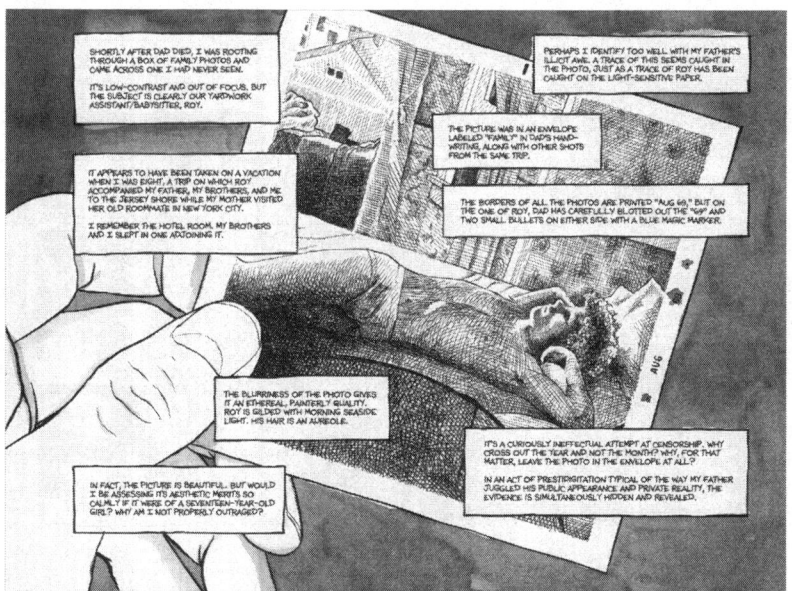

Figure 6.2 Pages 100–101 from *Fun Home: A Family Tragicomic* by Alison Bechdel. Copyright © 2006 by Alison Bechdel. Reprinted by permission of Houghton Mifflin Harcourt. All rights reserved.

roughly the center of the book,[8] which is particularly important in *Fun Home* because the text employs a circular structure so that the book in many ways spirals out of this image, but it also shows Bechdel responding to the image in multiple ways: contextualizing it in her family's history, assessing its aesthetic merits, trying to capture outraged shock, and so on. Most interesting of all, though, is how Bechdel uses the extra-large panel to depict a twice-life-size hand holding the photograph. As Watson points out, this hand invokes Bechdel's material body, as well as the reader's, whose hand similarly holds the book and gazes at the photograph of Roy (39–41). Bechdel here evokes a queer spectator, offering visual pleasure to the reader who can appreciate masculine beauty as Alison and Bruce, and Bechdel, do.

The New Queer Spectator

Bechdel does more in *Fun Home* than only depict a queer model of spectatorship, however. She also uses the formal elements of the graphic narrative to avow this queer spectatorial position and queer knowledge, in general. To do so, she also considers how it is that spectators, even knowing spectators, so often disavow the knowledge they have of homosexuality. Aaron has pointed out that while traditional models of spectatorship were always "obliquely queer" in the ways they invoked female transvestism and cross identification, the queer spectatorial position was always contained— understood to be temporary and at the same time disavowed (Aaron, "New Queer Spectator" 187). Judith Halberstam agrees, focusing on how despite the recent inclusion of a wider range of homosexual characters in mainstream representations, these characters are still generally treated comically or punished in some way to render the representation harmless to the supposedly heterosexual viewer (84–85).

Disavowing knowledge of homosexuality is linked to the process of "closeting," which Sedgwick has described as "the defining structure for gay oppression in this century" (71), as it seeks to uphold the binary constructions of Western patriarchal and heterocentrist discourse. "The closet" represents an attempt to police a strict gay-straight dichotomy, and within the logic of closeting, it is necessary for "straight" individuals to deny knowledge of homosexuality in order to maintain this dichotomy. However, as Sedgwick explains, "the closet" actually creates a myriad of queer subject positions, due to it being a complex constellation of interrelated social and psychological phenomena. As such, interrogating "the closet"—as Bechdel does in *Fun Home*—can be a difficult task, giving rise to multiple readings dependent on the viewer's subject positions and what Sedgwick has referred to as his or her own "homosexual/homophobic knowing" (97).[9]

In *Fun Home*, Bruce's homosexuality exists in the twilight between secrecy and reprimand because of social convention and homophobia. Bechdel is attentive in the text to who can see through his performance of heterosexuality and therefore "knows" about his homosexuality, and she considers how characters, especially her mother Helen as well as Bruce himself, nevertheless disavow their knowledge of homosexuality, even at great personal cost.

Bechdel foregrounds the issue of knowledge by employing an autobiographical avatar who is unable to see through Bruce's performance and fails to recognize his homosexuality. As a child, Alison defines herself largely in opposition to Bruce but without any awareness that her father is a closeted homosexual. Alison and her father are locked in a contest of wills because he attempts to impose conventional norms of femininity on her, while she derides him as a sissy. In other words, Bechdel presents them as "inverted versions of each other in the family . . . Alison's rejection of femininity as a compensation for her father's lack of manliness, and his insistence on her dressing and acting 'feminine' as a projection of his own desire to perform femininity" (Watson 39). However, Alison is a truly ignorant spectator; she does not recognize her father's lack of masculinity as a sign of homosexuality;[10] nor does she understand that he imposes femininity on her due to his own desire to perform femininity. At the pictorial and intradiegetic levels of narration, Alison understands Bruce only as an enforcer of feminine gender norms, and she sees this as an extension of his more general authoritarian parenting. For example, Alison repeatedly resists Bruce's attempts to make her appear feminine throughout the narrative, whether he is trying make her wear a matching neckline on a sweater, or barrettes, or pearls, but her resistance is part of a more general resistance she offers to what she refers to as his "curatorial onslaught" (14). Alison's failure to recognize Bruce's homosexuality, though it seems reasonable given her age, in fact drives much of the narrative of *Fun Home*, motivating Bechdel to reconstruct memories of her childhood so as to "resee" them through the lens of her adult knowledge.

Moreover, Bechdel illustrates that Alison's ignorance about her father's homosexuality is not due to a lack of awareness about homosexuality per se but simply a failure to recognize Bruce, specifically, as homosexual. Alison acknowledges her own lesbianism and is able to identify signs of homosexuality in others long before she learns about Bruce's closeted homosexuality. For example, during the family's trip (minus Helen) to New York during America's bicentennial celebration, Bechdel employs the equivalent of a shot/reverse shot sequence of panels to depict Alison's recognition of the prevalence of homosexuality in Greenwich Village. She first provides close ups on Bruce's and Alison's faces, which seem to look out of the panel at the reader; in the next panel, however, the reverse shot, the reader looks over Alison's shoulder at "a display of cosmeticized masculinity" (190). In her extradiegetic narration, Bechdel observes, "It was like the moment the manicurist in the Palmolive commercial informs her client, 'You're soaking in it.' The suspect element is revealed to be not just benign, but beneficial, and in fact, all pervasive" (190). Alison's sudden awareness changes her perspective on the entire trip to New York, prompting Bechdel to comment, "It was a gay weekend all around" (190). In this sequence, Alison's gaze is strongly linked to her father's, as the two stare at the group of men, and is contrasted to her brother's, who appears to the right of the panel staring at the fireworks display. Nevertheless, despite recognizing the pervasive homosexuality surrounding her in New York, Alison remains strangely oblivious to Bruce's homosexuality. Even when he leaves the children alone to go "out for a drink" at night, Alison's lack of awareness is signaled by the depiction of her sound asleep in the next panel (194). Alison's failure to recognize the implications of Bruce's own "cosmeticized masculinity" marks her as an ignorant spectator, rather than someone who has suppressed knowledge about homosexuality more generally.

Bechdel confirms that Alison is truly ignorant of Bruce's homosexuality instead of simply suppressing knowledge of it when Helen reveals Bruce's sexual history to Alison after she comes out to her parents at the age of 19. Alison is completely surprised (58–59), responding in the intradiegetic level of narration to her mother's revelation "Your father has had affairs with other men" (58) with "*Dad?* With other *men?*" and "Roy our babysitter?", and she is depicted as literally "floored" in that she comes to cradle the phone to her ear while lying on the floor in the fetal position (59, 79).

In contrast, Bechdel positions the reader of *Fun Home*, from the outset, as a knowing and complicitous observer. On the second page of the narrative, in an extradiegetic note, Bechdel informs the reader that her father is destined to die—"In our particular reenactment of this mythic relationship [between Icarus and Daedalus], it was not me but my father who was to plummet from the sky" (4)—and on page 16, she reveals that her father had a "dark secret," which is immediately revealed to be that he engaged in "sex with teenage boys" (17). By revealing her father's secret and fate so early in the book, Bechdel invites the reader to join her in scrutinizing and disassembling Bruce's attempts to pass as heterosexual.

In its focus on Bruce, *Fun Home* is about the spectacle of the closet and about the ways in which Bruce and Helen work together to perform a conventional, small-town, nuclear family. Bruce's secret identity is nevertheless ever present to the reader since Bechdel not only exposes it early in the narrative but also repeatedly uses extradiegetic commentary to draw the reader's attention to Bruce's performance of heterosexuality and the existence of his hidden identity. As a result, the reader shares Bechdel's gaze and perspective throughout the text; she explains that although "he didn't kill himself until I was nearly twenty," "his absence resonated retroactively, echoing back through all the time I knew him" (23), and in recreating her memories and family archive in *Fun Home*, Bruce's secret and death resonate throughout the story that Bechdel tells. Thus as readers, we watch how Alison and other characters interact with Bruce and are taken in by his performance of heterosexuality (on the pictorial and intradiegetic levels of narration), but we are constantly aware of Bruce's ambiguous identity. His passing is therefore rendered a failure in *Fun Home* since readers are never taken in by his performance of heterosexuality.

Bechdel's constant extradiegetic reminders about her father's passing also underline the queerness of the encounters between Bruce and Helen, as well as the reader's consciousness of it. For example, in Chapter 3, Bechdel recalls how her father would cultivate promising teenage boys "like orchids" by loaning books to them and offering them alcohol in his house, accompanying her extradiegetic narration with an image depicting Bruce entertaining Roy in his library, offering him books and a glass of sherry. Helen's intrusion with a reminder that their son John has been "waiting for you to pick him up from cub scouts for half an hour" (65) illustrates how fine a line exists between Bruce's appearance of heterosexual domesticity and illicit sexual behavior. Helen's failure to react to finding Bruce plying Roy with alcohol in the library also would suggest that she is ignorant of his intentions—except that only seven pages earlier, Helen revealed Bruce's long history of affairs with men to Alison, a history dating back to their engagement, so there is no doubt during this exchange that Helen understands what Bruce is doing in the library with Roy, and moreover the reader knows that Helen is aware and chooses to suppress this knowledge in the interest of keeping the household together (216). In *Fun Home*, these reminders serve to unsettle readers' fixed position of superior knowledge about Bruce's identity—their supposedly sharp contrast to the duped characters. By highlighting the characters' suppressed knowledge about Bruce, Bechdel forces the reader to see Bruce's attempt to pass as heterosexual as a failure.

At the same time, the text questions how much Bruce really understands about himself and implies that on some level he believes his own performance. During a high school English class that Alison takes with her father, she participates in a class discussion in which her father points out how the male teacher, Antolini Peters, makes a pass at the much younger Holden in *Catcher in the Rye*. Bechdel adds the extradiegetic note, "awesome capacity for cognitive dissonance" (199). And even after Bruce is outed to Alison and his family, he seems incapable of speaking openly. In the one discussion Alison and Bruce have about their "shared predilection," where Bruce shares his originary moment with Alison, Bechdel describes Bruce's story as a "shamefaced recitation" during which he fails to respond to Alison's attempts to identify with his experience. She indicates that "it was not the sobbing, joyous reunion of Odysseus and Telemachus. It was more like fatherless Stephen and sonless Bloom having their equivocal late-night cocoa at 7 Eccles Street" (221).

Through her extradiegetic narration, which often reminds readers about her father's closeted homosexuality or juxtaposes in some way Alison's and Bruce's experiences, Bechdel explicitly avows a queer perspective and ensures that readers cannot completely misunderstand the purpose of her text or misunderstand her as either vilifying or unequivocally celebrating her father. This avowal is particularly important in light of research within queer film theory that suggests that if a film leaves too much of the work of interpretation up to audiences, filmmakers risk spectators, seemingly deliberately, misreading signs of homosexuality (Benshoff 182). Given the necessarily collaborative nature of graphic narratives, the risk of being too ambiguous is great. Bechdel's frequent use of extradiegetic narration helps ensure that readers cannot completely misread her text or disavow the knowledge of homosexuality that they bring to bear in interpreting it, something that makes the popularity and appeal of *Fun Home* even more remarkable.

Bechdel also avows a queer spectatorial position by drawing on the reader's knowledge of homosexuality to complete closure, and in order to understand *Fun Home*, the reader specifically must perform closure by bringing to bear all of what Aaron refers to as "queer common sense" that he or she possesses. For example, Bechdel calls on the reader's queer common sense when she narrates the events surrounding Bruce's arrest and hearing for providing alcohol to a teenage boy. In a series of panels depicting the event and its aftermath (see Figure 6.3), she depends on the reader's ability to interpret Bruce's "cruising" in his car to pick up a teenage boy, Mark, with the excuse that they will look for Mark's brother together. Even in her extradiegetic narration, Bechdel does not explicitly challenge the official police report, which she reproduces, and which states "during the course of the evening, defendant purchased a six-pack of beer. Witness stated that Mr. Bechdel offered him a beer and he took it and drank it" (Fun Home 161).

In the aftermath, there is no contradiction to this report either. Helen describes the offense to Alison as "He bought a beer for a boy who wasn't old enough" (173), while Bruce simply confesses to Alison, saying, "I'm

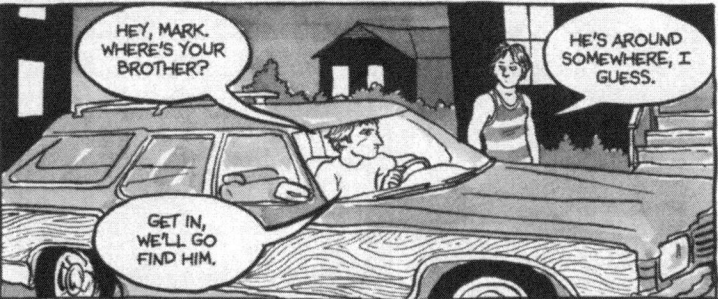

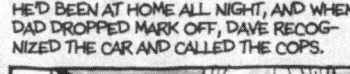

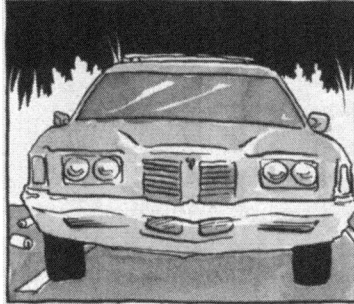
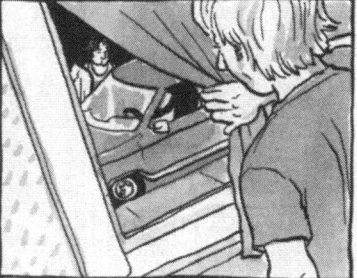

Figure 6.3 Page 161 from *Fun Home: A Family Tragicomic* by Alison Bechdel Copyright © 2006 by Alison Bechdel. Reprinted by permission of Houghton Mifflin Harcourt. All rights reserved.

bad. Not good like you" (153), and Bechdel notes that the judge also "stuck strictly to the liquor charge" though "a whiff of the sexual aroma of the true offense could be detected in the sentence," which includes counseling (180). In this instance, Bechdel assumes that readers will "read between the lines" of the event and make a connection between Bruce cruising in his car and cruising for young boys in order to detect the "sexual aroma" for themselves without her filling in any more of the gaps. In doing so, she implicates readers with possessing knowledge about cruising and pederastic relationships, knowledge readers might disavow but must employ in this scene in order to interpret and understand its importance to the narrative of *Fun Home*.

In *Fun Home*, the reader is already assumed to be a queer spectator, capable of cross identifying with characters on the basis of gender and sexuality. This position is in fact required in order to understand *Fun Home*, and it replicates Bechdel's own attempt to understand her father's complex and fraught identity and behavior, which requires her to cross boundaries of gender, age, and culture in order to empathize with his experience as a closeted homosexual man.

Expanding Women's Writing about Visuality

Bechdel's queering of spectatorship, using the medium of graphic narrative, represents an important evolution of women's writing about visuality. In the first place, her attention to the queer underpinnings of spectatorship usefully complicates the reductive binary opposition of male spectators and female objects of the gaze that is the basis for traditional models of spectatorship. In the second place, her use of the comics medium illustrates the power of this form to intercede in representational practices not only by making visual relations themselves visible but also by helping readers practice new ways of looking.

Though all the texts included in *Confronting Visuality* resist the "male gaze" and demonstrate that there are a variety of spectatorial positions women can inhabit that don't reduce only to "being looked at ness," they do not, for the most part, challenge the heterosexual bias of traditional models of spectatorship. However, queer theorists have long derided the heterosexual basis of Mulvey's model of spectatorship. For example, Ellis Hanson contends, "Queer theorists have already discovered that the heterocentric and exceedingly rigid structure of the look in Mulvey's analysis—patriarchal masculinity leering at objectified femininity—writes homosexuality out of existence" (13). Queer theory has worked to articulate the parameters for a "queer gaze," and the result has been increasing numbers of films (and indeed images, in general) that "make many forms of address to more than one audience and allow the possibility of multiple identifications by the spectator" (Evans and Gamman 32). The works of "new queer cinema" such as *Paris Is Burning* (1990), *Poison* (1991), and

Swoon (1992) were particularly committed to undoing the heterosexist basis of the gaze.[11]

Fun Home demonstrates the possibility for American women's literature to participate in this project of reworking the traditional spectatorial model. Though Bechdel is not the first to posit the importance of a queer spectatorial position, she does explore the possibilities of this position in new and unprecedented ways using graphic narratives. Her work illustrates that graphic narratives are well suited to exploring issues of visuality and gender and perhaps, out of necessity, put these issues at their center. As well, *Fun Home* participates in the work of confronting visuality by focusing on *how* we frame events and how we come to see them, in Bechdel's case, through the material artifacts of family. By making these visualization processes visible in unprecedented ways, Bechdel expands the range of women's writing about visuality significantly.

Conclusion

Confronting Visuality in the Digital Age

What emerges from examining women writers' engagement with issues of visuality is the need for contemporary audiences to possess a nuanced, critical media literacy. In order to be the type of literate person who can effectively engage contemporary media, the writers indicate that viewers must be able to connect what is depicted in the media to larger ideologies about race, gender, and sexuality. But perhaps even more important, viewers must be able to see what is *not* visualized, since important issues of race, gender, sexuality, and class remain hidden. However, though the writers stress the importance of seeing what is not visualized, they do not suggest that this is an easy task. In fact, if the accounts included in *Confronting Visuality* are not enough, the history of feminist media studies itself testifies to the challenge of recognizing what has not been visualized. This is evident, for example, in early models of spectatorship that did not take into account differences between women based on race and sexuality. As bell hooks asked incredulously in 1992, "Are we really to imagine that feminist theorists writing only about the image of white women, who subsume this specific historical subject under the totalizing category 'woman,' do not 'see' the whiteness of that image?" (*Black Looks* 124). While hooks attributed this oversight to the psychoanalytic bases of feminist film theory at the time, E. Ann Kaplan suggests that it is due more to the "powerful shaping force of the history of imaging," writing, "The inability to 'see' the racism in the films we were studying in relation to structures of the male gaze testifies to how looking is socially constructed: we had grown up with such images, regardless of our actual relations with people of other ethnicities, and thus could not see what was under our very eyes" (*Looking* 127).

In truth, it can be enormously difficult to see what is "under our very eyes" when we have been socialized not to see it, and philosopher Jacques Rancière argues that the very essence of politics is making visible what has been rendered unseen. In "Ten Theses on Politics," Rancière describes politics as a contest about what can become visible. He asserts the essential division between "the police" as the "symbolic constitution of the social" whose "essence is a certain manner of partitioning the sensible" and the politics, which is "first and foremost an intervention upon the visible and the sayable":

> "Move along! There is nothing to see here!" The police say that there is nothing to see on a road, that there is nothing to do but move along. It asserts that the space of circulating is nothing other than the space of circulation. Politics, in contrast, consists in transforming this space of "moving-along" into a space for the appearance of a subject: i.e., the people, the workers, the citizens: It consists in refiguring the space, of what there is to do there, what is to be seen or named therein. (Rancière)

Over and over again in the narratives included in *Confronting Visuality*, the writers assert "there *is* something to see here." There *is* an overlooked history of African Americans in the United States and African American girlhood in particular that speaks to the ongoing difficulties that black women face in the United States. There *is* a story about how mass media increasingly shape memory and perception, even those of "eyewitnesses" to historical events. There *are* biological limitations to seeing, and these limitations are subject to manipulation. There *are* ongoing legal disputes over Native American land that deserve recognition because Native Americans have not "vanished." Fetal images *are* difficult to interpret, and their role in pregnancy *is* complex and fraught. There *is* a repressed sexual history evident even in familiar domestic arrangements and texts. As they explore these and other difficult issues in their writing, women writers participate in what Rancière calls the "politics of dissensus," which "makes visible that which had no reason to be seen." The writers demand the right to look at what a range of authorities—governmental, institutional, and familial—seek to conceal, refusing to "move along" and accept that there is nothing to see so as to maintain the status quo of gender, race, and sexual relations.

Moreover, the writers also invite readers to refuse to move along with them. In this way, along with claiming the right to look, these works point to the importance of what Nicholas Mirzoeff refers to as "the right to be seen" ("Introduction" xxxiii). He explains, "The demand is to 'look' on that which authority holds out of sight, and to be seen to be doing so, from a place that is freely chosen" ("Introduction" xxxiii). Each of these writers has chosen literature as a highly visible, public position from which to be seen examining the social and political operation of visuality. They develop new narrative strategies in order to engage contemporary visualization technologies and practices and in doing so contribute to the development of a literary tradition that actively intervenes in visuality, by considering the role ideology plays in how visual images are constructed and by offering strategies readers can employ to recognize and resist visuality. In this sense, Toni Morrison's *The Bluest Eye*, Bobbie Ann Mason's *In Country*, Margaret Atwood's *The Handmaid's Tale* and *Oryx and Crake*, Louise Erdrich's *Shadow Tag*, Gish Jen's "Birthmates," Chitra Banerjee Divakaruni's "The Ultrasound," and Alison Bechdel's *Fun Home* constitute a cross-cultural literary corpus that has itself gone largely unseen by literary critics.

This tradition is especially relevant today as more traditional avenues of feminist critique struggle to respond to a postfeminist sensibility that "sutures" together feminism and antifeminism (Gill 270) and as feminist critics themselves are increasingly mired in "paralyzing debates" about the proper subject for critique (Van Zoonen 36). Moreover, the transition in Western culture to what has been widely called "the digital age" makes the need for critical engagements with media more pressing than ever before. Indeed the issues of transparency discussed in the context of medical imaging in Chapter 5 are magnified in digital environments because computers have come to be widely understood as "transparency machines" despite the multiple levels of mediation involved in their operation. As Wendy Hui Kyong Chun has discussed, "For computers to become transparency machines, the fact that they compute—that they *generate* text and images rather than merely represent or reproduce what exists elsewhere—must be forgotten" (65). In contrast to medical imaging, in which those who undergo imaging are often keenly aware of the mediating role played by the technician as well as the physician reading the images (whether that person is seen or not), computers are less likely to be perceived as involving any mediation but rather to merely represent. Alexander Galloway refers to this as a paradox inherent in any mediating technology, which is "obliged to erase itself to the highest degree possible in the name of unfettered communication, but in so doing it proves its own virtuosic presence as technology, thereby undoing the original erasure" (320).

Nevertheless, just as in medical imaging, behind the supposed transparency of computers hides ideology and the numerous choices that have been predetermined for computer users that not only shape the experience of using software and hardware but also shape users themselves. Chun focuses in particular on the work of software in fostering the rhetoric of transparency and describes how "software, or perhaps more precisely operating systems, offer us an imaginary relationship to our hardware: they do not represent transistors but rather desktops and recycling bins" (79). Moreover, software "interpellates a 'user' . . . So Mac users 'think different' and identify with Martin Luther King and Albert Einstein; Linux users are open-source power geeks, drawn to the image of a fat, sated penguin; and Windows users are mainstream, functionalist types perhaps comforted, as Eben Moglen argues, by their regularly crashing computers" (79). These "choices," however, "limit the visible and the invisible, the sayable and the unsayable" (79). Nevertheless, most computer users will not become aware of the ways their choices are constricted unless they find themselves at odds with the program's default settings.

Chun's work illustrates the extent to which the authority of the computer programmer and the ideological work of computing are rendered invisible to computer users, making this authority and ideology seem natural and therefore more difficult to recognize and critique. Similarly, contemporary technoculture can also obscure the operation of gender in digital environments and make critical examinations of gender in digital contexts challenging. On the one hand, categories such as gender, race, and sexuality seem to become increasingly irrelevant in digital contexts, especially because technoculture "cherishes a fetish for the transcendence of the material" (van Doorn, Wyatt, and Van Zoonen 434). Kaplan summarizes this optimistic vision of transcending material differences in digital environments: "Wouldn't it be neat if U.S. culture and people did not have to struggle with racial difference or oppressive gaze structures, or work toward new looking relations . . . because humans no longer functioned through embodied interaction but instead through cyberspace, where racial and gender markers can be hidden?" (*Looking* 292). And there is evidence that such transcendence is facilitated in cyberspace, for example, when male gamers adopt female avatars and seem to cross identify with a female spectatorial position in doing so (Cassell and Jenkins; Ouellette "When").[1]

However, the possibilities for and prevalence of cross identification in technoculture can obscure what seem to be some rather hard limits on the extent to which transcending materiality and embodiment does take place as well. For example, in the case of male gamers adopting female avatars, research indicates that frequently these men enforce the most traditional stereotypes about female sexuality in creating their avatars (Cassell and Jenkins 32). Niels van Doorn, Sally Wyatt, and Liesbet Van Zoonen explain that in fact technoculture "is continually haunted by the 'specter of embodiment' that enforces its law and governs our discourse. In the context of gender, this specter continues to enforce a discourse that links gender to a dichotomously sexed body, whether visible or not" (434).

We cannot, then, simply look to digital forms to solve the problems that persist regarding visualization and representation. As Kaplan notes, "Humans carry with them into cyberspace formations ongoing now. Even writers' imaginings in science fiction cannot avoid repeating well-worn female stereotypes" (*Looking* 292–93). There is ample evidence to support her claim in today's technoculture where, despite the opportunity to imagine completely alternative gender and sexual relations, digital texts are more likely to simply recycle patterns familiar from mediums such as film and television (or pornography).[2] And because computers masquerade as "transparency machines," these problems are likely magnified as it becomes increasingly difficult to recognize the ways both hardware and software mediate our entire experience in digital environments and how these machines encode assumptions about gender, race, and class into their operation and naturalize them in doing so.

When it comes to technoculture, we must not "move along" too quickly on the assurance that there is nothing to be seen. Consequently, women's writing about visuality might be regarded as a road map to use in navigating the less familiar terrain of cyberspace. Feminist critiques of technoculture face the same challenges as do critiques of women's images in mediums such as film and television. In fact, ongoing debates centered on, for example, whether *Tomb Raider*'s Lara Croft is a feminist icon or a "cyberbimbo" (Kennedy) strongly mirror the debates about *Mad Men* and *Game of Thrones* that I alluded to in this book's Introduction.[3] And ultimately, these debates do little either to resolve the problematic combination of feminism and antifeminism inherent in such postfeminist representations or to settle the question for feminist critics about what the basis for a critique of such images should be. Throughout this book, I have suggested that women's writing about visuality is well equipped to address these sorts of issues because it necessarily attends to larger contexts of visuality rather than narrower contexts of specific representations and can serve as a bridge between "professional feminism" and "popular feminism" in doing so (Stuart 30). The writers included in *Confronting Visuality* do not become bogged down by debates about whether a specific image is ultimately more positive or negative for women. Moreover, they acknowledge the complexity of women's relationships with images, at times highlighting explicitly contradictory readings of the same image—whether Shirley Temple or a fetal ultrasound. But in every case, they attend carefully to the contexts from which images of women emerge and the multiple, sometimes completely unexpected, effects they have on viewers. In moving forward into the digital age, these works suggest that rather than debating what the proper subject for feminist analysis should be, the focus should be on the more difficult and ultimately important questions about how visualization is related to subjecthood, how representation is related to subjectivity, and how particular narratives of femininity and ideals of beauty and sexuality become normalized and then internalized and adopted as our own.

Notes

Introduction

1. Critics such as Angela McRobbie and Andrea Stuart have observed that feminist theoretical trajectories shifted in the early 1990s as feminism split with "professional feminism" retreating to the academy, while "popular feminism" "comes at most of us through the media" (Stuart 30). However, what this split means is still hotly contested. Gill explains that critics have variously interpreted the emergence of "popular feminism," or what has come to be known as "postfeminism," as an "epistemological break" (250), a "historical shift" (251), or a backlash to feminism (253). Throughout this book, I follow Gill, who argues that postfeminism "is best understood not as an epistemological perspective, nor as a historical shift, and not (simply) as a backlash" but rather as a "sensibility" with "recurring and relatively stable themes, tropes and constructions that characterize gender representations in the media in the early twenty-first century" (254–55).
2. Judith Williamson refers to this genre of programming as "retro-sexist."
3. As Sady Doyle explains, *Game of Thrones* features "old-timey, misogynist knights and kings," while *Mad Men* focuses on old-timey, misogynist admen.
4. Andi Zeisler notes that "with every season of *Game of Thrones*, one question has become more insistent among in the blogosphere: 'Is *Game of Thrones* feminist?'" The same is also true for *Mad Men*. Primarily, the debates about these programs have occurred online, in blogs and online magazines, though several scholarly collections focused on *Mad Men* have been published as well. Although it is beyond the scope of this introduction to list all the articles devoted to this debate, a few of the most widely cited articles are listed here. For the debate on *Mad Men*, see Coontz, Gray, Kearns, Kim, Matlack, and Rine. For the debate on *Game of Thrones*, see Armstrong, Arthur, Morrissey, Mulhall, Salter, Watercutter, and Zeisler.

5. Recent critics have begun laying the groundwork for such critique. See Gill, Ross, Williamson, and Kearney for examples.
6. See the Centers for Disease Control's 2010 report "National Intimate Partner and Sexual Violence Survey" for figures charting rates of domestic and sexual violence against women (Black, et al., 13–19). See also the "Eating Disorders Statistics" provided by the National Association of Anorexia Nervosa and Associated Disorders. The American Society of Plastic Surgeons's "2012 Plastic Surgery Procedural Statistic" report documents the growing rate of plastic surgery among very young women.
7. See Kathleen Fitzpatrick's *The Anxiety of Obsolescence* (2006) for a discussion of how key contemporary male writers have responded to new media.
8. Martin Jay points out that "the pictorial turn has taken place, as observers have been quick to note, against the backdrop of the seemingly exponential increase of images in Western culture" (Jay, "Vision" 3–4).
9. Though the transition from an industrial, print-based society to one grounded in the information age took more than a century, according to the authors of *Mass Media and the Cultural Landscape*, "the electronic phase of the Information Age really boomed in the 1950s and 1960s with the arrival of television and its dramatic impact on daily life" (9). Richard Campbell, Christopher R. Martin, and Bettina Fabos explain that the move to the information age in America began in the 1840s with the development of the telegraph (8). Other "early signs" of the information age included "the rise of film at the turn of the twentieth century" and "the development of radio in the 1920s" (9).
10. The publication of *The Feminine Mystique* is arguably the starting point for modern, or second-wave, feminism. As Van Zoonen explains, the text led to the "revival of the women's movement which had been dormant since the successful struggle for women's suffrage" (26).
11. For example, in 1970, approximately a hundred activists from NOW, Media Women, New York Radical Feminists, and Redstockings, among others, organized a sit-in at the offices of *The Ladies Home Journal* to protest the way the mostly male staff represented women's issues and to demand, among other things, a female editor-in-chief and an onsite child-care center for employees. For a first-person account of the takeover by one of the activists involved, see Bikman.

12. Teresa de Lauretis and Judith Mayne also made note of the gap in feminist film theory regarding race, and bell hooks called on white feminists to remedy it in *Black Looks*.
13. It is worth noting that E. Ann Kaplan disagrees that psychoanalysis was responsible for the blind spots in early feminist models of spectatorship, though she acknowledges that early feminist theory did overlook issues of race and sexuality. She contends that "this claim ignores the groundbreaking work of Franz Fanon, the later writings of Joel Kovel and the current work of Jessica Benjamin, Michele Wallace, and Jane Flax, among others. Psychoanalysis can and should lead one directly to issues of race" (Kaplan, *Looking* 295). Instead Kaplan attributes the omission of race to "far broader historical, political, cultural and intellectual reasons than psychoanalytic methodology itself" (Kaplan, *Looking* xv).
14. For example, the study of advertisements—which as Karen Ross explains, has traditionally used "notions of woman and man as a simple analytical binary" and ignored "other kinds of marked differences such as race and ethnicity, often because introducing more than one variable (i.e. gender) into the mix could make analysis more ambiguous" (55)—has nevertheless increasingly seen the publication of studies that engage multiple identities. See Plous and Neptune; Durham; Duke; Covert and Dixon; Thomas and Treiber; and Holden.
15. This seems to stem, at least in part, from traditional divides between images and texts as well as between literary criticism and art history.
16. There is also a curious gap on this subject with regard to periodization. Although Mitchell identifies the pictorial turn as a contemporary phenomenon, most theoretical treatments of visual culture and literature focus on modernist or earlier literature, including Hinnov, Spengler, Sherrard-Johnson, Denisoff, Humm, Conway, and Jacobs.
17. As Annette Kuhn has explained, the "language of memory does seem to be above all a language of images," and it shares with dreams and fantasies the ability to condense and displace our desires and fears into powerful images (*Family Secrets* 160).
18. For example, there has been a heated debate between scholars about women's engagement with so-called women's genres, such as soap operas. This debate focuses on whether there is any possible space for female agency or transformation within narratives that, as Rosalind Coward puts it, "confirm men's power, women's subordination" (203). The fact that women frequently take pleasure from these narratives further complicates the question (Thornham 56).

For differing perspectives on the critical possibilities associated with women's engagement with soap operas, see Modleski, Brown, and Ang.

19. The National Endowment for the Arts has exerted considerable resources studying reading habits in the twenty-first century. Its 2004 report *Reading at Risk: A Survey of Literary Reading in America* labeled the state of reading in America "bleak," and its 2007 follow-up *To Read or Not to Read* suggested the situation was "alarming" (5).
20. See Birkerts and Nunberg.
21. See Lott, Hon, and Crain.
22. See Birkerts and Nunberg as well as the NEA studies *Reading at Risk* pg. vii and *To Read or Not to Read*.
23. Steven Johnson responded to the 2007 NEA study with an article in *The Guardian*, questioning the design of the study and its conclusions. And a 2012 PEW Research Center study found that e-readers may be leading to an increase in reading. It is also worth mentioning that recent work by N. Katherine Hayles demonstrates that though people may indeed be reading as much as ever before, what she terms "digital reading" is quite different from "print reading." Hayles argues that the move from print to digital reading is transforming individuals' "cognitive modes"—away from the "deep attention" required to engage in close reading and toward "hyper attention," with its concomitant "hyper reading," a practice that represents a survival strategy in the face of information overload (59–60). I would suggest that a number of the narrative innovations developed by the writers in *Confronting Visuality* are precisely intended to engage an audience accustomed to "hyper reading." This issue will be discussed in more detail, particularly in Chapter 3.
24. One result of the blurring of the visual and verbal has been to call into question traditional distinctions between these modes of communication. For example, in "There Are No Visual Media," Mitchell argues that even painting cannot rightly be labeled a "purely visual medium" (7). Similarly, composition scholars, Anne Frances Wysocki notable among them, have argued that there are no purely textual mediums since text itself has a clear visual dimension (evident in the choices writers face regarding fonts, white space, and page layout), and these characteristics are not distinct from content but constitute part of the content.
25. An incomplete list of awards that the authors and works included in this study have won includes the Nobel Prize, the PEN/Hemingway Award, Guggenheim Fellowships, the Booker Prize,

inclusion in *Best American Short Stories*, the Pushcart Prize, and Lambda Literary Awards.

Chapter 1

1. Critics have long considered issues of visuality in Morrison's writing although *The Bluest Eye* remains the text most discussed in relation to these issues. For discussions of film in *The Bluest Eye*, see Azouz, Gerster, and Fick. Articles that discuss issues of aesthetics include Moses and Hastings. See Simpson; Rand; and Yancy and Alcoff for discussions of issues of the gaze. For discussions of traumatic seeing in the novel, see Ledbetter, Bouson, and Dickerson. Scholars have also published a number of analyses of visuality in relation to *Beloved*; see, for example, McDermott, "Silence, Visuality, and the Staying Image"; Schreiber; Mao and Zhang; and Adams. In "Toni Morrison's *Tar Baby*: Re-Figuring the Colonizer's Aesthetics," Walther analyzes issues of visuality in relation to *Tar Baby*, and in "Out of Sight: Toni Morrison's Revision of Beauty," she considers a number of Morrison's works. Spohrer examines issues of visuality in *Jazz*, Krumholz investigates issues of visuality in *Song of Solomon*, and Stave addresses visuality in relation to *A Mercy*. See Guerrero for an analysis of all Morrison's works through 1990. See Wyatt for a focus on representation. Kolmerten, Ross, and Wittenberg's anthology on Morrison's works also includes several essays that foreground issues of the gaze.
2. Michael Awkward contends that the only novel to predate Morrison's synthesis of nationalism and feminism is Zora Neale Hurston's *Their Eyes Were Watching God* (66).
3. John N. Duvall describes the ongoing critical discussion about the issue of authenticity in *The Bluest Eye* in *The Identifying Fictions of Toni Morrison: Modernist Authenticity and Postmodern Blackness*. This issue will be discussed in more detail later in this chapter as well.
4. *The Bluest Eye* has been described as an important evolution of the traditional bildungsroman, which generally focuses on a single male hero who successfully navigates challenges to reach "maturity and the recognition of his identity and role in the world" (Abrams 121). *The Bluest Eye* represents what Laura Sue Fuderer refers to as the new, ironic bildungsroman, in which female characters suffer "an awakening to limitations" (4), though Anne Salvatore contends that through her strategy of paired characters, Morrison "offers an antithesis to

the horror ... she demonstrates that opposing forces will inevitably rise, even from supremely negative circumstances" (156).
5. Douglas suggests that because reviewers (often black male reviewers) recognized the context of the Black Arts movement in *The Bluest Eye*, they were less critical of the novel than of other novels by black women published during the same time (153). See also Dubey's *Black Women Novelists and the Nationalist Aesthetic* for more about the reception of black women writers by black aesthetic critics.
6. See Thornham and Van Zoonen for a discussion of early feminist engagement with images of women.
7. In fact, early feminist work later came to be viewed as reductionist for overlooking the role of race and other factors in visual relations. Jane Gaines was one of the first to observe this gap in feminist theory in "White Privilege and Looking Relations," and Teresa de Lauretis and Judith Mayne also commented on this oversight. bell hooks called on white feminists to rectify the situation in *Black Looks*.
8. Nicholas Mirzoeff has coined the phrase "critical visuality studies" to refer to "one of the four main areas of visual culture practice that can be identified at present in Anglophone contexts" and "the methological link between these areas" ("Introduction" xxix). In particular, critical visual studies is characterized by opposition to visuality as a "specific technique of colonial and imperial practice" and "claims the right to look at that which authority wishes to conceal" ("Introduction" xxx).
9. Samy Azouz describes the *eye* in the title as a "multiple pun: it is at once the eye that Pecola Breedlove covets most, the eye of a white deity, the eye of a surrogate camera, and the 'bluest I' that narrates Pecola's victimization, Claudia MacTeer."
10. The gaze did not become a popular critical concept in feminist media studies until the publication of Mulvey's "Visual Pleasure and Narrative Cinema" in 1975, though, as James Elkins has explained, the concept of the gaze had already begun to "revive" in twentieth-century thinking due to "Alois Riegl's descriptions of the Dutch group portrait; Jean-Paul Sartre's theory of seeing-as-being-seen; Merleau Ponty's account of embodied seeing" ("The End" 1). See Elkins's "The End of the Theory of the Gaze" for a historical overview of "the gaze" in nineteenth- and twentieth-century thinking.
11. Similarly, Morrison alludes to the famous 1951 "dolls study" conducted by Kenneth Clark and Mamie Clark. This study asked 16 black children in a Charleston segregated school to compare otherwise identical brown and white colored dolls. The children's spontaneous responses to the dolls often addressed racial difference in

terms of which doll was "pretty" compared to another doll, confirming the internalization of racial and gendered social messages of beauty. The study was used as evidence for the need to integrate schools in the *Brown v. Board of Education* court case. See Douglas for more on Morrison's engagement with the dolls study and Frever for a discussion of what makes Morrison's depiction of dolls "the most ground-breaking—and doll-breaking—image of the doll in woman-authored fiction of the twentieth-century, and perhaps of all time" (123).

12. See Douglas for a discussion of Morrison's engagement with "the national narrative of minority citizenship enshrined by *Brown v. Board of Education* in its overturning of *Plessy v. Ferguson*'s 'separation of segregationist logic'" (145). Douglas points out that "Pecola and Claudia go to an integrated school, and Claudia, at least, lives in an integrated neighborhood . . . But in what might be an ironic commentary on the premise of *Brown*—that black self-esteem is irreparably harmed when law sanctions social segregation, especially during elementary education—the pathology of self-loathing emerges forcefully in Pecola despite her partially integrated environment" (148–49).

13. This kind of self-imposed segregation by race continues to characterize primary and secondary schools today. See Beverly Daniel Tatum's *Why Are All the Black Kids Sitting Together in the Cafeteria* for a discussion of this.

14. Almost all of the critical works listed in note 1 of this chapter touch on Morrison's engagement with mass media images.

15. At one point, Morrison describes how "three pennies had bought her nine lovely orgasms with Mary Jane" (50).

16. Lucky's discussion of ancestral knowledge in *The Bluest Eye* articulates this dichotomy particularly clearly: "Failure to remain connected to [an African-American cultural aesthetic] and to ancestral wisdom proves devastating for Pauline Breedlove, China, Poland, Marie, and Geraldine; but for Mrs. MacTeer, who is hard-working, high-strung, and stern toward her children and others for whom she cares, the progressive employment of these modes securely grounds her in African-American traditions and practices" such as "signifying" (21). Moses extends this dichotomy into aesthetics, arguing that the Breedloves are associated with a "Shirley Temple aesthetic," while the MacTeers are associated with a "blues aesthetic."

17. Rosalind Gill has discussed how simply creating positive images has not led to an overall change in either the simultaneous creation of negative images or the social positioning of women. Instead

"constructions of gender" are characterized by "extraordinary contradictoriness" whereby "confident expressions of 'girl power' sit alongside reports of 'epidemic' levels of anorexia and body dysmorphia; graphic tabloid reports of rape are placed cheek by jowl with adverts for lap-dancing clubs and telephone sex lines; lad magazines declare the 'sex war' over, while reinstating beauty contests and championing new, ironic modes of sexism; and there are regular moral panics about the impact on men of the new, idealized male body imagery, while the re-sexualization of women's bodies in public space goes virtually unremarked upon" (1). Gill's point is clear: simply intervening at the level of images won't change their "sedimented meanings" (Felski 182).

18. Mirzoeff describes the importance of holding the moment in place as a potentially dangerous and revolutionary act, building on work by Jacques Rancière ("Introduction" xxxiii).
19. Duvall argues that the prostitutes are "as authentic as it gets in *The Bluest Eye*" because they "imagine a way to inhabit the African-American female body" (45). Certainly, Pecola does use the word "real" to refer to them (58), and in their embrace of physical processes such as eating and sex, they stand in such stark contrast to the "sugar-brown" girls. However, the commodification of the women's sexuality seems to deeply problematize their relationship to their bodies.

Chapter 2

1. This cognitive turn is being driven by advances in imaging technology that allow scientists to "see" the brain in new ways and have prompted new directions in interdisciplinary research between scholars in the humanities and sciences into "concerns of human life usually reserved for the liberal arts: consciousness, language, art, morality, love" (Ty 206). See Michelle Ty and Mark Turner for further discussion of this topic.
2. Mason's use of pop culture allusions in her writing has caused considerable debate among critics. Her work has been referred to derogatively as "shopping mall realism," a phrase coined by Joel Conarroe to refer to Mason's ubiquitous allusions to popular culture in her short fiction and novels. Conarroe complains that these allusions are "not altogether distinguished artifacts," with "little reverberations for anyone who prefers Mahler to Madonna" (7). Other critics have championed Mason's cause, however. Leslie White was one of the

first critics to explore the critical potential of Mason's use of popular culture; she argues that "no matter how banal, demeaning or forgettable, popular culture is formative, and in Mason's fiction it appears as the foreground on which her characters move" (70). More recently, critics have recognized the potentially subversive role that media and popular culture play in Mason's works. Marjorie Winther concludes that Mason employs references to popular culture to develop an "intricate prose pattern" (195), and Stephen doCarmo claims that she practices "'excorporation,' which is the 'tearing' or disfigurement of a commodity in order to assert one's right and ability to remake it into one's own culture" in order to demonstrate the possibility for a historical and political consciousness within mass-mediated culture (590).

3. See Elizabeth Wolfson for a thirty-year retrospective on the memorial that contextualizes its controversy within the political and cultural landscape of the early 1980s. According to Wolfson, "the first skirmish of the culture wars of the 1980s can be traced back to the public debate that broke out in reaction to Maya Lin's design for the Vietnam Veterans Memorial in Washington, D.C."

4. Critics have long discussed Mason's depiction of PTSD in *In Country*. Among early articles focused on this topic, Matthew Stewart stands out for his assessment of Mason's representation of the condition. More recent readings of *In Country* through the lens of trauma theory have been published by Hinrichsen; Michael Barry; Grewe-Volpp; and Sinead McDermott.

5. See Farrell, LaCapra, and Vickroy, *Trauma* for discussions of the important role that fiction plays in mediating trauma in contemporary culture.

6. See Kaplan, *Rocking* and Lewis for analyses of the relationship between MTV and gender in the 1980s. See Mair for a history of HBO, which documents the cable network's rise from failing pay cable service in the early 1970s to "the most successful pay television enterprise in the history of the world and a major profit center for Time Inc." by 1981 (42). See Tichi for a more thorough discussion of the influence of television on *In Country*'s form and content.

7. Critics have been divided over Mason's decision to highlight Sam's narrative perspective. Milton Bates, for example, argues that the novel is "framed in such a way as to preclude serious engagement with the conflict" (29). However, other critics such as Lowney and Dwyer consider how this perspective allows Mason to offer a different kind of war narrative.

8. Hirsch defines postmemory as the "second-generation memories of cultural or collective traumatic events and experiences" (22). Sinead McDermott, who analyzes *In Country* through the lens of this concept, explains that it is a "useful" term because "it draws our attention to the manner in which memories translate into history/ies and the role of textual artifacts (photographs, diaries, and letters, but also the artifacts of popular culture) in such translations" (8).
9. This phenomenon is not limited to images of Vietnam. Later in the novel, Sam's mother Irene comments that she likes a particular field because "it's just like England. I've seen pictures of England that look like this field" (163). Sam's paternal grandparents similarly perceive Italy through the lens of *That's Incredible*, as a place "I'd hate to live . . . with all those miracles they have" (193). Mason implies that American perceptions of foreign countries are largely shaped by television, which offers simplistic and reductionist visions of those countries and international issues.
10. Stewart notes that Mason's fictional representation of the behavioral aftereffects of the Vietnam War is so exact that "it seems as if Mason availed herself of the many psychological and sociological studies of the Vietnam veterans and then managed to embody all that she has learned in this one small group of fictional Kentucky veterans" (167).
11. See Michael Barry and O'Brien for analyses of natural symbols throughout *In Country*. Barry observes that "analysis of the novel's symbols rewards the kind of attention to detail that psychotherapists employ in interpreting the cases of their patients" and is another way in which Mason weaves images of repressed trauma throughout the novel (153).
12. In October 2001, the online journal *Senses of Cinema* called for reflections on the relation between cinema and reality in light of the events of Sept. 11, 2001. See Villella and Martin for these reflections, many of which explicitly explore the repetitious use of "it was like a movie" after Sept. 11.
13. The memorial was still steeped in controversy when Mason chose to locate the conclusion of her novel there. When then 21-year-old undergraduate architectural student Maya Lin's memorial design was selected in 1981, controversy erupted over its abstract style. Critics did not feel the memorial conveyed the heroism, patriotism, and honor inherent in most wars. They argued that placement of the memorial below ground level hid it from view, while its color further hinted at a feeling of shame, and they thought the memorial focused too much on death and loss. For example, veteran Tom Carhart famously commented as follows:

I don't care about artistic perceptions, I don't care about the rationalizations that abound. One needs no artistic education to see this design for what it is, a black trench that scars the Mall. Black walls, the universal color of shame and sorrow and degradation. Hidden in a hole in the ground, with no means of access for those Vietnam veterans who are condemned to spend the rest of their days in a wheelchair. Perhaps that's an appropriate design for those who would spit on us still. But can America truly mean that we should feel honored by that black pit? ("The Vietnam Wall Controversy")

In Country was the first literary representation of the memorial, and the film adaptation of *In Country* was the first to use the memorial as a location. Responses to the novel's ending range from critics who argue that the memorial "provides the culmination, the final stage of [Sam and Emmett's] rite of passage" (Gunn 70) to those who contend that Emmett and Sam's experience at the memorial is "the sort of pat ending typical of a television movie" (Stewart 177). The film's conclusion received similarly mixed reviews; see Corliss and Sterritt. Early in the novel, Sam asks Tom if he has been to Washington to see the memorial, and despite the fact that he has not seen it in person, he is able to describe its appearance, of which he is critical: "A big black hole in the ground, catty-cornered from that big white prick. Fuck the Washington Monument" (80). Sam's conversation with Tom not only reveals that both characters are familiar with the memorial but also primes Sam to interpret the memorial in the context of the Washington Monument as well.

14. Their viewing of the memorial may be interpreted as similar to the tourist that Walker Percy describes in "Loss of the Creature" who attempts to see the Grand Canyon but is prevented from doing so because the canyon "has been appropriated by the symbolic complex which has already been formed in the sightseer's mind." According to Percy, the canyon is as follows: "that which has already been formulated—by picture postcard, geography book, tourist folders, and the words Grand Canyon. As a result of this preformulation, the source of the sightseer's pleasure undergoes a shift. Where the wonder and delight of the [original observer] arose from his penetration of the thing itself, from a progressive discovery of depths, patterns, colors, shadows, etc., now the sightseer measures his satisfaction by the degree to which the canyon conforms to the preformed complex" (48).

15. Some critics such as Sinead McDermott and Brinkmeyer point to the fact that both Sam and Emmett seem open to transformation following this experience, with the final image of Emmett sitting before the wall when his "face bursts into a smile like flames" (245) suggesting the image of a phoenix rising from its ashes. Other critics, particularly those who adopt a perspective based on trauma theory, are more skeptical about the extent to which this visit will foster healing for either Sam or, especially, Emmett. In particular, Hinrichsen interprets the final scene as deeply unsettling rather than cathartic: "Coded within this moment of apparent enlightenment is an image of violence suggestive of the horrific political and historical realities of U.S. involvement in western imperialism, namely the widely-circulated photographs of self-immolation by Buddhist monks of the streets of Saigon" (246). For her, this moment seems intended to undo any sense of consolation achieved by the visit to the memorial. My own sense is that Mason intends both meanings for the final scene. The characters do seem to have experienced a degree of catharsis, but rather than signaling the end of their investigations into Vietnam, this redirects them to the larger, still unsettled, political contexts in which Vietnam occurred.

16. See Dwyer, Holstein, and Grewe-Volpp for this perspective on the conclusion of *In Country*.

17. For two weeks in 1983, Christo surrounded 11 of the islands in Biscayne Bay with 6.5 million square feet of floating pink woven polypropylene fabric covering the surface of the water and extending out 200 feet from each island into the bay (Church).

18. Throughout *In Country*, Sam perceives sexual relationships in terms of conquest, with the female body being essentially "conquered" by the male in the form of reproduction. Sam's attitude stems from the very real correlation between teenage pregnancy and limited social and economic opportunities, and pregnancy symbolizes for Sam the end of opportunities to pursue higher education and leave Hopewell. See Kinney for a more thorough discussion of issues of reproduction in *In Country*.

19. For example, Christo's 2005 project for New York City's Central Park "The Gates" was estimated to have attracted more than four million visitors during its two-week exhibition (New York City).

Chapter 3

1. See Sharon Wilson's "Eyes and I's" for a consideration of vision in all Atwood's works up to and including *Cat's Eye*. See also Laura Wright's "National Photographic" and Laurie Vickroy's "Seeking Symbolic Immortality" for more recent examinations of the visual in relation to *Surfacing* and *Cat's Eye*, respectively.
2. See Reingard Nischik's excellent volume *Engendering Genre: The Works of Margaret Atwood* for a comprehensive discussion of Atwood's body of work as well as the relationship between issues of gender and literary genre.
3. See Atwood, "A Feminist *1984*" for Atwood's first reference to her work as speculative fiction. The MaddAddam trilogy comprises *Oryx and Crake* (2003), *The Year of the Flood* (2009), and *MaddAddam* (2013), all of which are set in the same fictional dystopian future.
4. In my discussion of *The Handmaid's Tale* and *Oryx and Crake*, I follow Atwood's manner of capitalization.
5. Atwood visited Iran and Afghanistan during a 1978 trip with her family. Although Atwood has not written explicitly about the trip, Graeme Gibson recorded his impressions in a *Chatelaine* piece titled "Travels of a Family Man."
6. The novel is not as unique to the United States as was *The Handmaid's Tale*, however, because the distinctions between nation-states dissolve as the power of multinational corporations increases. While the novel emphasizes a growing divide between the First World and the Third World, identifiable characteristics of the United States and Canada are less distinct. The environmental devastation that characterizes the world of *Oryx and Crake* is felt by all the nations of the world, and the only difference between nations is their ability to guard their citizens from its impact.
7. I generally refer to the narrator as Jimmy because I focus primarily on his life prior to the apocalypse. He only takes the name Snowman when he assumes responsibility for the Children of Crake.
8. In *The Year of the Flood*, readers learn that a number of other individuals, including some of those who worked with Crake to create the virus, survived the cataclysm as well. In *The Year of the Flood*, they describe avoiding contact with Jimmy and the Crakers he is guarding, so he remains unaware of their existence for most of the novel, but he and the Crakers do join with them in the trilogy's final installment, *MaddAddam*. Because the protagonists in *The Year of the Flood* and *MaddAddam* live primarily in a commune that rejects technology and emphasizes survival skills, issues of visuality emerge less

forcefully in these final two novels than they do in *Oryx and Crake*, and when these issues do come up, they seem to reinforce rather than extend Atwood's consideration of visuality in *Oryx and Crake*.
9. Significantly, even though Moira is aware of the regime's agenda, she overestimates her own ability to act in response to it.
10. Atwood's fictional world thus questions Foucault's historic distinction between "spectacle" and "surveillance" by developing a dystopian scenario in which both forms of power are combined.
11. See Pamela Cooper and Linda Kauffmann for extended analyses of Foucault's ideas as they relate to *The Handmaid's Tale*.
12. Though the correspondence of photographs to reality has been questioned since the nineteenth century, photographs continued to exert what William Mitchell refers to as a "powerful 'reality effect'" (27) until recent technological innovations made the digital alteration of photographs easy and commonplace. Mitchell identifies a 1989 controversy over photographs of two Libyan MiG-23s as a pivotal moment in the contemporary debate over photographic realism. When the American ambassador to the UN used the photographs to "prove" that two Libyan planes were armed when they were shot down by American forces, the Libyan ambassador to the UN accused the United States of doctoring the photographs, claiming they were "directed in the Hollywood manner" (qtd. in Mitchell 23).
13. *Time* magazine's handling of O. J. Simpson's mug shot remains one of the most familiar examples of digital alteration. When both *Time* and *Newsweek* ran Simpson's mug shot as their cover images during the same week, it became obvious that *Time* had digitally altered the image to darken Simpson's skin color. And during the 2004 US election campaign, an image of John Kerry sitting on the platform during a Jane Fonda speech at an antiwar rally was distributed widely on the Internet in an attempt to discredit Kerry, though the image was later revealed to have been "faked" by combining two distinct photographs.
14. Lorraine York's *Margaret Atwood and the Labour of Literary Celebrity* includes a detailed account of Atwood's use of mass media and digital technology in the management of her public persona.

Chapter 4

1. Chippewa and Ojibwe are white-invented names for the people who called and, for the most part, continue to call themselves the Anishinabe (variously spelled). Erdrich uses all three terms in her writing.

I follow her use of the term *Ojibwe* in her novel *Shadow Tag*, the focus of this chapter. For more about the politics of tribal naming, see Vizenor, *People Named the Chippewa* 13–21.

2. For example, Robert Silberman has described the book in Native American literature as "a necessary evil" (111), while Karl Kroeber refers to the novel as "an Anglo-American literary structure that must prohibit any authentically Indian imaginative form" (18). Kathleen Brogan situates Erdrich's work in the context of bicultural translation and details the controversy surrounding this work in *Cultural Haunting* 36–38. Robert Stirrup describes the evolution of the concept of storytelling as it applies to Erdrich in *Louise Erdrich* 17–18.

3. See Vizenor, *Survivance* for a detailed discussion of this term, which combines elements of resistance and survival.

4. These issues are particularly pressing in Erdrich's 2008 novel *The Plague of Doves*. See Valentino for an extended discussion of how issues of sovereignty and patriarchy intersect in *The Plague of Doves*. For a consideration of issues of land and tribal sovereignty in Erdrich's earlier works, see Sarvé-Gorham.

5. Erdrich returns to this point even more forcefully in her 2012 novel *The Round House*, in which a deranged white man is driven to rape and murder to prevent his former lover from enrolling her child as a member of her tribe, a process that would require her to reveal the child's paternity.

6. One key distinction between Anglo and traditional Native American men and women is that the former often define themselves primarily through gender, whereas the latter are usually defined through tribal affiliation. In other words, an Anglo man or woman tends to think of himself or herself first as a man or woman and second as a member of a specific national, regional, or familial community, while a Native American man or woman is more likely to think of himself or herself first as a member of a specific tribe and then as a man or woman. Cultural historian Basil Johnston explains that traditionally this was particularly true for the Ojibwe, the tribe about which Erdrich writes, because Ojibwe identity is located primarily in extended family (totem) groups and community: "Men and women preferred to regard themselves as members of a totem and then a community. Strangers, when they met, always asked one another, 'Waenaesh k'dodaem?' (What is your totem?); only afterwards did they ask, 'Waenaesh keeni?' (Who are you?)" (59).

Thus for traditional Ojibwe, personal identity is the result of an interconnected web of relationships—with one's family, the community, and the larger world. However, as a German American and

Turtle-Mountain Chippewa descendant, Erdrich is not a traditional Ojibwe, and neither are her characters in *Shadow Tag*. Having had their traditional communities largely destroyed by Anglo domination, characters in Erdrich's novels must reformulate identity, family, and community. Most of Erdrich's characters, particularly her contemporary characters, experience a pull between Anglo gender norms, with their emphasis on individualism, and Native American gender traditions, with their concern for connection and harmony.

7. See Cohen, Bancroft, Charles, Frase, and Putnam.
8. Though ekphrasis was at one time used exclusively for poetry that described painting, the term has been expanded to refer to descriptions of art across various genres. Ekphrasis has also been subdivided into two types. The first is "actual" ekphrasis, in which writers describe real works of art. The second type is "notional" ekphrasis, which describes imaginary art. Homer's description of Achilles's sword in *The Iliad* and Keats's description of the urn in "Ode on a Grecian Urn" are probably the best known examples of notional ekphrasis. See James Heffernan's "Ekphrasis and Representation" and *Museum of Words* and W. J. T. Mitchell's *Picture Theory* for contemporary definitions and redefinitions of ekphrasis.
9. Critics have long recognized that particular characters in Erdrich's writing embody qualities associated with the windigo. See Strandness, Korpez, Mermann-Jozwiak, and Tharp for analyses of the windigo in Erdrich's earlier works. In her 2012 novel *The Round House*, Erdrich's characters themselves interpret the actions of another character as indicative that he is a windigo, and they justify his retributive murder on the basis of traditional laws concerning the windigo.
10. See Putnam and Cohen.

Chapter 5

1. It was not until the 1970s that medical imaging technologies entered the commercial marketplace and began to become commonplace in the practice of medicine. See Bettyann Kevles's *Naked to the Bone: Medical Imaging in the Twentieth Century* for a good history of medical imaging. Consequently, responses to medical imaging emerged in the 1980s as scholars attempted to theorize the impact of the new technologies on medical practice. Some examples of early scholarly responses to medical imaging that recognize the importance of gender as a context include Oakley, Haraway, and Petchesky. The 1990s saw the publication of several important critical works on medical

imaging. In 1992, *Camera Obscura* devoted two special issues to imaging technologies; though gender was not central in every article, it did receive attention. Also see Phelan and Cartwright, *Screening the Body*. Perhaps the most important text to give a sustained treatment to the role of gender in medical imaging is Treichler, Cartwright, and Penley's *The Visible Woman: Imaging Technologies, Gender, and Science*.
2. The essays included in *The Visible Woman* focus on the impact of a whole range of imaging technologies on women, not only those targeted specifically at women. But imaging technologies associated with women have also received considerable critical attention, particularly mammogram and fetal ultrasound. On mammogram, see Solomon.
3. The Guttmacher Institute reports that black women and Latinas account for 55 percent of abortions, while white women account for 36 percent of abortions, and 57 percent of women seeking abortions are classified "low-income" ("Facts on Induced Abortion").
4. State laws concerning the use of ultrasound in abortion counseling differ. The Guttmacher Institute reports that

- 12 states require verbal counseling or written materials to include information on accessing ultrasound services,
- 21 states regulate the provision of ultrasound by abortion providers,
- 2 states mandate that an abortion provider perform an ultrasound on each woman seeking an abortion and require the provider to show and describe the image,
- 6 states mandate that an abortion provider perform an ultrasound on each woman seeking an abortion and require the provider to offer the woman the opportunity to view the image,
- 9 states require that a woman be provided with the opportunity to view an ultrasound image if her provider performs the procedure as part of the preparation for an abortion,
- and 5 states require that a woman be provided with the opportunity to view an ultrasound image. ("Requirements for Ultrasound")

Chapter 6

1. I use the term *graphic narrative* for reasons that Hillary Chute and Marianne DeKoven outline in their introduction to the 2006 *Modern*

Fiction Studies special issue on graphic narratives. They define the term as "narrative work in the medium of comics," distinguishing it from the potentially problematic term *graphic novel* (767). Some critics have referred to *Fun Home* as an "autographic memoir" instead (see Watson), but these critics generally situate *Fun Home* in the narrower context of memoir, not the broader context of narrative that I consider in this chapter.

2. Marjane Satrapi's acclaimed 2003 graphic narrative *Persepolis* had previously ignited interest in issues of gender in graphic narratives in a global context. For more on the significance of *Persepolis*, see Chute, *Graphic Women* or Gilmore.

3. It has become conventional in critical discussions of *Fun Home* to use "Bechdel" to refer to the author outside the text and "Alison" to refer to her in-text avatar. Ann Cvetkovich explains that this practice is consistent with critical discussions of memoir in general (126).

4. The *Modern Fiction Studies* special issue indicated that graphic narrative is suitable for serious academic inquiry and was the first special issue on the graphic narrative within the larger field of modern and contemporary narrative. The formation of an MLA Discussion Group on Comics and Graphic Narratives in 2009 further signified the acceptance of graphic narrative as viable for serious study.

5. For more on *Fun Home* in the context of women's previous work in the genre of graphic narratives, see Chute, *Graphic Women*. For more on *Fun Home* in the context of memoir, see Michael Chaney's *Graphic Subjects*.

6. For example, Robyn Warhol notes that Scott McCloud's important work *Understanding Comics* develops "universal descriptions for the elements of comics. As a result, he does not attend to differences that gender and sexuality might make in one's approach to that art" (6). However, *Fun Home*, with an "aura of embodiment" (Warhol 6) that is resolutely gendered and sexualized, cannot be adequately explained by the existing gender-blind models of analysis in comics theory.

7. The outpouring of criticism on *Fun Home* has required critics, in particular literary critics, to develop new interpretive skills, a challenge Gillian Whitlock has described as follows: "Ironically, work on these most familiar texts require the acquisition of new interpretive skills for many of us. The vocabulary of comics represents figures and objects across a wide iconic range from the abstraction of cartooning to realism; its grammar is based on panels, frames, and gutters that translate time and space onto the page in black and white;

and balloons both enclose speech and convey the character of sound and emotion" (968).
8. Bechdel has referred to it as the book's "centerfold" (Chute, "An Interview" 1006).
9. Sedgwick uses the term *homosexual/heterosexual knowing* to describe a "form of knowledge that represents at the same time 'knowledge itself' and a diagnosable pathology of cognition . . . In a more succinct formula, paranoia" (97).
10. Indeed the equation of femininity with male homosexuality is reductive, as Bechdel acknowledges in an extradiegetic note (*Fun Home* 97).
11. *New queer cinema* is the name given by film theorist B. Ruby Rich to a wave of queer films that gained critical acclaim on the festival circuit in the early 1990s. Aaron explains that these films "represented the exciting prospect that lesbian and gay images and filmmakers had turned a corner. No longer burdened by the approval-seeking sackcloth of positive imagery, or the relative obscurity of marginal production, films could be both radical and popular, stylish and economically viable" ("New Queer Cinema" 3).

Conclusion

1. See Penley for a discussion of females identifying with male protagonists in digital texts.
2. See Martis and Jansz; Ouellette, "When"; Children Now; Dietz; Gailey; Beasley and Standley; and Kennedy.
3. Although this debate is common among bloggers, it has also been picked up by and is reflected in academic criticism as well. For this academic debate, see Kennedy; Walk; Cassell and Jenkins; Ouellette, "Two Guns"; Stasia; and Flanagan.

Works Cited

Aaron, Michele, ed. *New Queer Cinema*. New Brunswick, NJ: Rutgers UP, 2004. Print.
———. "New Queer Cinema: An Introduction." Aaron 3–15.
———. "The New Queer Spectator." Aaron 187–200.
Abrams, M. H. *A Glossary of Literary Terms*. New York: Holt, Rinehart and Winston, 1981. Print.
Adams, Rachel. "The Black Look and 'the Spectacle of Whitefolks': Wildness in Toni Morrison's *Beloved*." *Skin Deep, Spirit Strong: The Black Female Body*. Ed. Kimberly Wallace-Sanders. Ann Arbor: U of Michigan P, 2002. 153–81. Print.
American Society of Plastic Surgeons. *2012 Plastic Surgery Statistics Report*. ASPS National Clearinghouse of Plastic Surgery Procedural Statistics, 2012. Web. 26 July 2013.
Ang, Ien. "Melodramatic Imaginations: Television Fiction and Women's Fantasy." *Television and Women's Culture: The Politics of the Popular*. Ed. Mary Ellen Brown. London: Sage, 1990. 75–88. Print.
Armstrong, Jennifer. "*Game of Thrones*: Feminist or Not?" *Entertainment Weekly*. Entertainment Weekly, 18 Apr. 2011. Web. 7 July 2013.
Arthur, Kate. "9 Ways *Game of Thrones* Is Actually Feminist." *BuzzFeed Entertainment*. Buzzfeed, 17 Apr. 2013. Web. 3 Aug. 2013.
Atwood, Margaret. "Author Interview." *Margaret Atwood: Oryx and Crake*. Random, 3 Jan. 2003. Web. 17 Mar. 2006.
———. "A Feminist *1984*: Margaret Atwood Talks about Her Exciting New Novel." *Ms* 14 (Feb. 1986): 26. Print.
———. *The Handmaid's Tale*. New York: Fawcett Crest, 1985. Print.
———. "An Interview with Margaret Atwood: 20 Apr. 1983." By Jan Garden Castro. *Margaret Atwood: Vision and Forms*. Ed. Kathryn Vanspanckeren and Jan Garden Castro. Carbondale: Southern Illinois UP, 1988. 215–32. Print.
———. "An Interview with Margaret Atwood on Her Novel *The Handmaid's Tale*." *A Reader's Companion to* The Handmaid's Tale. Random, n.d. Web. 13 Mar. 2013.
———. *MaddAddam*. New York: Doubleday, 2013. Print.

———. *Oryx and Crake*. New York: Anchor, 2003. Print.

———. *Surfacing*. 1972. New York: Anchor, 1998. Print.

———. *The Tent*. New York: Doubleday, 2006. Print.

———. "Writing *Oryx and Crake*." *Margaret Atwood: Oryx and Crake*. Random, 3 Jan. 2003. Web. 4 Aug. 2005.

———. *The Year of the Flood*. New York: Anchor, 2009. Print.

August Wilson: Writing and the Blues. Dir. Kate Roth Knull. *World of Ideas/ The Moyer Collection Series*. Princeton: Films for the Humanities, 1988. Film.

Awkward, Michael. "Roadblocks and Relatives." *Critical Essays on Toni Morrison*. Ed. Nellie Y. McKay. Boston: G. K. Hall, 1988. 57–67. Print.

Azouz, Samy. "Cinema and Ideology in *The Bluest Eye* by Toni Morrison." *Americana: E-Journal of American Studies in Hungary* 4.2 (Fall 2008): n. pag. Web. 20 July 2013.

Baker, Houston A. *Blues, Ideology and, African-American Literature*. Chicago: U of Chicago P, 1984. Print.

Bambara, Toni Cade. "Commitment: Toni Cade Bambara Speaks." Bell, Parker, and Guy-Sheftall 230–49.

Bancroft, Colette. "*Shadow Tag* by Louise Erdrich." *St. Petersburg Times* 21 Feb. 2010: L.7. Print.

Barry, Ann. *Visual Intelligence: Perception, Image, and Manipulation in Visual Communication*. Albany: State U of New York P, 1997. Print.

Barry, Lynda. *The Good Times Are Killing Me*. 1988; rpt. New York: HarperPerennial, 1991. Print.

Barry, Michael. "Black Holes, Graveyards, and the Gravitational Force of What's Below: Mason's *In Country*." *PLL: Papers on Language and Literature* 49.2 (Spring 2013): 141–71. Print.

Barthes, Roland. *Image, Music, Text*. Trans. Stephen Heath. New York: Farrar, Straus, and Giroux, 1977. Print.

Bates, Milton J. "Men, Women, and Vietnam." *America Rediscovered: Critical Essays on Literature and Film of the Vietnam Era*. Ed. Owen W. Gilman Jr. and Lorrie Smith. New York: Garland, 1990. 27–63. Print.

Baudrillard, Jean. *Simulations*. Trans. Paul Foss, Paul Patton, and Philip Beitchman. New York: Semiotext[e], 1983. Print.

Beasley, Berrin, and Tracy Collins Standley. "Shirts vs. Skins: Clothing as an Indicator of Gender Role Stereotyping in Video Games." *Mass Communication and Society* 5.3 (2002): 279–93. Print.

Bechdel, Alison. *Are You My Mother?: A Comic Drama*. Boston: Houghton, 2012. Print.

———. *The Essential Dykes to Watch Out For*. Boston: Houghton, 2008. Print.

———. *Fun Home: A Family Tragicomic*. Boston: Houghton, 2006. Print.

Beck, Melinda, et al. "America's Abortion Dilemma." *Newsweek* 105 (14 Jan. 1985): 20–29. Print.

Bell, Roseann P., Bettye J. Parker, and Beverly Guy-Sheftall. *Sturdy Black Bridges: Visions of Black Women in Literature*. Garden City: Anchor, 1979. Print.

Benshoff, Harry M. "Reception of a Queer Mainstream Film." Aaron 172–86.

Berenstein, Rhona J. "Spectatorship as Drag: The Act of Viewing and Classic Horror Cinema." Williams 231–70.

Berlant, Lauren. "America, 'Fat,' the Fetus." *The Queen of America Goes to Washington City*. Durham, NC: Duke UP, 1997. 83–144. Print.

———. "National Brands/National Body: *Imitation of Life*." *Comparative American Identities*. Ed. Hortense J. Spillers. New York: Routledge, 1991. 110–40. Print.

Bikman, Minda. "The Ladies' Invasion of Man's Home Journal." *Village Voice* 26 Mar. 1970: 7–8, 24. Print.

Birkerts, Sven. *The Gutenberg Elegies: The Fate of Reading in an Electronic Age*. Boston: Faber and Faber, 1994. Print.

Black, Michele C., et al. "The National Intimate Partner and Sexual Violence Survey (NISVS): 2010 Summary Report." Atlanta: National Center for Injury Prevention and Control, Centers for Disease Control and Prevention, 2011. Web. 26 July 2013.

Bobo, Jacqueline. "*The Color Purple*: Black Women as Cultural Readers." *Female Spectators: Looking at Film and Television*. Ed. Deirdre Pribram. London: Verso, 1988. 90–109. Print.

Bordo, Susan. *Unbearable Weight: Feminism, Western Culture, and the Body*. 1993. Berkeley: U of California P, 2003. Print.

Bouson, J. Brooks. *Quiet as It's Kept: Shame, Trauma, and Race in the Novels of Toni Morrison*. Albany: State U of New York P, 2000. Print.

Brinkmeyer, Robert H., Jr. "Finding One's History: Bobbie Ann Mason and Contemporary Southern Literature." *Southern Literary Journal* 19.2 (Spring 1987): 22–33. Print.

Brogan, Kathleen. *Cultural Haunting: Ghosts and Ethnicity in Recent American Literature*. Charlottesville: U of Virginia P, 1998. Print.

Brown, Mary Ellen. *Soap Opera and Women's Talk*. London: Sage, 1994. Print.

Cairncross, Frances. *The Death of Distance: How the Communications Revolution Will Change Our Lives*. Boston: Harvard Business School P, 1997. Print.

Campbell, Richard, Christopher R. Martin, and Bettina Fabos. *Mass Media and the Cultural Landscape*. 8th ed. Boston: Bedford-St. Martins, 2011. Print.

Carby, Hazel. *Reconstructing Womanhood: The Emergence of the Afro-American Woman Novelist.* New York: Oxford UP, 1987. Print.
Cartwright, Lisa. *Screening the Body: Tracing Medicine's Visual Culture.* Minneapolis: U of Minnesota P, 1995. Print.
Caruth, Cathy. *Unclaimed Experience: Trauma, Narrative, and History.* Baltimore: Johns Hopkins UP, 1996. Print.
Cassell, Justine, and Henry Jenkins. *From Barbie to Mortal Kombat: Gender in Video Games.* Boston: MIT, 1998. Print.
Catlin, George. *Letters and Notes on the Manners, Customs, and Conditions of North American Indians.* 2 vols. New York: Dover, 1973. Print.
Chaney, Michael A., ed. *Graphic Subjects: Critical Essays on Autography and Graphic Novels.* Madison: U of Wisconsin P, 2011. Print.
Charles, Ron. "Book Review: *Shadow Tag* by Louise Erdrich." *Washington Post* 3 Feb. 2010: C.1. Print.
Children Now. "Fair Play? Violence, Gender, and Race in Video Games." *Children Now.* Children Now, 1 Dec. 2001. Web. 15 July 2013.
Chomsky, Noam. *Necessary Illusions: Thought Control in Democratic Societies.* Boston: South End, 1989. Print.
Chun, Wendy Hui Kyong. "On Software, or the Persistence of Visual Knowledge." Mirzoeff 65–85.
Church, Jok. "Christo and Jeanne-Claude F.A.Q." *Christo and Jeanne Claude.net.* Christo and Jeanne Claude, 6 Apr. 2005. Web. 13 Mar. 2013.
Chute, Hillary L. *Graphic Women: Life Narrative and Contemporary Comics.* New York: Columbia UP, 2010. Print.
———. "An Interview with Alison Bechdel." *Mfs: Modern Fiction Studies* 52.4 (Winter 2006): 1004–13. Print.
Chute, Hillary, and Marianne DeKoven. "Introduction: Graphic Narrative." *Mfs: Modern Fiction Studies* 52.4 (Winter 2006): 767–82. Print.
Cohen, Leah Hager. "Cruel Love." Rev. of *Shadow Tag*, by Louise Erdrich. *New York Times Book Review* 5 Feb. 2010: 1. Print.
Conarroe, Joel. "Winning Her Father's War." Rev. of *In Country*, by Bobbie Ann Mason. *New York Times Book Review* 15 Sept. 1985: 7. Print.
Conway, Alison. *Private Interests: Women, Portraiture, and the Visual Culture of the English Novel, 1709–1791.* Toronto: U of Toronto P, 2001. Print.
Coontz, Stephanie. "Why *Mad Men* Is TV's Most Feminist Show." *The Washington Post Opinions.* The Washington Post, 10 Oct. 2010. Web. 3 Aug. 2013.
Cooper, Pamela. "Sexual Surveillance and Medical Authority in Two Versions of *The Handmaid's Tale*." *Journal of Popular Culture* 28 (1995): 49–66. Print.

Corliss, Richard. Rev. of *In Country*, by Bobbie Ann Mason. *Time* 2 Oct. 1989: 90. Print.

Covert, Juanita J., and Travis L. Dixon. "A Changing View: Representation and Effects of the Portrayal of Women of Color in Mainstream Women's Magazines." *Communication Research* 35.2 (2008): 232–56. Print.

Coward, Rosalind. *Female Desire: Women's Sexuality Today*. London: Paladin, 1984. Print.

Crain, Caleb. "Twilight of the Books." *The New Yorker*. The New Yorker, 24 Dec. 2007. Web. 2 Aug. 2012.

Crawford, T. Hugh. "Imaging the Human Body: Quasi Objects, Quasi Texts, and the Theater of Proof." *PMLA* 111 (1996): 66–79. Print.

Cronin, Anne. *Advertising and Consumer Citizenship*. New York: Routledge, 2000. Print.

Cvetkovich, Ann. "Drawing the Archive in Alison Bechdel's *Fun Home*." *WSQ: Women's Studies Quarterly* 36.1–2 (Spring/Summer 2008): 111–28. Print.

Debord, Guy. *The Society of the Spectacle*. 1967. Trans. Ken Knabb. London: Rebel, 2006. Print.

Dee, Ruby. Rev. of *The Bluest Eye*, by Toni Morrison. *Freedomways* 11.3 (1971): 319. Print.

Denisoff, Dennis. *Sexual Visuality from Literature to Film, 1850–1950*. Basingstoke, England: Palgrave Macmillan, 2004. Print.

Derrida, Jacques. *Spurs: Nietzsche's Styles/Eperons: Les Styles de Nietzsche*. Trans. Barbara Harlow. Chicago: U of Chicago P, 1981. Print.

Dickerson, Vanessa D. "The Naked Father in Toni Morrison's *The Bluest Eye*." *Refiguring the Father: New Feminist Readings of Patriarchy*. Ed. Patricia Yaeger and Beth Kowaleski-Wallace. Carbondale: Southern Illinois UP, 1989. 108–27. Print.

Diehl, Joanne Feit. "Toward a Theory of Ekphrasis: The Female Tradition." Hedley, Halpern, and Spiegelman 43–54.

Dietz, Tracy L. "An Examination of Violence and Gender Role Portrayals in Video Games: Implications for Gender Socialization and Aggressive Behavior." *Sex Roles* 38 (1998): 425–42. Print.

Dijck, José van. *The Transparent Body: A Cultural Analysis of Medical Imaging*. Seattle: U of Washington P, 2005. Print.

Divakaruni, Chitra Banerjee. "The Ultrasound." *Arranged Marriage*. New York: Random, 1995. 203–30. Print.

Doane, Mary Ann. "Film and the Masquerade: Theorising the Female Spectator." *Femmes Fatales: Feminism, Film Theory, Psychoanalysis*. London: Routledge, 1991: 17–33. Print.

doCarmo, Stephen N. "Bombs from Coke Cans: Appropriating Mass Culture in Bobbie Ann Mason's *In Country*." *Journal of Popular Culture* 36.3 (Winter 2003): 589–99. Print.

Doorn, Niels van, Sally Wyatt, and Liesbet Van Zoonen. "A Body of Text: Revisiting Textual Performances of Gender and Sexuality on the Internet." Kearney 423–36.

Doty, Alexander. *Making Things Perfectly Queer: Interpreting Mass Culture*. Minneapolis: U of Minnesota P, 1993. Print.

Douglas, Christopher. "What *The Bluest Eye* Knows about Them: Culture, Race, Identity." *American Literature* 78.1 (Mar. 2006): 141–68. Print.

Doyle, Sady. "Mad Men, and the New Crop of Retro Sexist TV Shows." *Global Comment*. Slate, 14 Sept. 2011. Web. 5 Aug. 2013.

Draper, J. "'It's the First Scientific Evidence': Men's Experience of Pregnancy Confirmation." *Journal of Advanced Nursing* 39.6 (Sept. 2002): 563–70. Print.

———. "'It Was a Real Good Show': The Ultrasound Scan, Fathers and the Power of Visual Knowledge." *Sociology of Health and Illness* 24 (Nov. 2002): 771–95. Print.

Dubey, Madhu. *Black Women Novelists and the Nationalist Aesthetic*. Bloomington: Indiana UP, 1994. Print.

Duke, Lisa. "Black in a Blonde World: Race and Girls Interpretations of the Feminine Ideal in Teen Magazines." *Journalism and Mass Communication Quarterly* 77.2 (2000): 367–92. Print.

Durham, Meenakshi Gigi. "Myths of Race and Beauty in Teen Magazines: A Semiotic Analysis." *Women in Mass Communication*. 3rd ed. Ed. Pamela J. Creedona and Judith Cramer. Thousand Oaks, CA: Sage, 2007. 233–45. Print.

Duvall, John N. *Identifying Fictions of Toni Morrison: Modernist Authority and Postmodern Blackness*. Gordonsville, VA: Palgrave Macmillan, 2000. Print.

Dwyer, June. "New Roles, New History and New Patriotism: Bobbie Ann Mason's *In Country*." *Modern Language Studies* 22.2 (Spring 1992): 72–78. Print.

Dyer, Richard. *The Culture of Queers*. London: Routledge, 2002. Print.

Elkins, James. "The End of the Theory of the Gaze." *The Visual: How It Is Studied*. Academia.edu, Oct. 2002. Web. 20 Aug. 2013.

———. *The Object Stares Back*. New York: Simon, 1996. Print.

Ellison, Ralph. *Invisible Man*. New York: Vintage, 1952. Print.

Erdrich, Louise. *Conversations with Louise Erdrich and Michael Dorris*. Ed. Allan Chavkin and Nancy Feyl Chavkin. Jackson: UP of Mississippi, 1994. Print.

———. "Dartmouth Commencement Address." Dartmouth.edu, 9 June 2009. Web. 15 Jan. 2013.

———. "Dear John Wayne." *Jacklight: Poems*. London: Little/Abacus, 1984. Print.

———. *Love Medicine: New and Revised*. 1984. New York: Harper, 1993. Print.

———. *The Plague of Doves*. New York: Harper, 2008. Print.

———. *The Round House*. New York: Harper, 2012. Print.

———. *Shadow Tag*. New York: Harper, 2010. Print.

———. *Tracks: A Novel*. New York: Harper, 1988. Print.

———. "Whatever Is Really Yours: An Interview with Louise Erdrich." Interview by Joseph Bruchac. *Survival This Way: Interviews with American Indian Poets*. Ed. Joseph Bruchac. Tucson: U of Arizona P, 1987. 73–86. Print.

———. "Where I Ought to Be: A Writer's Sense of Place." *Louise Erdrich's Love Medicine: A Casebook*. Ed. Hertha D. Wong. New York: Oxford UP, 2000, 43–50. Print.

Erdrich, Louise, and Michael Dorris. "An Interview with Louise Erdrich and Michael Dorris." Interview by Kate Bonetti. *Missouri Review* 11.2 (1988): 79–99. Print.

Evans, Caroline, and Lorraine Gamman. "The Gaze Revisited, or Reviewing Queer Viewing." *A Queer Romance*. Ed. Paul Burston and Colin Richardson. London: Routledge, 1995. 13–56. Print.

Farrell, Kirby. *Post-Traumatic Culture: Injury and Interpretation in the Nineties*. Baltimore: Johns Hopkins UP, 1998. Print.

"Fat." *Frontline*. PBS. 3 Nov. 1998. Television.

Felski, Rita. *Doing Time: Feminist Theory and Postmodern Culture*. New York: New York UP, 2000. Print.

Fick, Thomas H. "Toni Morrison's 'Allegory of the Cave': Movies, Consumption, and Platonic Realism in *The Bluest Eye*." *Journal of the Midwest Modern Language Association* 22.1 (Spring 1989): 10–22. Print.

Fitzpatrick, Kathleen. *The Anxiety of Obsolescence: The American Novel in the Age of Television*. Nashville: Vanderbilt UP, 2006. Print.

Flanagan, Mary. "Hyperbodies, Hyperknowledge: Women in Games, Women in Cyberpunk, and Strategies of Resistance." *Reload: Rethinking Women and Cyberculture*. Ed. Mary Flanagan and Austin Booth. Cambridge, MA: MIT P, 2002. 425–54. Print.

Florén, Celia. "A Reading of Margaret Atwood's Dystopia, *The Handmaid's Tale*." *Gender, Ideology: Essays on Theory, Fiction, and Film*. Ed. Chantal Cornut-Gentille D'Arcy and Jose Angel Garcia Landa. Amsterdam: Rodopi, 1996. 253–63. Print.

Fong, Timothy. *The Contemporary Asian American Experience: Beyond the Model Minority*. Upper Saddle River, NJ: Pearson, 2002. Print.

Foucault, Michel. *Discipline and Punish: The Birth of the Prison*. Trans. Alan Sheridan. New York: Vintage, 1995. Print.

Frase, Brigitte. "*Shadow Tag* by Louise Erdrich." *Los Angeles Times* 30 Jan. 2010: 26. Print.

Freud, Sigmund. *Beyond the Pleasure Principle*. Trans. C. J. M. Hubback. London: Hogarth, 1948. Print.

Frever, Trinna S. "'Oh! You Beautiful Doll!': Icon, Image, and Culture in Works by Alvarez, Cisneros, and Morrison." *Tulsa Studies in Women's Literature* 28.1 (Spring 2009): 121–39. Print.

Friedan, Betty. *The Feminine Mystique*. 1963. London: Penguin, 1965. Print.

Friedberg, Anne. "Cinema and the Postmodern Condition." Williams 59–86.

Fuderer, Laura Sue. *The Female Bildungsroman in English: An Annotated Bibliography of Criticism*. New York: MLA, 1990. Print.

Fuller, Hoyt. "Towards a Black Aesthetic." Gates and McKay 1813.

Gailey, Christine Ward. "Mediated Messages: Gender, Class, and Cosmos in Home Videogames." *Journal of Popular Culture* 27 (1993): 81–97. Print.

Gaines, Jane. "White Privilege and Looking Relations: Race and Gender in Feminist Film Theory." *Cultural Critique* 4 (Autumn 1986): 59–79. Print.

Gallagher, Jean. *The World Wars through the Female Gaze*. Carbondale: Southern Illinois UP, 1998. Print.

Galloway, Alexander R. "Language Wants to Be Overlooked: On Software and Ideology." *Journal of Visual Culture* 5 (2006): 315–31. Print.

Gardiner, Judith Kegan. "Queering Genre: Alison Bechdel's *Fun Home: A Family Tragicomic* and *The Essential Dykes to Watch Out For*." *Contemporary Women's Writing* 5.3 (2011): 188–207. Print.

Gasche, Rodolphe. *The Tain of the Mirror: Derrida and the Philosophy of Reflection*. Cambridge, MA: Harvard UP, 1986. Print.

Gates, Henry Louis, Jr., and Nellie McKay, eds. *Norton Anthology of African American Literature*. New York: Norton, 1997. Print.

Gerster, Carole J. "From Film Margin to Novel Center: Toni Morrison's *The Bluest Eye*." *West Virginia University Philological Papers* 38 (1992): 191–200. Print.

Gibson, Graeme. "Travels of a Family Man." *Chatelaine* Mar. 1979: 36. Print.

Gill, Rosalind. *Gender and the Media*. Cambridge: Polity, 2007. Print.

Gilmore, Leigh. "Witnessing *Persepolis*: Comics, Trauma, and Childhood Testimony." Chaney 157–63.

Giroux, Henry. *Channel Surfing: Racism, the Media, and the Destruction of Today's Youth*. New York: St. Martin's, 1997. Print.

Gloeckner, Phoebe. *A Child's Life and Other Stories*. Berkeley: Frog, 1998. Print.

Goldman, Robert. *Reading Ads Socially*. New York: Routledge, 1992. Print.

Gozzi, Raymond, Jr. *The Power of Metaphor in the Age of Electronic Media*. Cresskill, NJ: Hampton, 1999. Print.

Gray, Jonathan. "Is *Mad Men* Feminist? Ask the Paratexts." *The ExtraTextuals*. The ExtraTextuals, 22 July 2013. Web. 10 July 2013.

Grewal, Gurleen. "'Laundering the Head of Whitewash': Mimicry and Resistance in *The Bluest Eye*." McKay and Earle 118–28.

Grewe-Volpp, Christa. "'Memory Attaches Itself to Sites': Bobbie Ann Mason's *In Country* and the Significance of the Vietnam Veteran's Memorial." *Amerikastudien/American Studies* 49.2 (2004): 173–89. Print.

Grundberg, Andy. "Ask It No Questions: The Camera Can Lie." *New York Times* 12 Aug. 1990 Sunday ed. sec. 2: 1, 2, 29. Print.

Guerrero, Edward. "Tracking 'the Look' in the Novels of Toni Morrison." *Black American Literature Forum* 24.4 (Winter 1990): 761–73. Print.

Guihau, Ma. "Checking Imbalance in Gender Ratio." *China Daily on the Web*, 26 May 2004. Web. 1 June 2007.

Gunn, Drewey Wayne. "Initiation, Individuation, *In Country*." *Midwest Quarterly* 38.1 (Autumn 1996): 59–71. Print.

Guttmacher Institute. "Facts on Induced Abortion in the United States." *Brief: Fact Sheet*. Guttmacher Institute, Aug. 2011. Web. 10 Mar. 2013.

———. "Requirements for Ultrasound." *State Policies in Brief*. Guttmacher Institute, 1 Mar. 2013. Web. 10 Mar. 2013.

Halberstam, Judith. *In a Queer Time and Place: Transgender Bodies, Subcultural Lives*. New York: New York UP, 2005. Print.

Hanson, Ellis. "Introduction: Out Takes." *Out Takes: Essays on Queer Theory and Film*. Ed. Ellis Hanson. Durham, NC: Duke UP, 1999. 1–22. Print.

Haraway, Donna. *Simians, Cyborgs, and Women: The Reinvention of Nature*. New York: Routledge, 1991. Print.

Hastings, Phyllis. "*The Bluest Eye* and the American Dream." *Literature and Black Aesthetics*. Ed. Dele Orisawayi and Ernest Emenyonu. Ibadan, Nigeria: Heinemann, 1990. Print.

Hausdoerffer, John. "The 'Nature' of Environmental Disaster: George Catlin's Lament as Eco-genocide." *Tamkang Review* 37.1 (Sept. 2009): 141–57. Print.

Hayles, N. Katherine. "Hyper and Deep Attention: The Generational Divide in Cognitive Modes." *Profession* 2007 (2007): 187–99. Print.

Hébert, Kimberly B. "Acting the Nigger: Topsy, Shirley Temple, and Toni Morrison's Pecola." *Approaches to Teaching Stowe's* Uncle Tom's Cabin.

Ed. Elizabeth Ammons and Susan Belasco. New York: MLA, 2000. 184–98. Print.

Hedley, Jane. "Introduction: The Subject of Ekphrasis." Hedley, Halpern, and Spiegelman 15–42.

Hedley, Jane, Nick Halpern, and Willard Spiegelman, eds. *In the Frame: Women's Ekphrastic Poetry from Marianne Moore to Susan Wheeler.* Newark: U of Delaware P, 2009. Print.

Heffernan, James A. W. "Ekphrasis and Representation." *New Literary History* 22 (1991): 297–316. Print.

———. *Museum of Words.* Chicago: U of Chicago P, 1993. Print.

Henninger, Katherine. *Ordering the Facade: Photography and Contemporary Southern Women's Writing.* Chapel Hill: U of North Carolina P, 2007. Print.

Hinnov, Emily M. *Encountering Choran Community: Literary Modernism, Visual Culture, and Political Aesthetics in the Interwar Years.* Selinsgrove, PA: Susquehanna UP, 2009. Print.

Hinrichsen, Lisa. "'I Can't Believe It Was Really Real': Violence, Vietnam, and Bringing War Home in Bobbie Ann Mason's *In Country*." *Southern Literary Journal* 42.2 (Spring 2008): 232–48. Print.

Hirsch, Marianne. *Family Frames: Photography, Narrative, and Postmemory.* 1997. Cambridge, MA: Harvard UP, 2002. Print.

Hockey, Jenny, and Janet Draper. "Beyond the Womb and the Tomb: (Dis) Embodiment and the Life Course." *Body and Society* 11.2 (2005): 41–57. Print.

Holden, Todd. "The Color of Difference: Critiquing Cultural Convergence via Television Advertising." *Interdisciplinary Information Sciences* 51.1 (1999): 15–36. Print.

Holstein, Suzy Clarkson. "Into the Swamp at Oblique Angles: Mason's *In Country*." *Mississippi Quarterly* 54.3 (Summer 2001): 327–36. Print.

Hon, Adrian. "The Long Decline of Reading." *Mssv.* Mssv.net, 28 Dec. 2008. Web. 25 July 2012.

hooks, bell. *Black Looks: Race and Representation.* Boston: South End, 1992. Print.

Humm, Maggie. *Modernist Women and Visual Cultures: Virginia Woolf, Vanessa Bell, Photography and Cinema.* New Brunswick, NJ: Rutgers UP, 2003. Print.

"Illegal Gender Selection." *ABC News Video.* ABCnews.com, 9 Nov. 2011. Web. 1 Mar. 2013.

Irigaray, Luce. *Speculum of the Other Woman.* Trans. Gillian C. Gill. Ithaca, NY: Cornell UP, 1985. Print.

Jacobs, Karen. *The Eye's Mind: Literary Modernism and Visual Culture.* Ithaca, NY: Cornell UP, 2001. Print.

James, Caryn. Rev. of *In Country*, by Bobbie Ann Mason. *New York Times* 15 Sept. 1989: C.6. Print.
Jameson, Fredric. "Postmodernism and Consumer Society." *Postmodern Culture*. Ed. Hal Foster. London: Pluto, 1985. 111–25. Print.
Jason, Philip K., ed. *Fourteen Landing Zones: Approaches to Vietnam War Literature*. Iowa City: U of Iowa P, 1991. Print.
Jay, Martin. *Downcast Eyes: The Denigration of Vision in Twentieth-Century French Thought*. Berkeley: U of California P, 1993. Print.
———. "Scopic Regimes of Modernity." *Vision and Visuality*. Ed. Hal Foster. Seattle: Bay, 1988. 2–25. Print.
———. "Vision in Context: Reflections and Refractions." *Vision in Context: Historical and Contemporary Perspectives*. Ed. Teresa Brennan and Martin Jay. New York: Routledge, 1996. 3–12. Print.
Jen, Gish. "Birthmates." *Ploughshares*. 1995. *The Best American Short Stories 1995*. Ed. John Updike and Katrina Kenison. Boston: Houghton, 1995. 110–25. Print.
———. "Gish Jen Passes Muster—Again." *Powells.com*, 17 June 1999. Web. 9 Dec. 2004.
Joannou, Maroula. "'Finding New Words and Creating New Methods': *Three Guineas* and *The Handmaid's Tale*." *Virginia Woolf and Fascism: Resisting the Dictators' Seduction*. Ed. Merry Pawlowski. New York: Palgrave Macmillan, 2001. 139–55. Print.
Johnson, Steven. "Dawn of the Digital Natives." *The Guardian*. Guardian News and Media, 6 Feb. 2008. Web. 15 July 2012.
Johnston, Basil. *Ojibwe Heritage*. New York: Columbia UP, 1976. Print.
Jones, Amelia. "Introduction." *The Feminism and Visual Culture Reader*. Ed. Amelia Jones. New York: Routledge, 2003. 1–9. Print.
Jones, Bessie, and Audrey Vinson. *The World of Toni Morrison: Explorations in Literary Criticism*. Dubuque: Kendell/Hunt, 1985. Print.
Kaplan, E. Ann. *Looking for the Other: Feminism, Film, and the Imperial Gaze*. New York: Routledge, 1997. Print.
———. *Rocking around the Clock: Music Television, Postmodernism, and Consumer Culture*. New York: Routledge, 1987. Print.
Karenga, Maulana. "Black Art: Mute Matter Given Force and Function." Gates and McKay 1972–77.
Kauffman, Linda S. *Special Delivery: Epistolary Modes in Modern Fiction*. Chicago: U of Chicago P, 1996. Print.
Kearney, Mary Celeste, ed. *The Gender and Media Reader*. New York: Routledge, 2012. Print.
Kearns, Megan. "*Mad Men* Week: Is *Mad Men* the Most Feminist Show on TV?" *Bitch Flicks*. Bitch Flicks, 30 Aug. 2011. Web. 3 Aug. 2013.

Kennedy, Helen W. "Lara Croft: Feminist Icon or Cyberbimbo?" *Game Studies: International Journal of Computer Game Research* 2 (2002): 1–12. Print.

Kevles, Bettyann. *Naked to the Bone: Medical Imaging in the Twentieth Century*. Reading, MA: Addison-Wesley, 1998. Print.

Kim, Yoonj. "*Mad Men* Actresses Reluctant to Call Peggy and Joan Feminists." *BitchMedia*. Bitch Media, 14 Apr. 2013. Web. 24 July 2013.

Kinney, Katherine. "'Humping the Bonnies': Sex, Combat, and the Female in Bobbie Ann Mason's *In Country*." Jason 38–48.

Kolmerten, Carol A., Stephen M. Ross, and Judith Bryant Wittenberg, eds. *Unflinching Gaze: Morrison and Faulkner Re-Envisioned*. Jackson: UP of Mississippi, 1997. Print.

Kominsky-Crumb, Aline. *Need More Love: A Graphic Memoir*. London: MQP, 2007. Print.

Korpez, Esra. "The Windigo Myth in *The Antelope Wife* and *Last Standing Woman*: The Evil Within and Without." *Comparative Critical Studies* 2.3 (Oct. 2005): 349–63. Print.

Kroeber, Karl. "Technology and the Tribal Narrative." Vizenor, *Narrative Chance* 17–38.

Krumholz, Linda J. "Reading in the Dark: Knowledge and Vision in *Song of Solomon*." McKay and Earle 106–12.

Kuhn, Annette. *Family Secrets*. London: Verso, 1995. Print.

———. "Women's Genres: Melodrama, Soap Opera, and Theory." *Screen* 25.1 (1984): 18–28. Print.

LaCapra, Dominick. *Writing History, Writing Trauma*. Baltimore: Johns Hopkins UP, 2001. Print.

Laflen, Angela. "'From a Distance It Looks Like Peace': Reading beneath the Fascist Style of Gilead in Margaret Atwood's *The Handmaid's Tale*." *Studies in Canadian Literature* 32.1 (2007): 82–105. Print.

Larrick, Nancy. "The All-White World of Children's Books." *Saturday Review* 11 Sept. 1965: 63–65, 84–85. Print.

Last, Jonathan V. "The War against Girls." *Wall Street Journal*. Dow Jones, 24 June 2011. Web. 18 Mar. 2013.

Lauretis, Teresa de. *Technologies of Gender*. Bloomington: Indiana UP, 1987. Print.

Leach, Laurie. "Conflict over Privacy in Indo-American Short Fiction." *Ethnicity and the American Short Story*. Ed. Julia Brown. New York: Garland, 1997. 197–211. Print.

Leary, William. "Study Finds Waste in Ultrasound Use." *New York Times* 16 Sept. 1993: A17. Print.

Ledbetter, James. "Merge Overkill: When Big Media Gets Too Big, What Happens to Debate." *Village Voice*, 26 Jan. 1996: 30–35. Print.

Ledbetter, Mark. "Through the Eyes of a Child: Looking for Victims in Toni Morrison's *The Bluest Eye*." *Literature and Theology at Century's End*. Ed. Gregory Salyer and Robert Detweiler. Atlanta: Scholars, 1995. 177–88. Print.

Lessing, Gotthold. *Laocoon: An Essay upon the Limits of Painting and Poetry*. 1766. Trans. Ellen Frothingham. New York: Noonday, 1961. Print.

Lewis, Lisa A. *Gender Politics and MTV*. Philadelphia: Temple UP, 1990. Print.

Lott, Jeremy. "Should English Departments Throw in the Towel?" *The Washington Times*. The Washington Times, 20 Mar. 2012. Web. 30 July 2012.

Lowney, John. "'Homesick for Those Memories': The Gendering of Historical Memory in Women's Narratives of the Vietnam War." *Burning Down the House: Recycling Domesticity*. Ed. Rosemary Marangoly George. Boulder, CO: Westview, 1998. 257–78. Print.

Lucky, Crystal J. "Ancestral Wisdom in Toni Morrison's *The Bluest Eye*." *Proteus: A Journal of Ideas* 21.2 (Oct. 2004): 21–26. Print.

Lupack, Barbara Tepa. "History as Her-Story: Adapting Bobbie Ann Mason's *In Country* to Film." *Vision/Re-Vision: Adapting Contemporary American Fiction by Women to Film*. Ed. Barbara Tepa Lupack. Bowling Green: Bowling Green State U Popular P, 1996. 159–92. Print.

Madsen, Deborah L., ed. *Louise Erdrich*. London: Continuum, 2011. Print.

Mair, George. *Inside HBO: The Billion Dollar War between HBO, Hollywood, and the Home Video Revolution*. New York: Dodd, Mead, 1988. Print.

Mallik, Rupsa. "A Less Valued Life: Population Policy and Sex Selection in India." Committee on Women, Population, and the Environment. Adelphi University, 1 Oct. 2002. Web. 13 Mar. 2013.

Mao, Weiqiang, and Mingquan Zhang. "*Beloved* as an Oppositional Gaze." *English Language Teaching* 2.3 (Sept. 2009): 26–34. Print.

Martis, Raynel, and Jeroen Jansz. "The Representation of Gender and Ethnicity in Digital Interactive Games." International Communication Association, New Orleans Sheraton, New Orleans, LA. 27 May 2004. Address.

Mason, Bobbie Ann. "Bobbie Ann Mason: 'I Had to Confront the Subject.'" Interview by Eric James Schroeder. *Vietnam, We've All Been There: Interviews with American Writers*. Westport, CT: Praeger, 1992. 164–79. Print.

———. "Bobbie Ann Mason's Border States." Interview by Mervyn Rothstein. *New York Times Book Review* 15 May 1988. Web. 13 Mar. 2013.

———. "Bobbie Ann Mason's *In Country* Evokes the Soul of Kentucky and the Sadness of Vietnam." Interview by Andrea Chambers. *People Weekly*. *Time* 28 Oct. 1985: 127–29. Print.

———. *In Country*. New York: Harper, 1985. Print.

———. "*PW* Interviews Bobbie Ann Mason." By Wendy Smith. *Publisher's Weekly* 30 Aug. 1985: 424–25. Print.
Matlack, Tom. "Is *Mad Men* a Feminist Show?" *The Huffington Post.com.* The Huffington Post, 13 July 2009. Web. 20 June 2013.
Mayne, Judith. "Feminist Film Theory and Criticism." *Signs* 11.1 (Autumn 1985): 81–100. Print.
———. "Paradoxes of Spectatorship." *The Film Cultures Reader.* Ed. Graeme Turner. New York: Routledge, 2002. 28–45. Print.
McCloud, Scott. *Understanding Comics: The Invisible Art.* New York: HarperPerennial, 1993. Print.
McDermott, Ryan P. "Silence, Visuality, and the Staying Image: The 'Unspeakable Scene' of Toni Morrison's *Beloved*." *Angelaki* 8.1 (Apr. 2003): 75–89. Print.
McDermott, Sinead. "The Ethics of Postmemory in Bobbie Ann Mason's *In Country*." *Journal of the Midwest Modern Language Association* 39.2 (Fall 2006): 5–21. Print.
McGrath, Charles. "Not Funnies." *New York Times Magazine* 11 July 2004: 24–33, 46, 55–56. Print.
McKay, Nellie, and Kathryn Earle, eds. *Approaches to Teaching the Novels of Toni Morrison.* New York: MLA, 1997. Print.
McLuhan, Marshall. *Understanding Media: The Extensions of Man.* New York: McGraw, 1964. Print.
McRobbie, Angela. "Post Feminism and Popular Culture." *Feminist Media Studies* 4.3 (2004): 255–64. Print.
Mehaffy, Marilyn Maness. "Fetal Attractions: The Limit of Cyborg Theory." *Women's Studies* 29 (2000): 177–94. Print.
Mermann-Jozwiak, Elisabeth. "'His Grandfather Ate His Own Wife': Louise Erdrich's *Love Medicine* as a Contemporary Windigo Narrative." *North Dakota Quarterly* 64.4 (1997): 44–54. Print.
Michaels, Meredith W. "Fetal Galaxies: Some Questions about What We See." *Fetal Subjects, Feminist Positions.* Ed. Lynn M. Morgan and Meredith W. Michaels. Philadelphia: U of Pennsylvania P, 1999. 113–32. Print.
Mirzoeff, Nicholas. "Introduction: For Critical Visuality Studies." Mirzoeff xxix–xxxviii.
———, ed. *The Visual Culture Reader.* 3rd ed. New York: Routledge, 2013. Print.
Mitchell, Lisa M. *Baby's First Picture: Ultrasound and the Politics of Fetal Subjects.* Toronto: U of Toronto P, 2001. Print.
Mitchell, W. J. T. *Picture Theory: Essays on Verbal and Visual Representation.* Chicago: U of Chicago P, 1994. Print.
———. "There Are No Visual Media." Mirzoeff 7–14.

Mitchell, William. *The Reconfigured Eye: Visual Truth in the Post-Photographic Era*. Cambridge, MA: MIT P, 1992. Print.
Modleski, Tania. *Loving with a Vengeance: Mass Produced Fantasies for Women*. New York: Methuen, 1984. Print.
Moi, Toril. *Sexual/Textual Politics: Feminist Literary Theory*. New York: Methuen, 1985. Print.
Morrison, Toni. *The Bluest Eye*. 1970. New York: Penguin, 2000. Print.
———. "Complexity: Toni Morrison's Women—An Interview Essay." Bell, Parker, and Guy-Sheftall 251–57.
———. "The Language Must Not Sweat: A Conversation with Toni Morrison." *Conversations with Toni Morrison*. Ed. Danielle Taylor-Guthrie. Jackson: UP of Mississippi, 1994. 119–28. Print.
———. *Playing in the Dark: Whiteness and the Literary Imagination*. 1992. New York: Vintage/Random, 1993. Print.
———. "The Site of Memory." *Inventing the Truth: The Art and Craft of Memoir*. Ed. William Zinsser. Boston: Houghton, 1987. 103–24. Print.
———. "Unspeakable Things Unspoken: The Afro-American Presence in American Literature." *Michigan Quarterly Review* 28.1 (Winter 1989): 1–34. Print.
Morrissey, Tracie Egan. "'Game of Thrones' George RR Martin Is 'Feminist at Heart.'" *Jezebel*. Gawker Media, 1 Apr. 2013. Web. 3 Aug. 2013.
Moses, Cat. "The Blues Aesthetic in Toni Morrison's *The Bluest Eye*." *African American Review* 33 (Winter 1999): 623–38. Print.
Mulhall, Elizabeth. "The Fans Doth Protest Too Much, Methinks: Is *Game of Thrones* Truly Feminist?" *Literati Co*. Literati Co., 22 Apr. 2013. Web. 3 Aug. 2013.
Mulvey, Laura. "Visual Pleasure and Narrative Cinema." *Screen* 16.3 (1975): 6–18. Print.
National Association of Anorexia Nervosa and Associated Disorders. "Eating Disorders Statistics." National Association of Anorexia Nervosa and Associated Disorders, Inc. n.d. Web. 26 July 2013.
National Endowment for the Arts. *Reading at Risk: A Survey of Literary Reading in America*. Research Division Report no. 47. National Endowment for the Arts, June 2004. Web. 1 Feb. 2013.
———. *To Read or Not to Read: A Question of National Consequence*. Research Division Report no. 47. National Endowment for the Arts, Nov. 2007. Web. 15 Feb. 2013.
Neal, Larry. "The Black Arts Movement." *The Drama Review: TDR* 12.4 (Summer 1968): 28–39. Print.
New York City. "Mayor Michael R. Bloomberg Announces $254 Million Economic Impact of the Gates on New York City." Department of Parks and Recreation Press Release, 3 Mar. 2005. Web. 5 Mar. 2013.

Nietzsche, Friedrich. *Thus Spoke Zarathustra: A Book for All and None.* Trans. Walter Kaufmann. New York: Penguin, 1978. Print.

Nischik, Reingard M. *Engendering Genre: The Works of Margaret Atwood.* Ottawa: U of Ottawa P, 2009. Print.

Noori, Margaret. "Review of *Shadow Tag.*" *Studies in American Indian Literatures* 22.2 (Summer 2010): 89–96. Print.

Nunberg, Geoffrey, ed. *The Future of the Book.* Berkeley: U of California P, 1996. Print.

Oakley, Ann. *The Captured Womb: A History of the Medical Care of Pregnant Women.* Oxford: Basil Blackwell, 1984. Print.

O'Brien, Timothy. "Oppositions in *In Country.*" *Critique* 41.2 (2000): 175–90. Print.

Okihiro, Gary. "Is Yellow Black or White?" *Asian Americans: Experience and Perspectives.* Ed. Timothy Fong and Larry Shinagawa. Upper Saddle River, NJ: Prentice-Hall, 2000. 63–78. Print.

O'Reilly, Andrea. "Maternal Conceptions in Toni Morrison's *The Bluest Eye* and *Tar Baby*: 'A Woman Has to Be a Daughter before She Can Be Any Kind of Woman.'" *This Giving Birth: Pregnancy and Childbirth in American Women's Writing.* Ed. Julie Tharp and Susan MacCollum-Whitcomb. Bowling Green: Bowling Green State U Popular P, 2000. 83–102. Print.

Ouellette, Marc. "'Two Guns, a Girl and a Playstation': Gender in the Tomb Raider Series." *TEXT Technology* 13.1 (2004): 157–84. Print.

———. "'When a Killer Body Isn't Enough': Cross-Gender Identification in Action-Adventure Video Games." *Reconstruction* 6.1 (Winter 2006): n. pag. Web. 10 Aug. 2013.

Paris Is Burning. Dir. Jennie Livingston. Miramax, 1990. Film.

Parmar, Pratibha. "That Moment of Emergence." *How Do I Look? Queer Film and Video.* Ed. Bad Object-Choices. Seattle: Bay, 1991. 11–31. Print.

Penley, Constance. "Brownian Motion: Women, Tactics, and Technology." *Technoculture.* Ed. Constance Penley and Andrew Ross. Minneapolis: U of Minnesota P, 1991. 135–62. Print.

Percy, Walker. "Loss of the Creature." *The Message in the Bottle: How Queer Man Is, How Queer Language Is, and What Has One to Do with the Other.* 1975. New York: Picador, 2000. Print.

Petchesky, Rosalind Pollack. "Fetal Images: The Power of Visual Culture in the Politics of Reproduction." *Feminist Studies* 13.2 (1987): 263–92. Print.

PEW Research Center. *The Rise of E-Reading.* Washington, DC: Pew Research Center's Internet and American Life Project, 2012. Print.

Phelan, Peggy. *Unmarked: The Politics of Performance.* London: Routledge, 1993. Print.

Plafker, Ted. "Sex Selection in China Sees 117 Boys for Every 100 Girls." *BMJ* 324 (25 May 2002): 1233. Print.

Plous, S., and Dominique Neptune. "Racial and Gender Biases in Magazine Advertising: A Content-Analytic Study." *Psychology of Women Quarterly* 21.4 (1997): 627–44. Print.

Poison. Dir. Todd Haynes. Zeitgeist, 1991. Film.

Pollock, Griselda. "What's Wrong with Images of Women?" *Representation and Photography: A Screen Education Reader.* 1977. Ed. Manuel Alvarado, Edward Buscombe, and Richard Collins. New York: Palgrave Macmillan, 2001. 76–86. Print.

"Preventing Gender-Based Sex Selection." Interagency Statement by OHCHR, UNFPA, UNICEF, UN Women, and WHO. United Nations Population Fund, 2011. Web. 1 Mar. 2013.

Putnam, Conan. "*Shadow Tag* by Louise Erdrich." *Chicago Tribune* 25 Mar. 2010: 12. Print.

Radner, Hilary. *Shopping Around: Feminine Culture and the Pursuit of Pleasure.* New York: Routledge, 1995. Print.

Radway, Janice. *Reading the Romance.* 1984. London: Verso, 1987. Print.

Rancière, Jacques. "Ten Theses on Politics." Trans. Rachel Bowlby. *Theory and Event* 5.3 (2001): n. pag. Web. 20 Aug. 2013.

Rand, Lizabeth A. "Female Discourse in *The Bluest Eye*—the Quest for Voice and Vision." *MAWA Review* 12.2 (Dec. 1997): 69–79. Print.

Rine, Abigail. "The Postfeminist Mystique: Or, What Can We Learn from Betty Draper?" *Pop Matters.* PopMatters Media, 15 Apr. 2013. Web. 27 June 2013.

Rodriguez, Richard. *Days of Obligation: An Argument with My Mexican Father.* New York: Penguin, 1993. Print.

Rogin, Michael. "'Make My Day!': Spectacle as Amnesia in Imperial Politics." *Cultures of United States Imperialism.* Ed. Amy Kaplan and Donald E. Pease. Durham, NC: Duke UP, 1993. 499–534. Print.

———. *Ronald Reagan, the Movie and Other Episodes in Political Demonology.* Berkeley: U of California P, 1987. Print.

Rohy, Valerie. "In the Queer Archive: *Fun Home.*" *GLQ: A Journal of Lesbian and Gay Studies* 16.3 (2010): 341–61. Print.

Ross, Karen. *Gendered Media: Women, Men, and Identity Politics.* Lanham, MD: Rowman and Littlefield, 2010. Print.

Ryan, Barbara T. "Decentered Authority in Bobbie Ann Mason's *In Country.*" *Critique* 31.3 (Spring 1990): 199–212. Print.

Sacks, Oliver. *An Anthropologist on Mars.* New York: Vintage, 1995. Print.

Said, Edward. "Homage to Joe Sacco." *Palestine.* Seattle: Fantagraphics, 2005. Print.

Salter, Jessica. "*Game of Thrones*'s George RR Martin: 'I'm a Feminist at Heart.'" *The Telegraph*. Telegraph Media Group, 1 Apr. 2013. Web. 26 July 2013.

Salvatore, Anne. "Toni Morrison's New Bildungsromane: Paired Characters and Antithetical Form in *The Bluest Eye*, *Sula*, and *Beloved*." *Journal of Narrative Theory* 32.2 (Summer 2002): 154–78. Print.

Satrapi, Marjane. *Persepolis: The Story of a Childhood*. Trans. Mattias Ripa and Blake Ferris. New York: Pantheon, 2003. Print.

Sarvé-Gorham, Kristan. "Games of Chance: Gambling and Land Tenure in *Tracks*, *Love Medicine*, and *The Bingo Palace*." *Western American Literature* 34.3 (1999): 276–301. Print.

Schiller, Herbert. "The Global Information Highway: Project for an Ungovernable World." *Resisting the Virtual Life: The Culture and Politics of Information*. Ed. James Brook and Iain Boal. San Francisco: City Lights, 1995. 17–33. Print.

Schreiber, Evelyn Jaffe. "Reader, Text, and Subjectivity: Toni Morrison's *Beloved* as Lacan's Gaze qua Object." *Style* 30.3 (Fall 1996): 445–61. Print.

Sedgwick, Eve Kosofsky. *Epistemology of the Closet*. Berkeley: U of California P, 1990. Print.

Sheckels, Theodore. *The Political in Margaret Atwood's Fiction: The Writing on the Wall of the Tent*. Farnham, UK: Ashgate, 2012. Print.

Sherrard-Johnson, Charene. *Portraits of the New Negro Woman: Visual and Literary Culture in the Harlem Renaissance*. New Brunswick, NJ: Rutgers UP, 2007. Print.

Shohat, Ella. "'Lasers for Ladies': Endo Discourse and the Inscription of Science." Treichler, Cartwright, and Penley 240–72.

Silberman, Robert. "Opening the Text: *Love Medicine* and the Return of the Native American Woman." Vizenor, *Narrative Chance* 101–20.

Simpson, Ritashona. *Black Looks and Black Acts: The Language of Toni Morrison in* The Bluest Eye *and* Beloved. New York: Peter Lang, 2007. Print.

Skeggs, Beverley. *Formations of Class and Gender*. London: Sage, 1997. Print.

Softing, Inger-Anne. "Carnival and Black American Music as Counterculture in Toni Morrison's *The Bluest Eye*." *American Studies in Scandinavia* 27.2 (1995): 81–102. Print.

Solomon, Alisa. "The Politics of Breast Cancer." *Camera Obscura: A Journal of Feminism and Film Theory* 28 (1992): 156–77. Print.

Sontag, Susan. *On Photography*. New York: Farrar, Straus, and Giroux, 1977. Print.

Spengler, Birgit. *Vision, Gender, and Power in Nineteenth-Century American Women's Writing, 1860–1900*. Heidelberg, Germany: Universitätsverlag, 2008. Print.

Spiegelman, Art. *Maus: A Survivor's Tale*. 2 vols. New York: Pantheon-Random, 1986–91. Print.
Spohrer, Erika. "Colonizing Consciousness: 'Race,' Pictorial Epistemology, and Toni Morrison's *Jazz*." *Amerikastudien/American Studies* 54.1 (2009): 79–98. Print.
Stabile, Carol. "Shooting the Mother: Fetal Photography and the Politics of Disappearance." Treichler, Cartwright, and Penley 171–97.
Stasia, Cristina Lucia. "'Wham! Bam! Thank You Ma'am!': The New Public/Private Female Action Hero." *Third Wave Feminism: A Critical Exploration*. Ed. Stacy Gillis, et al. Basingstoke, England: Palgrave Macmillan, 2004. 175–84. Print.
Stave, Shirley Ann. "Across Distances without Recognition: Misrecognition in Toni Morrison's *A Mercy*." *Toni Morrison's A Mercy: Critical Approaches*. Ed. Shirley Ann Stave and Justine Tally. Newcastle upon Tyne, England: Cambridge Scholars, 2011. 137–50. Print.
Sterritt, David. Rev. of *In Country*, by Bobbie Ann Mason. *Christian Science Monitor* 4 Oct. 1989: 11. Print.
Stewart, Matthew C. "Realism, Verisimilitude, and the Depiction of Vietnam Veterans in *In Country*." Jason 166–79.
Stirrup, David. *Louise Erdrich*. Manchester: Manchester UP, 2010. Print.
Strachan, Alex. "Gloria Steinem: 'This Generation of Women Is More Feminist Than We Ever Were.'" *National Post*. PostMedia Network, 8 Nov. 2010. Web. 25 July 2013.
Strandness, Jean. "When the Windigo Spirit Swept across the Plains." *Midamerica: The Yearbook of the Society for the Study of Midwestern Literature* 25 (1998): 36–49. Print.
Stuart, Andrea. "Feminism: Dead or Alive?" *Identity: Community, Culture, Difference*. Ed. Jonathan Rutherford. London: Lawrence and Wishart, 1990, 28–42. Print.
Sturken, Marita, and Lisa Cartwright. *Practices of Looking: An Introduction to Visual Culture*. New York: Oxford UP, 2001. Print.
Swoon. Dir. Tom Kalin. Fine Line Features, 1992. Film.
Tabbi, Joseph. "A Review of Books in the Age of Their Technological Obsolescence." *Ebr: The Electronic Book Review*. The Electronic Book Review, Winter 1995–1996. Web. 5 Aug. 2012.
Tatum, Beverly Daniel. *Why Are All the Black Kids Sitting Together in the Cafeteria: And Other Conversations about Race*. New York: Basic, 1999. Print.
Tharp, Julie. "Windigo Ways: Eating and Excess in Louise Erdrich's *The Antelope Wife*." *American Indian Culture and Research Journal* 27.4 (2003): 117–31. Print.

Thomas, M. E., and L. A. Treiber. "Race, Gender and Status: A Content Analysis of Print Advertisements in Four Popular Magazines." *Sociological Spectrum* 29.3 (2000): 357–71. Print.

Thornham, Sue. *Women, Feminism and Media*. Edinburgh: Edinburgh UP, 2007. Print.

Tichi, Cecilia. "Television and Recent American Fiction." *American Literary History* 1 (Spring 1989): 110–30. Print.

Travers, Peter. Rev. of *In Country*, by Bobbie Ann Mason. *Rolling Stone*. Rolling Stone, 1989. Web. 6 Apr. 2005.

Treichler, Paula A., Lisa Cartwright, and Constance Penley, eds. *The Visible Woman: Imaging Technologies, Gender, and Science*. New York: New York UP, 1998. Print.

Tuchman, Gaye. "Introduction: The Symbolic Annihilation of Women by the Mass Media." *Hearth and Home: Images of Women in the Mass Media*. Ed. Gaye Tuchman, Arlene Kaplan Daniels, and James Benét. New York: Oxford UP, 1978. 3–38. Print.

Turner, Mark. "The Cognitive Study of Art, Language, and Literature." *Poetics Today* 23.1 (2002): 9–20. Print.

Ty, Eleanor. *The Politics of the Visible in Asian North American Narratives*. Toronto: U of Toronto P, 2004. Print.

Ty, Michelle. "On the Cognitive Turn in Literary Studies." *Qui Parle: Critical Humanities and Social Sciences* 19.1 (Fall–Winter 2010): 205–19. Print.

US Food and Drug Administration (FDA). "Fetal Keepsake Videos." *FDA.gov*, 14 Aug. 2005. Web. 15 Feb. 2008.

Valentino, Gina. "'It All Does Come to Nothing in the End': Nationalism and Gender in Louise Erdrich's *Plague of Doves*." Madsen 121–35.

Vickroy, Laurie. "Seeking Symbolic Immortality: Visualizing Trauma in *Cat's Eye*." *Mosaic* 38 (June 2005): 129–44. Print.

———. *Trauma and Survival in Contemporary Fiction*. Charlottesville: U of Virginia P, 2002. Print.

"The Vietnam Wall Controversy, Round 3, October 1981–January 1982." *History on Trial*, Lehigh University Digital Library, n.d. Web. 20 Aug. 2013.

Villella, Fiona, and Adrian Martin, eds. *Terror, Disaster, Cinema, and Reality—a Symposium*. Spec. issue of *Senses of Cinema* 17 (Nov.–Dec. 2001): n. pag. Web. 6 Apr. 2005.

Viner, Katharine. "The Personal Is Still Political." *On the Move: Feminism for a New Generation*. Ed. Natasha Walter. London: Virago, 1999. 10–26. Print.

Vizenor, Gerald. *Narrative Chance: Postmodern Discourse on Native American Indian Literatures*. Norman: U of Oklahoma P, 1989. Print.

———, ed. *The People Named the Chippewa: Narrative Histories*. Minneapolis: U of Minnesota P, 1984. Print.

———. *Survivance: Narratives of Native Presence*. Lincoln: U of Nebraska P, 2008. Print.

Walk, Gary Eng. "Tail from the Crypt: Lara Croft Returns to Her Roots in the Fourth Installment of Tomb Raider." *Incite PC Gaming* Dec. 1999: 100–11. Print.

Walther, Malin LaVon. "Out of Sight: Toni Morrison's Revision of Beauty." *Black American Literature Forum* 24.4 (Winter 1990): 775–89. Print.

———. "Toni Morrison's *Tar Baby*: Re-Figuring the Colonizer's Aesthetics." *Cross-Cultural Performances: Differences in Women's Re-Visions of Shakespeare*. Ed. Marianne Novy. Urbana: U of Illinois P, 1993. 137–49. Print.

Warhol, Robyn. "The Space between: A Narrative Approach to Alison Bechdel's *Fun Home*." *College Literature* 38.3 (2011): 1–20. Print.

Washington, Mary Helen. *Invented Lives: Narratives of Black Women, 1860–1960*. New York: Doubleday, 1987. Print.

Watercutter, Angela. "Yes, Women Really Do Like *Game of Thrones* (We Have Proof)." *Wired*. Condé Nast, 3 June 2013. Web. 3 Aug. 2013.

Watson, Julia. "Autographic Disclosures and Genealogies of Desire in Alison Bechdel's *Fun Home*." *Biography* 31.1 (Winter 2008): 27–58. Print.

Werrlein, Debra. "Not So Fast, Dick and Jane: Reimagining Childhood and Nation in *The Bluest Eye*." *MELUS* 30.4 (Winter 2005): 53–72. Print.

White, Leslie. "The Function of Popular Culture in Bobbie Ann Mason's *Shiloh and Other Stories* and *In Country*." *Southern Quarterly* 26.4 (Summer 1988): 69–79. Print.

Whitlock, Gillian. "Autographics: The Seeing 'I' of the Comics." *Modern Fiction Studies* 52.4 (Winter 2006): 965–79. Print.

Williams, Linda, ed. *Viewing Positions: Ways of Seeing Film*. New Brunswick, NJ: Rutgers, 1994. Print.

Williamson, Judith. "Sexism with an Alibi." *Guardian*. Guardian News and Media, 31 May 2003. Web. 10 Aug. 2013.

Wilson, Sharon. "Eyes and I's." *International Literature in English: Essays on the Major Writers*. Ed. Robert L. Ross. New York: Garland, 1991. 225–35. Print.

Winship, Janice. "Sexuality for Sale." *Culture, Media, Language*. Ed. Stuart Hall, et al. London: Hutchinson, 1980. 217–23. Print.

Winther, Marjorie. "*M*A*S*H*, Malls and Meaning: Popular and Corporate Culture in *In Country*." *LIT* 4 (1993): 195–201. Print.

Wolfson, Elizabeth. "The 'Black Gash of Shame': Revisiting the Vietnam Veterans Memorial Controversy." *Art21*. Art21, Inc., 1 Nov. 2011. Web. 20 Aug. 2013.

Women Take Issue. Women's Studies Group, Centre for Contemporary Cultural Studies. London: Hutchinson, 1978. Print.

Wright, Laura. "National Photographic: Images of Sensibility and the Nation in Margaret Atwood's *Surfacing* and Nadine Gordimer's *July's People*." *Mosaic* 38 (Mar. 2005): 75–93. Print.

Wyatt, Jean. *Risking Difference: Identification, Race, and Community in Contemporary Fiction and Feminism*. Albany: State U of New York P, 2004. Print.

Wysocki, Anne Frances. "The Multiple Media of Texts: How Onscreen and Paper Texts Incorporate Words, Images, and Other Media." *What Writing Does and How It Does It: An Introduction to Analysis of Text and Textual Practices*. Ed. Charles Bazerman and Paul Prior. Mahwah, NJ: Lawrence Erlbaum, 2003. 123–63. Print.

Yancy, George, and Linda Martin Alcoff. *Black Bodies, White Gazes: The Continuing Significance of Race*. Lanham, MD: Rowman and Littlefield, 2008. Print.

York, Lorraine. *Margaret Atwood and the Labour of Literary Celebrity*. Toronto: U of Toronto P, 2013. Print.

Zeisler, Andi. "Does It Matter whether *Game of Thrones* Is Feminist?" *Bitch Media*. Bitch Media, 7 June 2013. Web. 3 Aug. 2013.

Zoonen, Liesbet Van. "Feminist Perspectives on the Media." Kearney 25–40.

Index

Aaron, Michele, 127, 131, 134, 138, 167
abortion, 105–6, 108, 165n3
   and mandatory ultrasounds, 165n4
   and sex selection, 113, 118
abstract citizenship, 25–26
advertising, 10, 31–32
aesthetics, 30–32
   See also mass media; visuality
Agent Orange, 45, 59
Amazon.com, 13
American Graffiti (film), 26
American New Right, 68
amniocentesis, 113, 115, 117–19
anxiety of obsolescence, 14, 150n7
Are You My Mother? (Bechdel), 124
Atwood, Margaret
   career, 66–67
   literary style, 66–67
   MaddAddam, 67, 161n3, 161n8
   and speculative fiction, 67, 75, 84, 161n3
   and technology, 162n14
   Tent, The, 66
   and the United States, 67–69, 80
   on writing, 65–66
   Year of the Flood, The, 161n3, 161n8
audience studies, 6–7
authenticity
   and African American culture, 22, 40–41, 153n3
   See also photography and authenticity

Baker, Houston A., 37
Bambara, Toni Cade, 36
Barnes & Noble, 13
Barry, Ann, 70–71
Barry, Lynda, 126
Barthes, Roland, 13–14
Baudrillard, Jean, 46–47
beauty. See *Bluest Eye, The* (Morrison)
Bechdel, Alison
   in American literature, 123–25
   Are You My Mother?, 124
   autobiographical avatar, use of, 124, 135, 166n3
   coming out, 123, 130–31
   critical reception, 125
   Dykes to Watch Out For, 124
   See also *Fun Home* (Bechdel)
Bentham, Jeremy, 73
Berlant, Lauren, 25–26, 31, 111
bildungsroman, 22, 153–54n4
"Birthmates" (Jen)
   abortion, 112, 116
   amniocentesis, 115, 117
   personhood, 114–15, 117
black aesthetic, 23, 39–49
   and female writers, 154n5
black arts movement, 22–25, 39–40, 154n5
black looks, 9
Black Looks (hooks), 24, 33, 143, 151n12
blindness. See *Handmaid's Tale, The* (Atwood)
blues aesthetic, 155n16
Bluest Eye, The (Morrison)
   advertising, 31–32
   aesthetics, 23, 28, 30–35, 38–40, 155n16

Bluest Eye, The (continued)
  and aurality, 35
  and authenticity, 22, 40–41, 153*n*3
  beauty, 22–23, 31, 33, 35, 38, 154*n*11
  as a black arts novel, 23
  and the blues, 35, 38–40
  and childhood, 26, 28, 36
  classification, 28–30, 33, 35
  consumer culture, 31, 34, 40–41
  and cultural citizenship, 25–26
  and dolls, 35, 38–39, 154–55*n*11
  as a female bildungsroman, 22, 153–54*n*4
  and femininity, 33–34, 41
  and feminism, 22–25
  funkiness, 40
  and integration, 29–30, 155*n*12
  and intraracism, 31–32, 40
  and mass media, 30–34, 39, 41
  and nostalgia, 25–26
  resistance to visuality, 36–39, 41
  separation, 28–30, 35
  See also World War II
Bobo, Jacqueline, 24
body image, 11, 25–26, 33–34
Bordo, Susan, 11
Bouson, J. Brooks, 21, 28, 153*n*1

Cairncross, Frances, 79
Carby, Hazel, 24
Cartwright, Lisa, 79, 164–65*n*1
Caruth, Cathy, 52
Catlin, George, 91, 93–94
Child's Life, A (Gloeckner), 126
Christo, 59–61, 160*n*17, 160*n*19
Chun, Wendy Hui Kyong, 145–46
Chute, Hillary, 124, 130, 165*n*1, 166*n*2, 166*n*5
classification, 28–30, 33, 35
  See also visuality
closeting, 124, 133–36, 138, 140
closure, in graphic narratives, 126, 138
cognitive turn, 156*n*1
comics theory. See *Fun Home* (Bechdel)

coming out, 123, 130–31
consumers
  consumer culture, 31, 34, 40–41, 43–49, 57, 60, 108
  of media, 4–5, 8, 12
cosmetic surgery, 4, 11, 150*n*6
counterculture, 47–48
critical visuality studies. See Mirzoeff, Nicholas
Cronin, Anne, 11, 32
cross gender identification, 8, 127–28, 132, 134, 140, 146, 167*n*1
cultural citizenship. See *Bluest Eye, The* (Morrison)
Currin, John, 92

"Dear John Wayne" (Erdrich), 86
Debord, Guy, 74–75, 84
deep attention. See Hayles, N. Katherine
deep metaphor. See metaphor
Degas, Edgar, 93
de Kooning, Willem, 92
de Lauretis, Teresa, 8, 24, 151*n*12, 154*n*7
DeLillo, Don, 14
Derrida, Jacques, 95–96
Dick-and-Jane readers, 25–27
Diehl, Joanne, 92
Discipline and Punish (Foucault), 72
dissensus, 144
Divakaruni, Chitra Banerjee, 107
  See also "Ultrasound, The" (Divakaruni)
Doane, Mary Ann, 8, 127
docile bodies, 11, 33, 73, 75
  See also Foucault, Michel
Doty, Alexander, 8
Draper, Janet, 115–16, 118
Duvall, John N., 37, 153*n*3, 156*n*19
Dykes to Watch Out For (Bechdel), 124

écriture féminine, 96
ekphrasis, 9, 15
  definition of, 164*n*8

and sexual difference, 92
See also *Shadow Tag* (Erdrich)
Elkins, James
  the gaze, 154*n*10
  usual seeing, 70–71
Ellison, Ralph. See *Invisible Man* (Ellison)
embodiment
  in *Fun Home*, 166*n*6
  and pregnancy, 111, 113
  and technoculture, 146
  and vision, 108, 117, 120, 154*n*10
epistemology of the closet, 124
Erdrich, Louise
  Anglo versus Native American gender norms, 88–89, 163–64*n*6
  Dartmouth Commencement Address, 85–86
  "Dear John Wayne," 86
  Love Medicine, 86
  and *mino bimaadiziwin*, 86, 89, 97
  myth of vanishing, 87–88, 93
  Native American literature, 85–86, 163*n*2
  Native American nationalism, 87–88, 101
  Plague of Doves, The, 163*n*4
  Round House, The, 163*n*5, 164*n*9
  Tracks, 100
e-readers, 152*n*23

Falwell, Jerry, 68
Felski, Rita, 8, 10, 156*n*17
female transvestism. *See* cross gender identification
Feminine Mystique, The (Friedan), 6–7, 24
feminism
  co-optation, 1–3
  and modern image culture, 6–7
  popular versus professional feminism, 2, 147, 149*n*1
  second-wave, 6, 24, 150*n*10
feminist media studies, 1–4, 6–7, 9, 154*n*10

and *Bluest Eye, The*, 23–25
and race, 143
fertility, 72
fetal imaging
  in advertising, 108
  in anti-abortion and mass media materials, 108–9, 120
  cultural context, 106, 118, 120
  diagnostic discourse on, 108–10, 117, 121
  and feminism, 108, 110–11, 119, 120–21
  mandatory ultrasounds, 105–6
  and personhood, 106, 110–11, 113–15
Fitzpatrick, Kathleen, 13–14, 150*n*7
Foucault, Michel
  and the spectacle of the scaffold, 72–73
  and surveillance, 72–74
Franzen, Jonathan, 14
Freud, Sigmund, 52, 96, 129
Friedan, Betty. See *Feminine Mystique, The* (Friedan)
Fun Home (Bechdel)
  as autobiography, 123–25, 166*n*1
  and comics theory, 125, 166*n*6
  critical reception, 125
  diegetic levels, 126–27
  and masculine beauty, 132, 134
  narrative innovations, 125–27
  queer model of looking, 125, 131–34
  spectacle of the closet, 135–36, 138

Gaines, Jane, 8, 24, 154*n*7
Gallagher, Jean, 86, 90
Game of Thrones, 2–3, 147, 149*n*3, 149*n*4
gaming, and gender, 146
Gardiner, Judith Kegan, 130–31, 133
Gasche, Rodolphe, 90
gaze, the
  history of, 154*n*10
  imperial gaze, 9

gaze, the (*continued*)
  in literature, 38
  male gaze, 8, 37, 90, 127–30, 140, 143
  objectification, 1, 3–5, 14, 23, 30, 91, 105, 128–29, 140
  oppositional gaze, 9
  queer spectatorship, 8
  and race, 22–25
genetic engineering, 69
Gibson, Graeme. *See* "Travels of a Family Man" (Gibson)
Gill, Rosalind, 1–4, 6, 145, 149*n*1, 150*n*5, 155–56*n*17
girlhood, 26, 30–31, 35–37, 47, 82, 129
Giroux, Henry, 26
global village, 79–80
Gloeckner, Phoebe. *See Child's Life, A* (Gloeckner)
graphic narratives
  closure in, 126, 138
  definition of, 165–66*n*1
  diegetic levels, 126–27
  and literary studies, 125, 166*n*4
  and looking relations, 125–26, 128, 131
  and memoir, 125–26
Grewal, Gurleen, 27
Guttmacher Institute, The, 105–6, 165*n*3, 165*n*4

Handmaid's Tale, The (Atwood)
  and Afghanistan, 68, 161*n*5
  blindness in, 65, 68–71
  fertility, 72
  and historical amnesia, 74
  and Iran, 68, 161*n*5
  and panopticism, 73
  reviews of, 67
  and spectacle, 72–73
  and the Third Reich, 84
  and totalitarianism, 68
  and visual literacy, 76–78, 83–84
Haraway, Donna, 108, 120–21, 164*n*1
Harlow, Jean, 33

Hayles, N. Katherine, 152*n*23
HBO, 46, 157*n*6
Henninger, Katherine, 4, 9–10, 12
Hirsch, Marianne, 49, 57, 158*n*8
hooks, bell, 8–9, 24, 33, 143, 151*n*12, 154*n*7
Hopper, Edward, 92
hyperreality, 46–47
  See also Baudrillard, Jean; *In Country* (Mason)

identification
  with images, 11, 33–35, 54
  with literary characters, 4, 57, 74, 126
  See also cross gender identification
images
  divide between image and text, 5, 13–15, 84, 125, 131, 151*n*15, 152*n*24
  and feminism, 1, 6–10, 24, 143, 147, 155*n*17
  as a form of ownership, 90–91, 93–94
  legacy of women's images, 4, 10–12, 32–34, 41
  the problem of the image, 67–69, 75, 80–81, 162*n*13
  proliferation of images, 6, 11, 79–80, 150*n*8
  reading images critically, 5, 11–12, 15, 92, 145
  and visuality, 4–5, 24–25, 30–31, 35
  See also fetal imaging; graphic narratives; *In Country* (Mason): and perception
Imitation of Life (film), 31
imperial gaze, 9
incest, 37
In Country (film), 49–50
  reviews of, 159*n*13
In Country (Mason)
  and catharsis, 44, 57–58, 160*n*15
  and consumer culture, 43–49, 57, 60

critical reception, 156–57n2, 157n4, 159–60n13
hyperreality, 46–47
and perception, 43–44, 53, 55, 57, 61, 158n9
and post-traumatic stress disorder, 44–45, 51, 55, 157n4
teenage pregnancy, 45, 160n18
television in, 43–47, 50–57, 60
and trauma, 44, 47, 49, 51–52, 55, 57, 61, 157n4, 157n5, 158n8, 158n11, 160n15
and the Vietnam Veterans Memorial, 44, 57–59, 157n3, 158–59n13, 159n14, 160n15
and the Washington Monument, 58–60, 159n13
See also Christo; HBO; *M*A*S*H*; MTV
information age, 159n9
intraracism, 31–32, 40
invisibility, 4–5, 21–22, 31, 37, 72–73, 100, 107, 118, 120, 143–46
See also myth of vanishing
Invisible Man (Ellison), 37
Irigaray, Luce, 90, 95–96

Jameson, Fredric, historical amnesia, 74
Jay, Martin
on the pictorial turn, 150n8
on specularity, 86, 90–91, 95–96
Jen, Gish, 107
See also "Birthmates" (Jen)
Jewison, Norman, 49–50
See also In Country (film)
Jones, Amelia, 6

Kaplan, E. Ann, 9, 47, 143, 146, 151n13, 157n6
Karenga, Maulana, 40
Kevles, Bettyann, 164n1
Kitaj, R. B., 92
Kmart realism, 15
See also In Country (Mason)

Knight, Etheridge, 23
Kominsky-Crumb, Aline, 126
Kuhn, Annette, 7, 151n17

Larrick, Nancy, 36
Last Picture Show, The (film), 26
Ledbetter, James, 79
legacy of women's images, 4, 10–12, 32–34, 41
Lessing, Gotthold, 13
Lin, Maya, 157n3
Love Medicine (Erdrich), 86
Lucretia (Rembrandt), 91–92

MaddAddam (Atwood), 67, 161n3, 161n8
Mad Men (television show), 2–3, 147, 149n3, 149n4
Madsen, Debra, 86–87
male gaze, 8, 37, 90, 94, 127–30, 140, 143
mammogram, 105, 165n2
Mary Jane (candy), 12, 26, 34, 155n15
M*A*S*H, 12, 46, 50–55
Mason, Bobbie Ann
critical reception of, 156–57n2, 157n4, 159–60n13
and minimalism, 44
and the regional renaissance in American literature, 43–44
See also In Country (Mason)
mass media
and aesthetics, 23, 28, 30–35, 38–40, 155n16 (*see also* visuality)
and consumer culture, 4–5, 8, 12, 31–32, 34, 40–41, 43–49, 57, 60, 108
and decline of literature, 13–14, 81–84
globalization of, 67–69, 79–80, 82–83
and human perception, 43–44, 53, 55, 57, 61, 158n9
and metaphor, 15, 44, 53–56
as mixed media, 14–15

mass media (*continued*)
   and postfeminism, 1–5, 9, 145, 147, 149n1
   and race, 30–34, 39, 41, 87, 107
   and reality: as an escape from, 33–34; hyperreality, 46–47, 49, 158n12; photographic realism, 80, 82, 162n12
Maus (Spiegelman), 124
Mayne, Judith, 8, 24, 151n12, 154n7
McCloud, Scott, 126, 166n6
McLuhan, Marshall, 79
Mehaffy, Marilyn, 108–9
metaphor, 15, 44, 53–56
   See also popular culture: allusions to
mino bimaadiziwin, 86, 89, 97
Mirzoeff, Nicholas, 4, 25, 28, 30, 36–37, 144, 154n8, 156n18
Mitchell, Lisa, 106, 114
Mitchell, William, 80, 162n12
Mitchell, W. J. T., 6, 14, 92, 152n14, 164n8
moral majority, 68
Morrison, George, 93
Morrison, Toni
   bearing witness in the works of, 21, 26
   Playing in the Dark, 21, 26
   on writing, 21, 36
   See also Bluest Eye, The (Morrison)
Moynihan Report, The, 28
Mr. Bojangles, 31, 39
MTV, 46–48, 54, 157n6
Mulvey, Laura. *See* "Visual Pleasure and Narrative Cinema" (Mulvey)
music
   the blues, 35, 38–40, 155n16
   1960s counterculture, 47–48
myth of vanishing, 87–89, 93

National Endowment for the Arts, 22, 23, 152n19
Native Son (Wright), 27
Neal, Larry, 23
new queer cinema, 140, 167n11

Nietzsche, Friedrich, 95–96
nostalgia, 25–26

oppositional gaze, 9
Oryx and Crake (Atwood)
   the crisis of the image in, 68–69, 78–81
   death of distance in, 79–81
   and genetic engineering, 69
   and global terrorism, 83–84
   and the global village, 79–80
   and spectacle, 74–75, 84

panopticism, 73
Parmar, Pratibha, 8
perception, 43–44, 53, 55, 57, 61, 75, 158n9
Percy, Walker, 159n14
Persepolis (Satrapi), 125, 166n2
personhood
   in "Birthmates," 113–14, 117
   and fetal imaging, 106, 110–11, 113–15
   and "The Ultrasound," 114, 119–20
Petchesky, Rosalind, 108, 110, 119, 164n1
photography and authenticity, 80–81, 83, 162n12, 162n13
   See also Sontag, Susan
Picasso, Pablo, 92–93
pictorial turn, 6–7, 13–14, 150n8, 151n16
Plague of Doves, The (Erdrich), 163n4
Playing in the Dark (Morrison), 21, 26
politics of the visible, 107, 111
Pollock, Griselda, 1
popular culture, 3, 22, 25–26, 41
   allusions to, 44–45, 52, 61, 156–57n2, 158n8
   See also mass media
pornography, 75, 80–82, 128, 147
portraiture, 87, 89–91, 93
postfeminism, 1–4, 9, 145, 147, 149n1
postmemory, 49, 57, 158n8

post-traumatic stress disorder (PTSD), 44–45, 51, 55, 157n4
psychoanalytic theory, treatment of sexuality and race in, 8, 143, 151n13
Pynchon, Thomas, 14

queer
  definition of, 127
  and spectatorship, 8, 125, 131–34

Radner, Hilary, 9
Radway, Janice, 7
Rancière, Jacques, 143–44, 156n18
Rauschenberg, Robert, 92
Reading at Risk: A Survey of Literary Reading in America, 152n19, 152n22
reading practices, 5, 13–15, 152n19, 152n22, 152n23
  and *Handmaid's Tale, The* (Atwood), 77
reflection, 89–91, 95–96
regional renaissance in American literature, 43–44
Rembrandt Harmenszoon van Rijn, 91, 94
resexualization of women's bodies, 3
retro-sexism, 149n2
Rich, B. Ruby, 167n11
Rodriguez, Richard, 87
Rogin, Michael, 26, 74
romance
  female readers of, 7
  and lesbianism, 131
  and media narratives, 55
Round House, The (Erdrich), 163n5, 164n9

Sacks, Oliver, 70
Said, Edward, 126
Satrapi, Marjane. See *Persepolis* (Satrapi)
Schiller, Herbert, 79

Sedgwick, Eve Kosofsky, 124, 134, 167n9
separation, 29–30
  See also visuality
Shadow Tag (Erdrich)
  and bearing witness, 89, 97–98, 100
  and dissimulation, 96
  ekphrasis, 91–92, 100, 164n8
  and George Catlin, 91, 93–94
  and incorporation, 99–100
  reflection, 89–91, 95–96
  the windigo, 94, 97, 164n9
Shohat, Ella, 109
shopping malls, 43, 45, 59, 61, 156n2
Skeggs, Beverley, 9, 33
software, 145–47
Sontag, Susan, 80
spectacle
  and Debord, 74–75, 84
  and Foucault, 72–73
  See also *Handmaid's Tale, The* (Atwood)
spectacle of the closet, 136
spectatorship
  critical spectatorship, 75, 81, 83
  models of, 6–7
  and psychoanalysis, 8, 143, 151n13
  and race, 8, 24, 35, 143, 151n13
  and sexuality, 8, 125, 127–28, 134, 140
  See also "Visual Pleasure and Narrative Cinema" (Mulvey)
specularity, 86–87, 89–91, 95–96
speculative fiction, 67, 72, 75, 84, 161n3
Spiegelman, Art, 124
Steinem, Gloria, 2–3
sterility, or male sexual dysfunction, 54–55, 68, 72
Stuart, Andrea, 2, 147, 149n1
Surfacing (Atwood), 67
Surrounded Islands (Christo), 59
surveillance
  and Foucault, 72–74
  See also *Handmaid's Tale, The* (Atwood)

"Symbolic Annihilation of Women by the Mass Media, The" (Tuchman), 7

technoculture, 146–47
television, 2–3, 46–48, 50–57, 60, 75, 77, 79, 87, 89, 105, 108, 147, 150n9, 157n6, 158n9, 159n13
   cable, 46–48, 54, 157n6
   and gender, 2–3, 46, 157n6
   See also *In Country* (Mason)
Temple, Shirley, 26, 34–35, 38–39, 41, 147, 155n16
Tent, The (Atwood), 66
"Ten Theses on Politics" (Rancière), 144
Their Eyes Were Watching God (Hurston), 153n2
Thornham, Sue, 1, 11, 24, 32–33, 151n18, 154n6
Tomb Raider (video game), 147
To Read or Not to Read, 152n19, 152n22
totalitarianism. See *Handmaid's Tale, The* (Atwood)
transparency machines, 145, 147
trauma
   catharsis, 57, 157n5
   in the context of gender, 36–37
   and psychoanalysis, 52, 158n11
   television mediation of, 44, 47, 49, 51–52, 55, 57, 61
   trauma theory, 157n4, 160n15
   traumatic seeing, 153n1
   See also postmemory; post-traumatic stress disorder
"Family Man" (Gibson),

of *Invisible Man*

and embodied vision, 108, 117, 120
feminist rhetoric in, 119–21
fetal imaging, 106, 108, 112–15, 117–21
personhood, 114, 119–21
quality baby, 118–19
sex selection, 113, 118
"Unspeakable Things Unspoken" (Morrison), 26
usual seeing, 70–71

van Dijck, José, 109
Van Zoonen, Liesbet, 3, 7, 9–10, 145–46, 150n10, 154n6
Velázquez, Diego, 92–93
Vietnam, 44, 46, 50–52, 56
Vietnam veterans, 49, 52, 55, 57, 157n3, 158–59n13
   and post-traumatic stress disorder (PTSD), 44, 57–59, 157n3, 158–59n13, 159n14, 160n15
Vietnam Veterans Memorial, 44, 57–59, 157n3, 158–59n13, 159n14, 160n15
violence, 28, 48, 57, 81, 84, 91, 108, 112, 160n15
   sexualized, 2, 3, 150n6
Visible Woman: Imaging Technologies, Gender, and Science, The (Treichler, Cartwright, and Penley), 165n1, 165n2
visuality
   components of, 4–5, 28–32, 35
   definition of, 4, 154n8
   and feminism, 4–9
   and gender, 5, 10, 126
   and literary studies, 1–2, 5, 9, 147
   and power, 21, 25, 72, 86–87
   resistance to, 13, 15–16, 22, 35–41, 92, 125, 143–45
   See also Mirzoeff, Nicholas
visual literacy, 76–77, 143
   See also spectatorship: critical spectatorship
visual metaphor. See metaphor

"Visual Pleasure and Narrative Cinema" (Mulvey), 7–8, 24, 127, 140, 154n10
Vizenor, Gerald, 86, 163n1, 163n3
Vogue (magazine), 10

Wallace, David Foster, 14
Warhol, Robyn, 126–27, 131, 166n6
Washington, Mary Helen, 24
Washington Monument, 58–60, 159n13
Watson, Julia, 128, 132, 134–35, 166n1

Werrlein, Debra, 26–28, 39
Whitlock, Gillian, 166n7
Williamson, Judith, 2–3, 149n2, 150n5
windigo, 94, 97, 164n9
Withers, Jane, 35
Women and Film (journal), 7
Women's Studies Group of the Centre for Contemporary Cultural Studies at Birmingham (CCCs), 7
World War II, 22, 26–27, 31, 36
Wyeth, Andrew, 92
Wysocki, Anne Frances, 152n24

States of America